Navigating the Labyrinth

Navigating the Labyrinth

Perspectives on India's Higher Education

Edited by

Devesh Kapur
Pratap Bhanu Mehta

Orient BlackSwan

NAVIGATING THE LABYRINTH: PERSPECTIVES ON INDIA'S HIGHER EDUCATION

ORIENT BLACKSWAN PRIVATE LIMITED

Registered Office
3-6-752 Himayatnagar, Hyderabad 500 029, Telangana, India
e-mail: centraloffice@orientblackswan.com

Other Offices
Bengaluru, Bhopal, Chennai, Guwahati,
Hyderabad, Jaipur, Kolkata, Lucknow, Mumbai,
New Delhi, Noida, Patna, Visakhapatnam

Paperback Reprint, 2019

027193

ISBN 978-93-5287-276-3

Typeset in
ITC Berkeley Oldstyle Std 10.5/12.6
by Le Studio Graphique, Gurgaon 122 001

Printed in India at
Yash Printographics, Noida

Published by
Orient Blackswan Private Limited
3-6-752, Himayatnagar, Hyderabad 500 029, Telangana, India
e-mail: info@orientblackswan.com

Contents

Abbreviations

AICTE	All India Council for Technical Education
AICTE Act	All India Council for Technical Education Act, 1987
ASSOCHAM	Associated Chambers of Commerce and Industry of India
BPLR	Benchmark Prime Lending Rate
CAG	Comptroller and Auditor General
CII	Confederation of Indian Industries
DEC	Distance Education Council
DGET	Directorate General of Employment and Training
FDI	Foreign Direct Investment
FICCI	Federation of Indian Chambers of Commerce and Industry
GER	Gross Enrolment Ratio
IGNOU	Indira Gandhi National Open University
IISER	Indian Institutes of Science, Education and Research
ITI	Industrial Training Institutes
KII	Knowledge-intensive Industries
KIS	Knowledge-intensive Services
MCI	Medical Council of India
MES	Modular employable skills
MHRD	Ministry of Human Resource Development
MoLE	Ministry of Labour and Employment
MoRD	Ministry of Rural Development
MSDE	Ministry for Skill Development and Entrepreneurship
MSE	Ministry for Skill Development and Entrepreneurship
MSMEs	Micro, Small and Medium Enterprises
NASSCOM	National Association of Software and Service Companies

NCHER	National Commission for Higher Education and Research
NCTE	National Council for Teacher Education
NCVT	National Council for Vocational Training
NDA	National Democratic Alliance
NEEM	National Employability Enhancement Mission
NEFC	National Education Finance Corporation
NOS	National Occupational Standards
NPA	Non-performing assets
NSDA	National Skill Development Agency
NSDC	National Skill Development Corporation
NSDF	National Skill Development Fund
NSQF	National Vocational Education Qualifications Framework
OBCs	Other Backward Castes
OJT	On-job training
PITI	Private Industrial Training Institutes
PPP	Purchasing Power Parity
RPL	Recognition of Prior Learning
SDIS	Skill Development Initiative Scheme
SSC	Sector Skill Councils
STAR	Standard Training Assessment and Reward Scheme
UGC	University Grants Commission
VET	Vocational education and training
VTPs	Vocational Training Providers
WTO	World Trade Organization

Tables and Figures

Tables

FIGURES

— one —

Introduction

Devesh Kapur and *Pratap Bhanu Mehta*

For much of the twentieth century, physical capital—its growth and distribution—was central to debates on economic development. In more recent years, however, human capital has been seen as increasingly central. This book focuses on one facet of human capital—higher (or tertiary) education—whose complex role in economic and social change is precisely what makes it such a politically charged issue in countries like India, which are undergoing rapid change.

Higher education encompasses a vast terrain of institutions and goals. Its instrumental goals (learning, skilling, advancing research and innovation) and normative goals (better citizens, fairer and more resilient societies) make this sector a linchpin of a modern economy and society. A vibrant higher education system matters for long-term democratic stability, if it can promote greater social mobility and economic progress through linking with labour markets, training personnel to staff and build institutions, and creating knowledge. Higher education underpins national development not only by building economic competitiveness, but also by developing and cultivating a wider intellectual milieu and promoting democratic ideals.

And with nearly a million young people joining higher education annually, the urgency of India's challenge in this sector is manifest. This book is an attempt to understand the complexity of the challenges facing Indian higher education, an issue whose economic and political salience has been receiving increasing academic attention.[1]

This introductory chapter first provides a brief historical overview of higher education in India and its recent rapid expansion that has resulted in massification. It then focuses on four key challenges: quality, access, financing, and internationalisation. A common factor underlying these challenges is the severe governance weaknesses plaguing Indian higher education, which can be best understood through a political economy framework. Finally, the chapter concludes by outlining the book and summarising the contributed chapters, which help to shed light on these challenges and on possible solutions.

Historical Overview

The modern university in India is a Western import dating back to the establishment of three universities in the British 'presidency' towns of Calcutta, Bombay and Madras in 1857, as the colonial government looked to educate a class of Indians who could staff the growing bureaucracy. By 1882, India had four universities (with the addition of Punjab University in Lahore) and 67 colleges, which grew by the turn of the century to five universities and 145 colleges, with 18,000 students (almost all male). While initially the colleges were founded by missionaries, by this time those funded and managed by Indians were the majority. The system was decentralised, with much of the funding coming from private Indian sources. For instance, Punjab University (India's first teaching university) was created in 1882 after local elites and businesses raised money, following the refusal of the colonial government to provide funds. Calcutta University led the way to create chairs funded by private industry, attracting outstanding scholars such as C. V. Raman and S. Radhakrishnan. Between 1914–22, just 6.5 per cent of the budget of the College of Science came from public money. By 1922, there were 14 universities and 167 colleges, with 46,000 students under the control of elected provincial authorities, with little role for the national government. In 1947, when India became independent, 21 universities and 496 colleges were in operation.

Pre-independence India had a larger number of secondary and post-secondary students than several industrialised countries (such as France), even though primary school enrolment rates in India were abysmally low. By 1931, India's literacy rate was just 8.6 per cent, and this small number of literates was highly educated. More than 10 per cent of them could read and write in English, a second language, even as the vast majority of Indians could not read or write in any language. India had the most Nobel Prizes in Asia prior to independence (and while Indians continued to garner Nobel Prizes in subsequent years, the post-independence Nobel laureates were all based abroad).

India's present-day higher education challenges need to be understood in the context of its weak record in human development, which is paradoxical, given the predictions that democratic governments are more likely to invest in universal education than authoritarian ones. But India's weak record in primary education belies this prediction. Why this has been the case is a separate story, but it has had consequences for higher education in India, in that the absence of a broad egalitarian base has shifted distributional politics to the apex (higher education), to the detriment of both base and apex.

EXPANSION AND MASSIFICATION

The data in Table 1.1 gives a sense of the scale of change in Indian higher education over the past six-plus decades. While India's population grew nearly four-fold over this period, enrolment in higher education grew *60-fold*. Most of this expansion has come in the new millennium, driven primarily by low-quality private-sector institutions that focus on professional education, which has allowed increased access to all social groups, albeit some more than others. In the 13 years from 2000–01 to 2013–14, the number of colleges increased from 12,806 to 39,671, *an average of nearly 40 new colleges per week over this period*. In 2013–14 alone, 2,467 new colleges opened—nearly seven per day (including weekends!).

TABLE 1.1: A Snapshot of Indian Higher Education

	1950–51	*1980–81*	*2000–01*	*2013–14*
GER (Gross Enrolment Ratio) (%)	0.4		8.1	21.1
Universities	30	133	256	666
Colleges	695	4,722	12,806	39,671
Students (million)	0.4	2.75	8.4	23.8
Girls per 100 boys	13	36	58	80
Teaching staff (million)	0.024	0.19	0.41	1.05

Source: University Grants Commission.

On the demand side, four principal factors have driven this rapid growth. The first is simply demographic. With more than 30 per cent of the population below the age of 15 and more than five million people entering the 15–24 age group annually, India's demographic momentum alone is massive. Between 1991–2010, the population increase in the 15–64 age group was 249 million; between 2010–30, it will increase by an additional 230 million.

Second, this demographic education bulge is more prepared for higher education. The achievement of near-universal primary enrolment, resulting from a combination of public funding (notably, the *Sarva Shiksha Abhiyan* or 'Education for All Programme') and private efforts, led to substantially higher secondary school enrolments. This was further boosted by the *Rashtriya Madhyamik Shiksha Abhiyan* ('National Secondary School Programme'), launched in 2009 with a commitment of Rs 20,000 crore during the Eleventh Five-Year Plan.

Third, India's rapid economic growth as well as greater integration into the global economy has raised the demand for people with knowledge and skills. A simulation study in 2000 to predict the demand for education if India became as open to trade as China found that such an opening would increase the demand for primary education by 12 per cent, for secondary education by 31 per cent, and for higher education by 64 per cent (Wood and Calandrino 2000). By this time, India had begun to integrate itself into the global economy, and this period also marked the onset of 'massification' of its higher education. Education is now a big business sector, with value addition in education services in India rising from $6.9 billion to $44.6 billion between 1990–2012.[2]

Finally, demand for higher education is being driven by major changes in the aspirations of the population, as well as by state policy. In India, the stated goal is to move from a current enrolment of approximately 21 per cent of its college-age population to 30 per cent by 2020. In terms of absolutes, India already has the second-highest number of students (after China) enrolled in tertiary education.

The supply response has been taking place at four different levels. The first—and the most important in quantitative terms—is the rapid expansion of private colleges (and increasingly, private universities), largely affiliated with state-level universities, especially in professional education.

The second has been the efforts of the central government to expand the supply of national-level higher education institutions during the Eleventh Five-Year Plan. This included establishing 15 new central universities, including the conversion of three state universities to central universities; eight new Indian Institutes of Technology (IITs); seven new Indian Institutes of Management (IIMs); five new Indian Institutes of Science Education and Research (IISERs); two new Schools of Planning and Architecture (SPAs); 10 new National Institutes of Technology (NITs); and 20 new Indian Institutes of Information Technology (IIITs). Plans were also announced to build one new 'model college' in each of the 374 educationally backward districts (whose gross enrolment ratio [GER] for higher education was less than the national average). Within two years of the Narendra Modi-led National Democratic Alliance (NDA) government coming to power in 2014, an additional six new IITs and seven IIMs were approved, so that 23 IITs and 20 IIMs were in existence by 2016. In addition, large sums were committed to elite vanity projects like SAARC University and Nalanda University.

Nonetheless, while the central institutions are the leading higher education institutions within the country, about 94 per cent of all students enrolled in government institutions are enrolled in colleges and universities run by state governments. In the 12th Five-Year Plan period, a new Centrally Sponsored Scheme, the *Rashtriya Uchchatar Shiksha Abhiyan* (RUSA), was launched to try to improve the quality of state universities and colleges by channelling funding through new State Higher Education Councils.

Finally, an important initiative in higher education has been a new emphasis on 'skilling'. This has opened up the institutional landscape of higher education, allowing for new pathways to both enter and exit higher education, as the chapter on community colleges by Manish Sabharwal and Srinivasan Kannan illustrates. The National Skill Development Agency (NSDA) was created in 2013 with the target of providing skills to 500 million people by 2022. Currently, the Government of India is funding skill development activities through dozens of schemes spread across multiple ministries. These programmes provided skill development for 17.34 million young people from 2011–13. While some of this training is conducted through government Industrial Training Institutes (ITIs), most of the training is being delivered by private Vocational Training Providers (VTPs) and Assessing Bodies, with the central government ministries providing funds to state governments for reimbursement of training and assessment costs, respectively.

What exactly are the outcomes of this massive programme will be an area of fertile research in the future. Megha Agarwal's chapter sheds some light on this by emphasising the need to find ways to improve the skills of the vast majority of India's labour force, which is in the unorganised sector. Her focus is on the supply side, in particular the regulatory framework as an enabler of quality and the funding mechanisms that enable access.

While there has been a massive increase in the supply of and demand for higher education, the vast majority of Indian college students are enrolled in private and state institutions of poor quality, with no research facilities and a dearth of qualified faculty. Although private higher education institutions are *de jure* non-profit, they are *de facto* commercial and profit-maximising. There have, however, been new (albeit few) private entrants of higher quality, supported by philanthropy—harking back to pre-independence India. Federal higher education institutions (the so-called central universities) continue to attract better students due to their better funding, greater autonomy from politics, selection criteria (competitive national exams), relatively modest fees (and generous scholarships and easy loans for needy students), and some commitment to research. After an initial burst in the 1950s and 1960s, there was a hiatus for nearly three decades before a new expansion of central universities opened in the 2000s. However, most students in public universities are in state, not central universities. By 2014, more than half of all students in higher education were enrolled in private institutions, the vast majority affiliated to state universities.

This massive expansion also appears to be somewhat divorced from the demand side emanating from labour markets. In their chapter, Jeemol Unni and Sudipa Sarkar shed light on one of the central questions facing higher education in India: Is there a demand for persons with higher education, or are we witnessing a situation of education inflation with a mismatch between degrees and emerging job requirements?

THE 'TRILEMMA' OF INDIAN HIGHER EDUCATION

With nearly a million Indians projected to enter the working age each month for the next two decades, India simply does not have the luxury of time to recreate the Western experience of brick-and-mortar universities. Indian higher education faces a 'trilemma' in trying to simultaneously address scale, cost and quality issues (Kapur 2011).

There is little disagreement that India needs to do much more in higher education—expand overall numbers, enhance access and improve quality. But this consensus becomes quickly contentious when it comes to addressing the fundamental trilemma: how to reconcile scale (or size), costs and quality. Notwithstanding intention and rhetoric, the policymaker has autonomy to choose only two of the three goals. Choose any two, and the third becomes automatically fixed: if the primary goals are to keep a check on costs and improve quality, then one cannot expand coverage rapidly; if, on the other hand, the key goals are rapid expansion while controlling costs, then quality will suffer. And if one wants to expand coverage and improve quality, costs will balloon, leading to the prosaic but critical question: Who pays? While all governments face this trilemma, it is more acute in India's case because of the sheer scale and rapidity of expansion.

India has addressed this trilemma by focusing on scale and costs, with quality the inevitable casualty. The 'massification' of Indian higher education was made possible by establishing thousands of new private colleges, with the bulk of expansion in professional and technical education, such as engineering, business, pharmacy, and the like. Little is known about what students learn in these institutions, and anecdotal accounts suggest that barely a tenth or so are providing any real skills.

The cost challenge was met by shifting the burden of expansion to private-sector providers and thereby to students, who in turn were granted ample loans by the financial system. As the chapter by K. P. Krishnan points out, higher education loans by the banking sector rose more than 200-fold in less than 15 years (and, including non-banking financial companies [NBFCs], by even more). Since most of these loans are held by public-sector banks, it remains to be seen what their fiscal implications may turn out to be.

The rapid expansion had a clearly positive effect on an issue that has bedevilled Indian higher education: access for hitherto marginalised social groups. In 1990, India was reeling in the aftermath of a policy decision by a minority government to sharply increase affirmative action in government jobs and education, as recommended by the Mandal Commission. A decade later, in the post-Mandal era, the divisiveness over the expansion of reservations became muted, since the system's expansion meant that the pressures of gaining admission to some colleges were no longer as acute. Indeed, as recent research has pointed out, *conditional on completing high school* there is little difference in access by social group, except for Muslims (Basant and Sen 2013). But of course, politicians are not concerned with improving the quality and completion rates at the high-school level.

Key Challenges

Quality

While at face value the huge expansion of Indian higher education appears to have addressed the rapidly rising demand, much of the system is of woeful quality, whether measured by learning or research outcomes. According to former Prime Minister Manmohan Singh, the Indian university system 'is, in many parts, in a state of disrepair .... In almost half the districts [340] in the country, higher education enrolments are abysmally low, almost two-thirds of our universities and 90 percent of our colleges are rated as below average on quality parameters...'.[3] The former Human Resource Development (HRD) minister, Arjun Singh, called higher education the 'sick child of education', omitting of course any discussion on the role of his ministry in deepening its malaise.[4] Why, despite India's robust growth and a legacy of one of the better higher education systems in developing countries, is quality so weak? Is it an inevitable casualty of rapid expansion, or did the quality deterioration occur much earlier, especially in the state universities in the 1970s?

Various indicators employed to study the quality of higher education in India, such as research output, infrastructure and placement of graduates, point to multiple weaknesses. No Indian university appears in any of the top-200 lists of the leading world university ranking surveys (Times Higher Education, Quacquarelli Symonds and Shanghai Jiao Tong University). Two Indian universities figure in the top 400 of the 2016–17 Times Higher Education list (the Indian Institute of Science, Bangalore, and IIT-Bombay) and another three (all IITs) in the top 500, while just one made it to the Shanghai Ranking's top 500 in 2016 (Indian Institute of Science). Note that even these few are dominated by engineering and technology-focused institutions, a sorry testament to the extreme weakness of broad-based universities in the country.

The contrast with China is stark. In 1990, India's gross domestic product (GDP) (on a purchasing power parity [PPP] basis) was 83 per cent that of China's, while the number of publications was double that of China's. By 2011, India's GDP was 43 per cent that of China's, but the ratio of publications was less than 30 per cent (Table 1.2). Clearly, despite rapid economic growth and expansion of higher education over the past two decades, India has severely underperformed relative to China on a key performance indicator of higher education: scientific publications. Drawing on international comparisons, Sachi Hatakenaka's chapter makes the case that India's focus on narrowly specialised research institutions instead of multidisciplinary research universities has not served it well on the research front. Hatakenaka suggests that it is far better to focus on

TABLE 1.2: Publication Trends, 1990–2011

	China		*India*		*United States*	
	No. of publications	*No. of highly cited articles*	*No. of publications*	*No. of highly cited articles*	*No. of publications*	*No. of highly cited articles*
1990	6,104		12,346		130,559	
2001	25,730	174	15,522	103	150,817	2,894
2011	122,672	980	36,456	191	184,253	3,137

Source: Xiea, et al. 2014..

quality improvement in research and on reforming existing doctoral education rather than on a grand quantitative expansion, and this is more likely to occur in a policy environment that allows institutional diversity while rewarding innovation among institutions.

The problems are even more acute in the social sciences. While the number of economics departments in Indian universities grew from 72 in 1971 to 119 in 2001, its quality dropped severely. The number of Ph.D.s produced by one of India's premier economics faculties, the Delhi School of Economics, dropped from about 4.5 per year in the 1970s and 1990s to barely 1.5 per year in the noughties. As an official review of Indian social sciences put it, 'an even more serious problem [than funding] is the severe, and increasing, shortage, of qualified researchers. Even research institutes and universities that have a good reputation for quality are faced with a decline in both the number and quality of Ph.D. students' (The Indian Council of Social Science Research 2007).

The shortage of faculty is ubiquitous across fields. A survey by the Pay Review Committee of India's University Grants Commission (UGC) in 2008 found that 44.6 per cent of sanctioned positions of lecturers at the university level and 41 per cent at the college level were vacant (University Grants Commission 2008). In December 2008, the Indian government approved a pay hike of 70 per cent for the nearly half-million faculty in universities and colleges across the country. However, the across-the-board salary increase did not make any link between academic productivity and salaries—understandably, given the fierce resistance this would have met from a vocal interest group, namely faculty. If one adds to this the UGC rules stating that faculty in public institutions should automatically be promoted based on length of service and have a common salary structure linked to the civil service salaries set by the Pay Commission, it comes as little surprise that faculty have essentially acquired the status and behavioural attributes of *babus*.

The poor quality of Indian higher education is evident across the board, whether in doctors whose diagnostic skills are less than quacks (Das, et al. 2012); the inability of the Indian Statistical Service, a cadre of the federal government that over the decades has produced one of the best government statistics among developing countries, to fill even two dozen positions from thousands of applicants; the difficulties facing newspaper editors in finding young people who can write correct English prose; or Delhi University's Hindi department, which has had to sharply lower its admission standards since most of the hundreds of applicants cannot write a proper essay in their mother tongue even after a college degree.

Why is Quality So Poor?

There are several reasons why Indian higher education—and its universities in particular—are in such a parlous state. The first is structural and stems from a decision made in the 1950s to create separate research institutions outside the university system. Over time, as universities became politicised, researchers fled the university system and migrated to public institutions under the umbrella of the Council of Scientific and Industrial Research (CSIR), the Department of Atomic Energy, the Indian Space Research Organization, and the Indian Council of Social Science Research (ICSSR). The bifurcation of research from teaching and the in-breeding of faculty gradually led to an entrenchment of mediocrity.

A second reason is that the massive growth has been accompanied by extreme fragmentation. The average size of an Indian college is less than half that of colleges in China. The penchant for setting up narrowly specialised institutions and wide dispersion means that instead of leveraging agglomeration economies, India has been paying a penalty for fragmentation diseconomies.

However, the most acute weakness plaguing India's higher education system is a crisis of governance, both at the regulatory level and within the university. In 2007, then Prime Minister Manmohan Singh (who was previously a professor at Delhi University) lamented, 'I am concerned that in many states university appointments, including that of vice-chancellors, have been politicised and have become subject to caste and communal considerations, there are complaints of favouritism and corruption.'

The core of the governance problem lies in the nature of the highly centralised state regulation of higher education that seeks to micromanage who can teach what, to whom, and at what cost. Table 1.3 gives an overview of the statutory regulators of Indian higher education. Its effects can be gauged from the bleak assessment of former cabinet member Kapil Sibal: 'There is not such a thing as

UGC (University Grants Commission), there is not such a thing as AICTE (All India Council for Technical Education), there is not such a thing as MCI (Medical Council of India) [in the western world]. They [have] destroyed our entire efforts to take education forward.'[5]

TABLE 1.3: Statutory Regulators in Indian Higher Education

Function	*Institution*
Universities	*University Grants Commission (UGC)*
All aspects of 'technical education', including engineering/technology and management	*All India Council for Technical Education (AICTE)*
Medical education	*Medical Council of India (MCI)* *Central Council of Indian Medicine* Pharmacy Council of India Indian Nursing Council Dental Council of India
Legal education	Bar Council of India (BCI)
Teaching	*National Council for Teacher Education (NCTE)*
Architecture	Council of Architecture

Note: Regulators in italics are pre-approval bodies, while the ambit of the others is confined to the recognition of professional qualifications in their respective disciplines.

While there is much truth in this statement, few countries have a central ministry, ministers and bureaucrats as involved in higher education decision-making as India, and whose choices of regulators have in the first place singularly undermined these institutions. The Ministry of Human Resource Development combines multiples roles, from policy formulation to funding to regulation, through an extremely top-down—and often arbitrary—approach. The picture is even worse in the states since higher education enrolments are still dominated by state universities, which require approvals by state legislatures. (Private universities also require legislative approval by either the Parliament or state legislatures, but in addition, need recognition by the UGC to operate.) As with most issues related to human capital in India, while public attention focuses on the role of the central government, in the aggregate, states play a greater role.

And when it comes to higher education, states have, with very few exceptions, played a uniformly feeble if not unsavoury role.

Even though Indian states differ considerably in economic performance and the political parties that dominate them, somewhat inexplicably, when it comes to state universities, virtually all are poorly governed. The state universities charge little and teach little, yet there is likewise little political pressure or leadership to undertake painful reforms. And the consequences are becoming apparent. The maximum number of new colleges opened in any state in 2013–14 was in Madhaya Pradesh—five new colleges every week. Yet, during this time, one of India's worst higher education scandals (Vyapam) was unfolding, driven by the reality that despite the huge expansion in higher education in that state, students are still desperate to get into the few institutions that have any signalling value in labour markets.

The apex statutory body regulating higher education in India is the University Grants Commission (UGC), whose approval is mandatory for the creation of any new university. Its rules, regulations and guidelines are binding on all universities, but exclude technical and professional education. The UGC's mandatory rules for teacher recruitment and promotion have ensured that they will never be able to attract and retain talent in sufficient numbers for a serious research culture to take root. A weak leadership has meant that it is ready to bend to whichever political wind is blowing, as exemplified by the fiasco of Delhi University's attempt to introduce a semester system.

The executive branch—both at the centre and the states—often overrides the regulators and even flouts the courts. To take one example: in 2003, the Supreme Court of India ruled that the MCI (Medical Council of India) was the only authority that could recommend an increase in student strength or a renewal of permission for medical colleges. That order had directed the central government 'not to grant any further permission without following the procedure prescribed under the Indian Medical Council Act'. In 2008, the MCI denied permission to two medical colleges to take new students, based on a report by a government-appointed lawyer stating that their facilities were 'inadequate'. The very same day, the Health Ministry permitted these same two private medical colleges to take in more students! Little wonder, then, that a report prepared by the National Institute of Public Finance and Policy on 'black money' generated in India, submitted to the Indian government (which had officially commissioned it) in December 2013, estimated that the capitation fees collected by private colleges on management quota seats in professional courses was approximately Rs 5,953 crore in 2013. With so much money at stake, it is not surprising that officials in virtually every higher education regulatory institution, be it the AICTE, MCI, National Council for Teacher Education (NCTE), etc., have been indicted for corruption.

The failure of the principal regulator, the UGC, together with its parent ministry, the HRD Ministry, has inflicted grievous wounds on Indian higher education, whether approving thousands of dubious colleges or scores of questionable universities, most run by politicians or their networks. A government committee set up in 2009 to review the functioning and academic standards of 'deemed universities' found 44 institutions unfit for the status and another 44 deficient on several counts, including 13 public universities and 31 private. Unsurprisingly, nearly half of these had links to politicians, who were in turn linked to constituent parties of the United Progressive Alliance (UPA) government. However, the UGC, which had granted them the status in the first place, decided to keep these cases 'in abeyance', which meant that the institutions kept the deemed tag by default. As for the 44 institutions found unfit by the review panel, they obtained a stay order from the Supreme Court, whose own role in Indian higher education is not inconsiderable, as the chapter by Devesh Kapur and Madhav Khosla argues.

The regulatory morass—together with multiple failures in the internal governance of higher education institutions in India—has led to increased litigation, and the courts have become the regulator of last resort, in a manner of speaking. The chapter by Kapur and Khosla in this volume examines the role of the Supreme Court, but the High Courts also exercise their writ jurisdiction from time to time, and together they have created 'higher education' jurisprudence. But, as with many other complex policy issues, the courts are a poor remedy for addressing the failures of the executive branch and indeed, as Kapur and Khosla demonstrate, often make matters worse.

Higher education is the last refuge of the 'license raj', with severe political, administrative and regulatory interference in virtually every aspect of the sector, be it admissions policies, internal organisation, fees and salaries, and the structure of courses and funding. The resulting rent-seeking behaviour is an inevitable consequence of centralised, detailed administrative regulation and bureaucratic control. While the private sector has massively ramped up supply, the quality of most new private-sector colleges (many linked to politicians) leaves much to be desired. Their governance problems may be different from public institutions, but are no less acute. This is more by design than happenstance, as a highly centralised regulatory system deliberately allows money-making institutions that prey on students to come up, while making it exceedingly difficult for genuine education providers to enter. The adverse consequences are manifest on many dimensions.[6]

First, the process of regulatory approvals diminishes the capacity of private investment to respond to market needs. Second, the regulatory process produces an adverse selection in the kind of entrepreneurs who invest, since the success of a project depends less upon the pedagogic design of the project than upon the ability to manipulate the regulatory system. As a result, private investment in higher education is driven principally by profit-making goals, and not by education as a public trust. Consequently, private-sector investment has been confined to professional streams, bypassing the majority of students and also suffering severe governance weaknesses, raising doubts as to its ability to addresses the substantial and latent demand for quality higher education in the country. Third, there are significant market failures in acquiring physical assets that are necessary for institutions, especially land. Fourth, since regulatory approvals are extremely rigid with regard to infrastructure requirements (irrespective of costs or location) and an insistence on academic conformity to centrally mandated course outlines, degree structures and admissions policies, this system, which is so large, leaves virtually no room for innovation and creativity. Fifth, a key element of a well-functioning market, competition, is distorted by not allowing foreign universities to set up campuses in India, limiting benchmarking to global standards. And finally, the central element of a well-functioning market, informational transparency, is woefully inadequate.

A third reason for the quality of Indian higher education being so poor lies in the key cleavages and drivers of Indian politics. As

Arjun Singh, former cabinet minister for higher education, argued, 'Inclusion and access with equity are the core issues that confront us today.'[7] With higher education a key battleground for distributional conflicts (and not just in India), it is not surprising that quality emerges as the inevitable collateral damage to the larger 'core' issues.

There is sufficient awareness of the problems afflicting Indian higher education at the highest levels of the Indian government, as evident from the quotes cited above from a range of key cabinet members. Why, then, has the Indian state not acted upon and addressed them? One reason may be that higher education is arguably one of the most difficult sectors to reform—and not just in India. University employees (both faculty and administration) and students are among the most vocal and well-organised political groups in any country. Even as unions have weakened in virtually all aspects of economic activity, public educational institutions remain a rare exception. Direct exit options—such as shutting down poorly performing departments or colleges—sharply increase the risks of an immediate political reaction.

The regulatory approach has been 'command and control', and universities are beset with direct and detailed prescriptions, with laws, rules, regulations, guidelines, and policies set by the government and multiple regulatory bodies. Underlying this model is a deep-rooted distrust of allowing universities autonomy, even after their initial approval. That distrust has been so disempowering as to have contributed to the very mediocrity and poor governance among most Indian universities that it was meant to overcome, but ironically it has become the rationale for continued control.

As Pankaj Chandra argues in his chapter in this volume, a critical but much-neglected challenge besetting Indian higher education institutions is the weaknesses in internal governance, and a key stakeholder—faculty—has much to answer for. The travails of the proposed four-year programme of Delhi University, one of the most visible public universities in India, are a stark illustration of the sheer bankruptcy of regulation and internal governance. Several years ago, in another of India's oldest universities, the University of Mumbai, when aspiring politician Aditya Thackeray of the right-wing Shiv Sena political party called for removing Rohinton Mistry's book *Such A Long Journey*, the alacrity with which the ruling Nationalist

Congress Party (NCP)-Congress alliance in Maharashtra endorsed the Shiv Sena's stand was matched only by an almost instantaneous notification of the ban by the university's vice-chancellor, indicative of his alleged proximity to a political party.

The regulatory structures governing Indian higher education were created for a system that has grown more than 100-fold since the time that it was put into place and the overall regulatory system was part of the overall system of Indian planning. Today, in the case of public institutions, scale effects dwarf the limited capacity of centralised systems of oversight and control. To take an example: a key feature of the institutional design of all central universities is to have the President of India as a Visitor, and for state universities, the governor of that state (first enshrined in the Model Act Committee of the Government of India, 1964). The Visitor's role was meant to exercise the power of enquiring into the affairs of the university, but was to be used in exceptional cases. But the sheer expansion of the system has meant that ex officio status simply leads to more attention span deficits. Indeed, if these constitutional functionaries actually attended all governing council meetings of the many institutions that they are supposed to supervise, they would have little time for anything else. In the 1950s, when India had a handful of central universities, the apolitical and distinguished stature of the office of the President added a lustre to these institutions. But by 2014, the President was to be the Visitor of 114 central institutions, ranging from central universities to NITs, IITs, IISERs, etc., under the administrative control of the Ministry of HRD; as well as other higher education institutions under the administrative control of the Ministries of Shipping, External Affairs, Agriculture, Sports, Textiles, and Chemicals and Fertilisers. Moreover, it is hardly a state secret that the quality of politicians who now find their way to governorships or even to the presidency is a long way from when these policies were put into place nearly half a century ago. The effects of these arrangements on the institutions, or for that matter on the discharge of the multiple other responsibilities of the country's highest constitutional office, need better understanding.[8]

Under the UPA government, attempts were made to overhaul the regulatory structures governing higher education, moving away from intrusive inspection-based processes to accountability through independent third-party validation, mandatory self-disclosures, and objective evaluation schemes. These proposals were ostensibly meant to encourage the state to take a more differentiated approach towards a highly variegated higher education sector, with a more hands-off 'promotional and evaluative' role for the set of upper-tier institutions, a more engaged 'steering role' in mid-tier institutions, and active regulation confined to lower-tier institutions; and at the same time, end the artificial separation between the regulation of 'technical' education from other fields. Accreditation was seen as a central plank of these reforms to ensure that poorly performing institutions were dealt with swiftly.

A series of bills was introduced in Parliament to this effect (although all stalled there). These included the National Accreditation Regulatory Authority for Higher Educational Institutions Bill, which sought to make accreditation by independent agencies mandatory for all higher education institutions; the Education Tribunals Bill to create a central tribunal and state-level tribunals to resolve disputes relating to institutions, faculty, students, and regulatory authorities; and the National Commission for Higher Education and Research (NCHER) Bill, to create an umbrella 'super' regulatory authority which would subsume the principal higher education regulators (UGC, AICTE, NCTE, and the Distance Education Council [DEC]).

As one of us argued, the drafts were 'so awful, so contrary to common sense and sensible regulatory principles' that they simply reinforced 'the impression that there was still a great deal of arbitrariness in the way government functions', and 'the fundamental infirmity in the present system: that the HRD ministry knows best, and has the license to bypass established process' (Mehta 2010). Instead of a carefully circumscribed dispute resolution mechanism, the Tribunals Bill appeared to grant the tribunal the power to adjudicate everything, from affiliation-related matters to service conditions to student grievances, with the last issue clearly best addressed through better in-house mechanisms. And by staffing the education tribunals with retiring Indian Administrative Service (IAS) officers, it not only violated the norms of judicial representation laid out by the Supreme Court, but also sent a depressing message about the value of academic autonomy and norms.

A different path to improving quality has been to create accreditation systems such as the National Assessment and Accreditation Council and the National Board of Accreditation, autonomous bodies set up by the UGC and the All India Council of Technical Education (AICTE), respectively. However, accreditation is voluntary, with about one-fifth of the colleges and less than one-third of all universities being accredited. An important driver in the decision to separate the National Board of Accreditation from the AICTE was to meet the requirements of the Washington Accord, an international agreement for recognising engineering degrees of signatory countries, which requires the accreditation body to be separate from the agency giving approval to engineering institutions (India was accorded membership in 2014).

The inability to regulate at the college/university level exposes a centralised regulatory structure that simply cannot cope with the sheer size of the system, and even more so when it is poorly staffed. Regulation might work better if it shifts from an input-based model to an outcome-based one. The creation of an All India Bar Examination, conducted by the Bar Council of India, marked the first time that a profession in India (other than the exams of the Institute of Chartered Accountants of India and the Institute of Cost Accountants of India) has attempted to shift to an output-based model of quality control. By creating a check for eligibility rather than expertise, it emphasises that students who graduate from law schools must possess a certain degree of legal knowledge, as well as the need to create a common set of standards across the country in this profession (Khosla 2010). If the exam standards are maintained, over the long run it should result in the improvement of law schools throughout India (but this is precisely why the experiment has faced much resistance).

The lack of institutional autonomy and poor academic governance have made it increasingly difficult for higher education to attract talent, especially since (unlike in the past) talent has alternatives. In many cases, talent has been driven out and, as individuals at the upper end of human capital distribution leave, the remaining pool is of poorer quality. This not only prompts the more talented to also consider leaving, but also discourages those who left earlier from returning, ensuring that mediocrity becomes entrenched in these institutions. While salaries are an issue, a poor overall academic environment is a much more acute impediment. In most government institutions, the focus is on process rather than performance; appointments are politicised; and autonomy in administration, financing and academic content is minimal. Resources are an undoubted constraint, but more flexible rules, access to modest research resources, and a work environment that encourages innovative practices and research can achieve much.

Access

Access is deeply intertwined with the much larger question of social justice, and few issues have been more contentious in Indian higher education policy than those related to social justice. There is fierce disagreement over the nature and form of affirmative action in higher education, and whether the goal of increasing access can be better achieved than with fixed quotas (or 'reservations') based on seemingly unchanging ascriptive identities. Despite its slow pace, the hierarchies and conditions that informed the original intent of affirmative action policies in India are undergoing gradual transformation; yet policies remain structured around seemingly immutable identities, most notably caste, with little attention to other axes of marginalisation, whether religion, parental education, or income.

Debates on affirmative action as *the* means to increase the representation of socially marginalised groups have been so contentious that, for many decades, they dominated virtually every other issue in Indian higher education. While the framers of India's constitution were deeply concerned with the ideals of social justice and equality, these progressive ideas ran contrary to the pervasive and deeply rooted social hierarchy and severe discrimination in India's caste system. In order to redress centuries of discrimination against India's lowest castes (the Scheduled Castes or Dalits) and indigenous peoples (the Scheduled Tribes), the Indian constitution enshrined the most comprehensive system of compensatory discrimination for these groups, known as 'reservations'. Seats in federal and state legislatures and jobs in civil services and state-owned enterprises were reserved in proportion to their share of the population. The same was the case in public higher education institutions (except in those run by minorities).[9]

The fundamental need for reservations was obvious in post-independence India. Indeed, given India's manifest inequalities, there continues to be a strong case for affirmative action there. Given the continued deep-rooted prejudices in Indian society, sustained and protracted efforts at social inclusion are fundamentally necessary for higher education to serve as an engine of opportunity (Deshpande and Zacharias 2013). But the issue of how to put a laudatory principle into action while balancing multiple goals and multiple constituencies has proven to be much harder.

Like the infant-industry argument, affirmative action programmes tend to take on a life of their own, as more and more groups press their claims to avail the benefits. The Indian constitution contains a clause allowing the federal and state governments to make 'any special provision for the advancement of any socially and educationally backward classes of citizens or for the Scheduled Castes and Scheduled Tribes'. Over time, the expansiveness and ambiguity of the clause 'any socially and educationally backward classes of citizens' opened a Pandora's box. While affirmative action has had some success in reducing inter-group inequality, it has tended to amplify intra-group inequalities. Broad social categories like 'Scheduled Castes', 'Scheduled Tribes' and 'Other Backward Castes' tend to gloss over the fact that these are themselves extremely heterogeneous categories that contain their own internal hierarchies. Consequently, the benefits of reservations are disproportionately garnered by some sub-groups. Finally, perhaps the most inimical impact is that these policies have resulted in enormous political energy and effort being spent on including increasingly more social groups, rather than improving and expanding the quality of supply by focusing on primary and secondary education. The last is especially important for economically weaker groups, since a weak foundation of cognitive and non-cognitive skills in early childhood makes it much harder to take advantage of higher education opportunities.

Debates on affirmative action are, of course, by no means unique to India. There continue to be widely divergent views on the role of higher education in society. Governments increasingly want universities to be 'engines of social justice' on the one hand, as well as 'handmaidens of industry' or 'implementers of the skills agenda' on the other. Recently, Alison Richard, Cambridge University's vice-chancellor, said that while institutions such as hers 'try to reach out to the best students, whatever their background', and that 'one outcome of that is that we can help to promote social mobility', nevertheless, 'promoting social mobility is not our core mission. Our core mission is to provide an outstanding education within a research setting' (Shepard 2008). And even if social mobility is an important goal, how should group rights be balanced against individual rights?

The effects of affirmative action policies on higher education have been extremely contentious, from its supposed 'crowding out' effects on better prepared students from non-reserved categories to the possible effects on less well-prepared students in the reserved categories in elite institutions. However, a study of affirmative action in engineering colleges in Maharashtra finds that affirmative action policy has increased attendance among targeted students, improving exams results, and with little adverse effects on graduation rates, especially for SCs, STs and women, but less for OBCs (Bagde, et al. 2016). Advocates highlight the important 'role model' effect of such programmes for disadvantaged groups and the many positive payoffs of diversity, while critics argue that these programmes perpetuate stereotypes. What criteria (or sunset clauses) should be used to phase out these programmes? There is little agreement on even the most basic questions. Under what conditions do such programmes entrench identity politics or instead gradually erode them? Then there are practical questions of how to implement these programmes. To what extent should governments use control or incentive mechanisms to oversee such programmes? What should be the policy at private institutions, given their growing importance? And how should the design of such programmes reflect not only the normative aspects, but also the reality of how political considerations will impact implementation?

In 2006, in an attempt to bolster its electoral base among India's largest social group, the Congress-led UPA government extended reservation benefits to the 'Other Backward Classes' (OBCs) in educational institutions run by the federal government. There are ongoing disputes about the statistical data used by the Government of India and Indian states to offer reservation benefits to these groups, especially since the possibility of entitlements has led to increasingly more social groups claiming that they are more backward than the others. Sundaram (2006) argues that representation of a social group can only be judged by a comparison of its share in enrolments at a given level of education with its share in the population eligible for entry into that level of education, rather than the population as a whole. By this criteria, for India's OBCs (and especially for over 70 per cent of them who are above the poverty line), their extent of under-representation in enrolments in Indian universities was less than 5 per cent (based on an analysis of the NSS 55th round surveys for 1999–2000). Affirmative action programmes that are based on identity rather than income or poverty—especially for a social group such as India's OBCs, whose social and economic conditions reflect the average in the country—risk the better-off within the group monopolising all of the privileges, with little benefit to the vast majority *within* that group.

Studies show that, once the likelihood of completion of high school is taken into account, the under-representation of socially marginalised groups in higher education is much less in the aggregate (but can still be substantial in elite institutions). The likelihood of undertaking higher education increases dramatically for marginalised groups, conditional on crossing the threshold of high school education. In India, this increase is particularly sharp for women and in rural areas. All socio-religious groups except upper-caste Hindus and 'other minorities' are under-represented. However, this declines once flow (rather than stock) measures are considered (suggesting improvements over time), and declines significantly when we compare across only the eligible population, that is, those who have completed high school.

A policy regime that keeps reservations for the designated groups, but which restricts benefits to two generations of a household would both allow economic gains and the development of cultural capital within households, while also ensuring that the benefits of these policies would spread more widely to other households within the group. And, given that the chances of participation in higher education increase significantly with parental education and are highest when the parents have a college-level education, this would indicate that giving preference to children whose parents have not gone to college (and then to those whose mothers have not gone to college) would provide a refreshing opportunity to broaden the debate on affirmative action to include other axes of marginalisation that deter access. It would also gradually shift affirmative action criteria to those that are—at least in principle—both fair and non-ascriptive, and thereby further the goal of higher education as a ladder of social mobility.

If the problem of access is largely due to prior economic and social disabilities—in particular, learning and completion at the secondary-school level—the lack of tracing studies that follow outcomes of 'reserved' candidates compared to the rest is a further impediment to fully understanding the benefits of this strategy. The limited evidence available suggests that admission alone would be insufficient to equalise career outcomes. One analysis based on data from one of India's most elite institutions, IIM-Ahmedabad, found that graduates who came through affirmative action (SC or ST) earned significantly lower wages (between one-fifth and one-third) than those admitted in the general category (Chakravarty and Somanathan 2008). However, this difference disappeared when the (lower) Grade Point Averages of SC/ST candidates were accounted for, suggesting that the wage differences could be due to the (on average) weaker academic performance of SC/ST candidates. This has little to do with intrinsic capabilities but rather appears to be the result of poor quality of schooling prior to entering higher education, the weakness of remedial programmes, and little effort to better integrate the student body as a whole so as to leverage peer-based learning. These findings highlight a singular weakness in Indian public policy, namely an obsession with inputs, but little regard to outcomes.

Financing

Higher education systems around the world are grappling with costs. Developing countries like India that are rapidly scaling up face several additional—and concurrent—challenges: how to reconcile scale (or size) with quality, access and costs. Access, discussed above, is somewhat easier to achieve when there is rapid expansion, and in some ways, the huge expansion of Indian higher education has diffused the access issue at the aggregate level, at least. But rapid expansion inevitably means that aggregate expenditure on higher education will balloon, leading to the prosaic but critical question: Who pays? While all governments face this challenge, it is more acute in India's case because of the rapid expansion in coverage and the existing low quality of higher education in the country.

Of the two main goals of higher education—teaching and research—the first is (largely) a private good whose gains can be appropriated by students through increased lifetime incomes. However, students may be financially constrained and, especially for low-income students, financial costs can be insurmountable. Consequently, publicly supported scholarships and loans are critical to ensuring access for students from lower-income households. Research—and especially university research—is largely a public good whose gains cannot be appropriated privately, and therefore needs substantial public funding. It is therefore not surprising that all of the great research universities in the world (including private universities) receive the majority of their funding from public sources.

At the time of independence, India had a dismally low level of literacy (barely 18 per cent in 1950). Nonetheless, between the early 1950s and early 1970s, the share of primary education in public expenditure dropped, while spending on higher education increased from one-quarter to one-third of the education budget. By the early 1970s, as the economy languished, unemployment among university graduates grew and became one of the drivers of social unrest and political turmoil during this period. As a result, for the next quarter-century, higher education spending and growth stagnated, and the gross enrolment ratio barely grew by 2–3 per cent as India's economy remained closed.

Since the mid-1970s, the share of total government spending on elementary education has been between 35–50 per cent; on secondary education, between 20–30 per cent; and on higher education, between 13–18 per cent. Between 1980 and 2000, education spending increased from nearly 3 per cent of GDP to 4.3 per cent. It declined to 3.3 per cent in 2004, before again increasing to 4.2 per cent in 2011–12. Much of the recent increase in public spending has come from the central government, but even so, the states account for three-fourths of total public education spending (Ministry of Human Resource Development 2013). However, the 'massification' of Indian higher education has resulted primarily from the immense expansion of the private sector, largely in undergraduate colleges, but those that are still predominantly affiliated to state universities.

As a result, increasingly large numbers of students are self-financing. As the chapter by K. P. Krishnan in this volume argues, this trend began when a 'New Educational Loan Scheme' was formulated at the turn of the millennium. In 2004–05, more liberal rules further boosted education lending, making it possible to borrow up to Rs 10 lakh for domestic education and Rs 20 lakh for studying in foreign colleges. From barely Rs 300 crore at the beginning of the decade, the educational loan portfolio jumped to Rs 4,000 crore in 2005, and then shot up to about Rs 40,000 crore in 2010 (with about two million accounts and an average loan size of Rs 2 lakh), climbing further to Rs 57,700 crore in 2013. Banks (and especially public-sector banks) initially provided funds only for overseas education, but soon expanded to loans for students studying in reputed Indian institutions. Subsequently, they gradually began funding students attending second-tier institutions and slowly even lower-quality colleges, as competition increased. Most recently, they have tied up directly with institutes to have a guaranteed clientele. As with many aspects of higher education, courts have complicated the picture. In a curious decision, the Madras High Court ruled that nationalised banks cannot deny education loans to students obtaining lower marks on the grounds that, since the government has prescribed only 35 per cent for admission to SC/ST students, the bank could not insist on higher cut-offs (in this case, 45 per cent).

Unsurprisingly, this massive increase has been accompanied by mounting non-performing assets (NPAs) in education loans. Banks cannot ask for any collateral for loans up to Rs 4 lakh, which is where the problem seems to be growing. The full implications of this massive expansion will not be known for many years, but there are reasons to be worried. A proposed National Education Finance Corporation (NEFC) will primarily refinance the banks that give education-related loans, guaranteeing 75 per cent of the defaults for loans made to weaker sections and 50 per cent of the defaults on loans between Rs 4.5–12 lakh, while there would be no guarantee on loans above Rs 12 lakh.[10] The expansion of scholarships and loans has certainly increased access widely, but access to what? If the access is to poor-quality education, then the ability to repay is low. And, to the extent that these poor-quality education institutions are owned by politicians, in the end this may simply end up being a large transfer from the public exchequer to connected politicians.

Internationalising Higher Education

With a national economy that is becoming more globally integrated and a rising global profile, India's higher education might have been expected to follow suit in becoming more international as well. Yet, if anything, this is another contentious issue that has generated more heat than light.

A self-confident leadership of post-independent India had actively courted international collaborations as it set about creating the new IITs and IIMs. A less heralded, but equally successful, international collaboration occurred in the development of nine state agricultural universities in the 1960s, in collaboration with US land-grant universities. Subsequently, the insecurity of Indian intellectual thought has made it more suspicious of foreign institutions. Unlike China, where foreign universities have partnered particularly with China's top public universities, the controls in India have been much more onerous.

A country can participate in international higher education in multiple ways. The World Trade Organization's (WTO) General Agreement on Trade in Services (GATS) framework on cross-border higher education is a globally accepted standard that distinguishes between four distinct mechanisms (Table 1.4): Mode 1: Cross-border supply; Mode 2: Consumption abroad; Mode 3: Commercial presence; and Mode 4: Presence of natural persons.

The international component of India's higher education has been historically dominated by Mode 2 and, to a much more modest extent, Modes 3 and 4. The former comprises the decision by tens of thousands of students to seek higher education abroad and personally finance their studies abroad (or look for financing through scholarships). While historically this has been the mechanism whereby India's political, business, scientific, and bureaucratic elites (exemplified by the leadership of India's nationalist movement, including Gandhi, Nehru, Ambedkar, Bose, and Patel) sought to augment their human capital, it has now broadened to India's middle

TABLE 1.4: Modes of Supply of Services under the WTO's General Agreement on Trade in Services (GATS)

GATS mode of supply	*Description*	*Examples from higher education*
Mode 1. Cross-border supply	Delivery of education services from exporting country A to importing country B	Distance education, tele-education, education testing services, education via Internet; Massive Open Online Courses (MOOCs)
Mode 2. Consumption abroad	Movement of students from importing country B to exporting country A to obtain education services	Indian students studying in foreign universities and foreign students studying in India
Mode 3. Commercial presence	Establishment of local unit of institution from exporting country A to importing country B	Foreign university and college offerings through branch campuses or subsidiaries of institutions, franchising, twinning/ articulated arrangements, etc.
Mode 4. Presence of natural persons	Temporary movement of teachers, lecturers and education personnel from country A to country B to provide education services	Teacher exchange programmes; joint research programmes; post-doctoral fellowships

classes, who face severe supply constraints in the availability of quality higher education institutions within the country, but now have the financial resources to purchase higher education abroad. It is important to note here that this leg of internationalisation of Indian higher education is primarily driven by household decisions, and is largely independent of government policies (other than government failures that have made it highly difficult for quality institutions to thrive in India).

Nonetheless, the sheer scale and needs of Indian higher education, the limited capacity of students to pay the high fees of foreign providers, and the marked caution on the part of the best research universities to set up new overseas branch campuses means that while the number of Indian students going abroad will continue to grow, the numbers will remain modest (2–3 per cent) relative to the number of students studying in higher education institutions within the country. Overseas education will cater to niche groups of students, especially from upper-class families or in specific fields of study or specific education levels, especially at the postgraduate level. Nonetheless, given the severe supply-demand imbalance of quality higher education institutions within the country, even these (relatively) modest numbers mean that Indian students are spending substantial amounts of money on purchasing higher education abroad (approximately $5.5 billion, as per a Ministry of Human Resource Development report from March 2011), relative to public expenditures on higher education within the country.

The second leg of the internationalisation of India's higher education has been driven by a variety of efforts to attract foreign higher education institutions to operate within India itself. In the 1950s and 1960s, the government made concerted efforts to work with foreign governments and invite leading institutions around the world to help set up high-quality Indian institutions. The best examples of this were the IITs, IIMs and agriculture universities. In the case of the IITs, each of the early schools was assisted in its first years through links with leading science and technology institutions to set up research laboratories and academic programmes. A less heralded, but nevertheless successful, example—albeit active for only a couple of decades—is that of the international linkages that helped to build Indian agriculture universities. In 1960, India decided to create State Agricultural Universities (SAUs), based on land-grant universities in the United States, which were directly responsible to the states and outside the control of the Ministry of Education.

Regrettably, the self-confidence and cognitive openness to the benefits of international linkages that characterised the Government of India's thinking about Indian higher education in the 1950s and 1960s waned over the following three decades. But an ill-judged Foreign Educational Institutions Bill failed to address a fundamental tension. The policies to attract international universities are not too different from those to build good domestic universities in India, just as foreign direct investment (FDI) does not come into a country if its domestic capital is unwilling to invest. Any special benefits will simply tilt the playing field against domestic institutions, which are already suffering from an egregious regulatory system and terrible internal governance. If foreign institutions are to be attracted, they need to be given considerable autonomy. But how can a democracy justify special privileges for foreign institutions while it ties the hands of domestic ones?

Nonetheless, much of the opposition to the entry of foreign institutions is sui generis. High costs, and therefore fees, alone would ensure that foreign providers would only occupy niche markets. But the most puzzling question is why Indian intellectuals and policymakers would rather see Indian students spend billions of dollars consuming higher education abroad rather than invite foreign institutions within the country, so that at least some of the funds are spent in-country. As for commercialisation, it is difficult to imagine how foreign institutions could do worse than what thousands of private Indian institutions are brazenly doing.

However, perhaps the most promising channel for internationalising higher education is one that has been virtually absent until now, namely cross-border supply (or Mode One). The onset of Massive Open Online Courses (MOOCs) holds the possibility of vastly expanding the supply of high-quality education at an affordable price in emerging economies like India, and already Indian students have emerged as one of the largest subscribers to such courses. MOOCs are a disruptive technology with potentially far-reaching effects on higher education, and whether (and how) India should leapfrog and embrace it is still an open question (for a detailed discussion, see Alcorn, et al. 2015).

Instead, the Indian government has engaged in grandiose pretensions that reaffirm its impoverished thinking on internationalising Indian higher education. It announced a grant of Rs 25 crore to Oxford University for the Indira Gandhi Centre for Sustainable Development in Somerville College. By 2011, it had created (through the Indian Council for Cultural Relations) 92 chairs in universities around the world; committed a projected $300 million in capital costs for the South Asia University, not including a 100-acre plot of land in a prime locality of south Delhi; and was in the hock for spending another Rs 2,500 crore to support Nalanda University, which, while in principle has international stakeholders, will in the end be financed largely by the Government of India.

Yet, at the same time, India has refused to pick lower-hanging fruit: allowing universities and institutes to recruit talent globally—with flexibility in contracts and pay; removing the proscription on Persons of Indian Origin (PIOs) from conducting 'research'; creating National Visiting Professorships—especially in S&T fields—as China has done, and leveraging them to train faculty and graduate students in India; reducing the high transaction costs of holding conferences in India by making it easier for foreign scholars and students to obtain visas; leveraging the potential of MOOCs by subsidising the translation of some course material into multiple Indian languages; making broadband cheaply accessible across the country; and ensuring that the regulatory frameworks for credentialing are simple and transparent. More than anything else, India needs to bring talent into India, whether individuals or institutions, rather than fritter away scarce resources on more new vanity projects.

Book Outline

The above discussion has described the range of challenges that Indian higher education is currently facing, the various considerations that animate the crises in higher education, and the solutions that are currently being debated. The conference from which this volume has emerged aimed to contribute to ongoing debates on higher education in India by delving into some of the aforementioned issues: the challenges, the factors that have contributed to amplify or attenuate these challenges, and possible pathways out of the morass. The chapters in this volume contribute in different ways to these debates.

Apoorvanand's deeply poignant and heartfelt story of the decline of a college in north Bihar brings out the challenges facing Indian higher education better than reams of data and statistics. His human tale is a work of remarkable introspection. Part memoir, part institutional history, the chapter forces us to see the struggles and triumphs of universities through the ways in which they are lived. A better understanding of the daily battle lived within an average college might be the most significant lesson for the future of higher education reform. The chapter is also a testimony, both to higher education's higher calling in cultivating the mind and to the critical role that the humanities play in bringing this about—and no less to the loss of both when higher education is reduced to a crude instrumental role.

Higher (or post-secondary) education covers a vast terrain, ranging from the research university to teaching colleges to institutes that impart skills through certification and diplomas rather than college degrees. The next three chapters in the volume focus on each of these three institutional mechanisms. Sachi Hatakenaka's detailed chapter situates the Indian experience in building university research and graduate education within an international context. The core concern which the chapter addresses is how to deepen research and research training within the higher education system. The most important element, Hatakenaka argues, is the establishment of multidisciplinary research universities—a sobering counter to the expansion of narrowly specialised research institutions. Rather than support the current expansion of Ph.D. education, Hatakenaka suggests that it is far better to focus on improving the quality of research and reforming existing Ph.D. education instead of embarking on a grand quantitative expansion. This reform must involve a move away from the Ph.D. as merely a kind of informal apprenticeship towards a programme that caters to the demand for higher skills. Hatakenaka also explores the importance of distinguishing between universities and national research institutions, and the need to build basic research capacity and develop research universities. Finally, Hatakenaka's chapter predicts that India's future solutions are unlikely to be simple and top-down, solutions that aim to magically work for every single institution in the country. Given the diversity of India's challenges, it is essential to create a policy environment that rewards innovation among institutions, and enables them to bring different strengths and perspectives to the overall mosaic of higher education in the country. This would also encourage competition, and push institutions towards more effective and innovative forms of action.

For the vast majority of India's population that still lives in rural and small-town India, the promise of higher education continues to be a distant mirage. While the market economy places greater demands on the skills of employees, India's rural population has hardly any access to education that would equip it with skills. One answer might be community colleges, the subject of Manish

Sabharwal and Srinivasan Kannan's chapter. The community college, they argue, 'can provide the necessary support with its potential for a variety of programmes ranging from credential-based academic offerings in vocational and technical domains, to capacity building and life skills-oriented community education initiatives.' In addition to providing an education that serves as its own end, community colleges provide students with the skills necessary to gain employment, and thereby offer a kind of remedial education that puts such students on par with university graduates seeking baccalaureate recognition. Sabharwal and Kannan examine the role of community colleges in supporting micro, small and medium enterprises, and as a supportive mechanism for work-related learning. Together, these benefits make a powerful case in support of community colleges. Through this study, they help us appreciate the promise of this emerging model of higher education in India, which can potentially provide new rampways to both enter and exit higher education.

Megha Aggarwal's chapter addresses another dimension of higher education's role in skill development in India. While on the one hand, a significant proportion of educated youth face employment difficulties, on the other hand, the private sector faces difficulties in finding skilled workers. Aggarwal addresses this paradox and identifies important ways in which it can be addressed. A strong system for skill development or vocational education and training is particularly important, Aggarwal argues, given that 90 per cent of the labour force currently operates in the unorganised sector. Without addressing this, India's much talked-about demographic dividend will atrophy. Aggarwal's focus is on the supply side, laying special emphasis on the kinds of initiatives that have attempted to remedy the problem of skill development in India. After examining various initiatives, the chapter considers critical institutional issues that need to be addressed for both private and government-led skill development, in particular the regulatory framework as an enabler of quality and the funding mechanisms that enable access.

A critical but often forgotten issue in debates on higher education is its links with labour markets. In their chapter, Jeemol Unni and Sudipa Sarkar remedy this and view the demand side of the equation. They investigate whether the demand for higher education is increasing more in certain professions, the extent to which technology and knowledge-intensive industries create demand linkages for workers in occupations requiring higher education, and whether the effect of having a graduate degree on the probability of being in technology and knowledge-intensive industries differs between occupations. In addressing these questions, the chapter sheds light on one of the central questions facing higher education in India: Is there a demand for persons with higher education, or are we witnessing a situation of education inflation with a mismatch between degrees and emerging job requirements?

The fastener that links demand with supply is a banal but essential ingredient: money. K. P. Krishnan addresses the financing of higher education in India. Although as a percentage of its GDP, India spends an amount on higher education that is comparable to other countries, on a per-student basis, it is far lower. Krishnan explores interventions in higher education policy that are essential given the limitations on public budgets, such as increasing student fees or loan schemes. In an attempt to harmonise the conflicting aims of limiting public expenditure and improving access to students from underprivileged households and communities, Krishnan examines the current education model operative in India, and suggests options that can address the twin goals of access and affordability.

At the heart of the travails of Indian higher education is governance, and the final two chapters focus on different aspects of this critical and deeply problematic issue. The first examines the role of an institution whose increasing presence in governance in India extends far beyond higher education, namely the courts. Even as courts have emerged as an important actor in the regulation of Indian higher education, very little is understood about their role. The chapter by Devesh Kapur and Madhav Khosla analyses empirical patterns in both litigation and adjudication in higher education cases since the inception of India's Constitution (1950–2009). The data collected shows the number of higher education cases as a percentage of constitutional cases, the average bench strength hearing such matters, the parties which litigate (the central government, state governments, private university, and so on), and the frequency of particular issues litigated in higher education cases (reservations, fees, disciplinary action, and so on). In addition to analysing this data, Kapur and Khosla highlight how the judiciary has, since the early 1990s, regulated higher education and private educational institutions by insisting that higher education has a chartable purpose, and that institutions cannot engage in 'profiteering'. The authors explore the foundations and implications of this judicially invented regulatory requirement. Through this and other examples, the chapter highlights the extent to which the Indian Supreme Court's regulatory interventions have shaped this sector.

The chapter by Kapur and Khosla demonstrates that, in recent years, the predominant higher education issues being litigated in the Supreme Court are not those related to regulation, but rather to issues *internal* to the university. The breakdown in internal governance has been one of the most disturbing and striking developments in Indian higher education over the years. In his chapter on 'Governance in Higher Education', Pankaj Chandra addresses this issue and explores how we should understand the meaning of governance and the special role it plays in academic institutions. The chapter considers how to categorise matters of governance among a range of factors that impact higher education. In particular, Chandra investigates the role that governance-related issues play in determining the quality of higher education and in shaping a learning environment. Existing forms of governance, Chandra argues, threaten the provision of quality education and precipitate tensions that institutions are unable to effectively resolve. Reflecting upon the range of governance failures that currently mark Indian universities, from bureaucratic control to self-preservation by faculty to poor leadership, Chandra's conclusions are a sobering reminder that the university would need to be entirely reimagined and rebuilt if quality is to be restored.

NOTES

1. Recent studies include Agarwal 2009, 2013; and Tilak 2013.
2. For more data, visit the National Science Foundation website, www.nsf.gov. The present data has been taken from NSF, 'Science and Engineering Indicators 2012', Table 6.4, and 'Science and Engineering Indicators 2014', Table 6.5.
3. Prime Minister Manmohan Singh's address at the 150th Anniversary Function of the University of Mumbai, 22 June 2007, available at http://pmindia.nic.in/lspeech.asp?id=555.
4. http://inhome.rediff.com/news/2007/oct/10arjun.htm.

5. *Business Standard*, 'Sibal Pitches for FDI in Education', 9 July 2008. Available at http://www.business-standard.com/india/storypage.php?autono=328167.

6. The next paragraph draws on Kapur and Mehta 2008.

7. http://inhome.rediff.com/news/2007/oct/10arjun.htm.

8. For a recent study on this subject, see Kumar, et al. 2015.

9. Article 15 of the Indian Constitution prohibits discrimination based on religion, race, caste, sex, and place of birth.

10. Minutes of the State Education Ministers Conference, held on 18 June 2010.

References

Agarwal, P., *Indian Higher Education: Envisioning the Future* (New Delhi: Sage Publications, 2009).

——— (ed.), *A Half Century of Indian Higher Education: Essays by Philip Altbach* (New Delhi: Sage Publications, 2013).

Alcorn, B., G. Christensen and D. Kapur, 'Higher Education and MOOCs in India and the Global South', *Change: The Magazine of Higher Learning* 47 (3), 2015, 42–49.

Bagde, S., D. Epple and L. Taylor, 'Does Affirmative Action Work? Caste, Gender, College Quality, and Academic Success in India', *American Economic Review* 106 (6), 2016, 1495–1521.

Basant, R. and G. Sen, 'Access to Higher Education in India: An Exploration of Its Antecedents', Indian Institute of Management-Ahmedabad Working Paper No. 2013–05–011, 2013.

Chakravarty, S. and E. Somanathan, 'Discrimination in an Elite Labour Market? Job Placements at the Indian Institute of Management-Ahmedabad', Indian Statistical Institute Discussion Paper No. 08–01, 2008.

Das, J., et al., 'In Urban and Rural India, a Standardized Patient Study Showed Low Levels of Provider Training and Huge Quality Gaps', *Health Affairs* 31 (12), 2012, 2774–84.

Deshpande, S. and U. Zacharias (eds), *Beyond Inclusion: The Practice of Equal Access in Indian Higher Education* (New Delhi: Routledge, 2013).

Kapur, D., 'Addressing the Trilemma of Higher Education', *Seminar* 617, 2011, 87–92.

Kapur, D. and P. B. Mehta, 'Mortgaging the Future? Indian Higher Education', *Brookings-NCAER India Policy Forum* 4, 2008, 101–57.

Khosla, M., 'Testing India's Lawyers', *India in Transition*, 16 August 2010.

Kumar, C. R., *The President of India and the Governance of Higher Education Institutions* (New Delhi: Universal Law Publishing Pvt. Ltd., 2015).

Mehta, P. B., 'No HR in HRD', *Indian Express*, 8 September 2010.

Ministry of Human Resource Development, *Analysis of Budgeted Expenditure on Education 2009–10 to 2011–12* (New Delhi: Government of India, 2013).

Shepard, J., 'Cambridge mission "not social mobility"', *The Guardian*, 10 September 2008.

Sundaram, K., 'On Backwardness and Fair Access to Higher Education', *Economic and Political Weekly* 41 (50), 2006, 5173–82.

The Indian Council of Social Science Research, 'Restructuring the Indian Council of Social Science Research: Report of the Fourth Review Committee', 2007.

Tilak, J. B. G. (ed.), *Higher Education in India: In Search of Equality, Quality and Quantity* (New Delhi: Orient BlackSwan, 2013).

University Grants Commission, *Report of the Committee to Review the Pay Scales and Service Conditions of University and College Teachers* (New Delhi: UGC, 2008).

Wood, A. and M. Calandrino, 'When the Other Giant Awakens: Trade and Human Resources in India', *Economic and Political Weekly* XXXV (52–53), 2000, 4677–94.

Xiea, Y., C. Zhangc and Q. Laia, 'China's rise as a major contributor to science and technology', *Proceedings of the National Academy of Sciences*, 16 June 2014.

— *two* —

A College in Search of a 'Saga'

Apoorvanand Jha

Prologue

The story of higher education in Bihar is told in terms of decline and decay. It is common knowledge that universities are starved of funds, with more than half the teaching posts in colleges and universities lying vacant (in many cases, for more than two decades); laboratories are dysfunctional and libraries are dying. Release of funds to the universities and payment of salaries to the teachers make front-page news. One of the main jobs of the universities and the government is to fight the hundreds of suits that teachers have been filing in the High Court to sort out service-related matters, including their seniority, length of service, fixation and regular payment of salary, release of pension, and other retirement benefits. Vice-Chancellors are appointed and summarily removed at the will of the Governor, who is also the Chancellor of the universities of Bihar. The tension between the Chancellor and the education department of the government has created bizarre situations like Vice-Chancellors being appointed by the Chancellor and their financial powers seized by the government, following which the Vice-Chancellors move to the courts for relief. News of principals and Vice-Chancellors being hauled up, dismissed, or even arrested on various charges no longer shocks the people of Bihar. All this has forced the students of Bihar to look towards places like Delhi and Bangalore to pursue their higher education. Students who do not have the wherewithal to go to such places are enrolled in various courses, but appear only at the time of examinations. People in Bihar seem to be convinced of the futility of college and university education. A lack of basic facilities like electricity and the poor quality of school education in most towns of

Bihar forces teachers to leave their families and children in Patna, or in a place close by. As a result, they do not live in their duty stations or spend increasingly less time there. Many of them keep visiting politicians or people who matter to try and get transferred to either Patna or places near it.

To tell all this in a language of cold statistics concerning student enrolment, faculty, allocation of funds, etc., did not seem adequate to me. Moreover, it would reveal little that was new. An analysis of the educational policies that successive governments have been following is also long overdue. The role of courts in matters of higher education in the context of Bihar remains to be examined. Bihar is known for its strong teachers' movement. I found it surprising that no serious study has been done on this issue or on the changing pattern of student politics, which is often blamed for the chaos that mars the campuses of Bihar. The link between caste politics and education has also not been explored. This is distressing, especially in light of the rise and consolidation of the politics of backward castes and Dalits in Bihar. Observers and students of higher education in India have always complained about the lack of documentation and research in this field. This is also true of Bihar.

When I started thinking about the cause of this sorry state of higher education in Bihar, a question arose: Can we describe it using the language of decline? Decline presupposes a high point. Was there ever a high point in Bihar? Or one can also ask: Why and how were these institutions of higher learning, colleges and universities, created in the first place? Whose aspirations did they reflect? Why did they start crumbling over a period of two or three decades, which is a very short duration in the life of an institution? What has been the relationship of these institutions with other social institutions? Who takes ownership of these institutions? In other words, what is their life story? Unfortunately for people like me, there is an acute dearth of such stories.

In this desert, *Knowledge, Power and Politics* (edited by Mushirul Hasan, 1998), a collection of studies of institutions of higher learning in India, for example Delhi College, St. Stephen's College, Presidency College, etc., is a rare flower. I found 'The College by a River: Patna College' in this collection, which stirred my own memories of the college where I had spent my student years. The poignant tale of Patna College, told with feeling by a man of letters, showed me the way (Mukherjee 1998). In the meantime, I also read Burton Clark's *The Distinctive College*, a masterly account of the historical development of three colleges, Antioch, Reed and Swarthmore, situated in a distant land, the United States of America (Clark 1970). His theory of 'Organisational Saga', developed from his research on these colleges, looked very powerful to me. It helped me understand the reason for the durability of an organisation as a living being. More often than not, the reasons for the success or failure of a college or an educational institution are sought in their structures or in their rational aspects. Clark, however, said:

> ... a needed corrective is more research on the cultural and expressive aspects of organisations, particularly on the belief and sentiments at broad levels of organization.... An Organizational saga is a collective understanding of unique accomplishments in a formally established group. The group's definition of the accomplishment, intrinsically historical but embellished through retelling and rewriting, links stages of organisational development (Clark 1972: 178).

Clark stated that the group adds emotional charge to the story; this explains not only how certain means lead to certain ends, but also why an organisation becomes a beloved place for a group of people. The Saga, according to Clark, is a strong purpose conceived and enunciated by a person or a group. Organisations established at the instance of some higher authority to fulfil some demands do not develop a saga. While even utilitarian organisations may develop a weak saga, a saga generally takes its own time to evolve. It must have some initiators, but there should also be people to inherit it, and make their own affective additions to it.

What I understood after reading Clark was that organisations that are treated as living beings and are beloved to a set of people have a greater chance of surviving and enduring with a sense of the purpose for which they were created. Second, organisations have their own time. A saga can evolve only over a period of time. This time is two-fold: historical time, which is independent of a particular organisation; and internal time, which may or may not co-relate or coincide with the outside time. This internal time gives the organisation its unique rhythm. But to have one's own rhythm, you also need to have individuals who not only invent rhythm, but keep practising it. Turning my attention to the colleges and universities of Bihar, I felt that there were institutions which had this seed of saga within them. However, it had failed to take root. In some cases, a weak saga developed. To develop, a saga also needs a receptive soil. This soil, to me, is the outside society. Institutions live and function in relation to this. It is therefore very important to understand the relationship between an institution—in our case, a college—and society.

It is said that human beings create everything in their own image. Societies too create institutions in their own image, constantly attempting to mould any institution that does not reflect it. Demands are placed on them and there is a constant pressure to respond to the changes occurring outside, in historical time. The institutions are asked to keep pace with these changes. This is bound to disturb the internal rhythm of the institution. With the loss of this rhythm, institutions lose their uniqueness.

I decided to tell the story of two colleges, Patna College and DAV College, Siwan. They are very different from each other. DAV College is located in a mofussil town of Bihar while Patna College is situated in Patna, the capital of Bihar, a city with a rich history. The former, however, is a part of my childhood and early youth memories as my father taught here for more than three decades; I, too, spent two of my post-secondary college years in this college. I joined Patna College for my undergraduate studies. I can claim to have seen the good times of these colleges and to also have seen them collapsing in pain. This chapter will not provide any analytical insights; it merely tries to present their narratives, with an emphasis on their relationship with their surroundings.

I had long conversations with my father, his colleagues, my teachers and old students of the DAV College, Siwan. The characters in this narrative are not fictional.[1] Unfortunately, as I have said earlier, there is little documentation of the process of establishing educational institutions in Bihar. In its absence, it is only memories which come to your aid. In many cases, they may not be reliable. This is therefore not a historical account of the institutions of higher education in Bihar, nor is it an authentic biography of the two colleges. It should be read more as a memoir of someone who, for more than three decades, was part of the lives of the two colleges, and who is now looking back at them from a distance. Using the category of 'Organisational Saga', I have tried to see if these colleges do have something like a saga. What I found is that they have failed to develop their saga. Hence the title of the chapter.

> I gave up trying to visualise what will happen to my college when I am no longer around, not even to hear or lament. Perhaps, late on some not too far August or September night, when the water is high, the college will simply jump into the river. The Ganga will neither pause nor look back; it has seen too much already.

Thus concludes Sujit Mukherji's affectionate recollection of Patna College, a college that he graduated from, and then spent a few years teaching at. His association with the college goes even farther back as his father had also taught here for more than eight years. Sujit is now no more. The college continues to lie where he had left it. The Ganga has receded further from Patna College. Does it still qualify as 'a college on the river bank', as Sujit would have liked for it to be known? Do memories of the Ganga ever stir its soul?

I too have known Patna College for more than three decades. In 1981, I joined this college as an undergraduate student. Hope was still in the air. Clutching that ray of hope, like thousands before me, I had come to Patna College from a small town in Bihar called Siwan. Patna College and Science College used to be the ultimate destinations for youth wishing to pursue education in liberal arts or the sciences. Allahabad University was another attraction, but mainly for those who aspired to go into the Indian Administrative Services. Banaras Hindu University was another possibility for a good undergraduate experience. *Dilli* was still some distance away. Bangalore was nowhere on the horizon of 'higher' or 'technical' education.

Sujit Mukherji would not have thought of writing these pensive words then. He could still recall his association with Patna College in a futuristic vein. Writing about his teacher Kalimuddin Ahmad, who taught English and was a critic in Urdu, he said:

> Kalim Saheb narrowly escaped being taught by my father, but Kalim Saheb's children—at least Azhar and Farida—did not escape me. In between, my next elder brother Subhas and I (and several in-laws, like my wife) partook of the feast of being taught by Kalim Saheb. I shall therefore have no hesitation in turning over my children, should the opportunity arise to the tutelage of Azhar and Farida. This is one way I can requite a fraction of what I owe to Kalim Saheb.

It would take another decade and a half for Sujit to visualise his beloved college as committing suicide. Or was it his wish? Perhaps he did not want his college to be forced to endure the ignominy he witnessed it suffering. The fate of his college, however different it might be from other colleges, was to be decided by human beings, mostly by those who did not carry with them the feel of the *parampara* (tradition) of the institution to which he felt existentially bound. Politicians, bureaucrats, vice-chancellors, principals, even teachers who have never been part of the journey that shapes a dream into an institution take over, and the dream starts falling apart.

I try to visualise institutions as organic beings. Rooted in the soil that nurtures and sustains them, their lives depend on its quality. Apart from the soil, the ecology they are part of impacts not only their growth, but also their very survival. They have been seen by many as rational organisations created through a charter, supposedly to respond to some social or national need and governed by some objective set of rules and regulations. I would like to treat them as emotional beings that exist in a universe of relationships, drawing life from them and in return energising them.

Patna College lived a full life because there was a happy and thriving Science College and a robust Patna Medical College flanking it. You had to traverse some distance on the Ashok Rajpath to reach the Bihar National College (B. N. College), which was never the first choice of students but which did have an academic air about it. There was a culture of give and take between these colleges and institutions. Students of Patna College could go to the annual Saraswati Puja festival organised by the Medical College students, which included inter-college drama, debate and music competitions, an opportunity that students of different colleges looked forward to eagerly. Friendships across disciplines and institutions were formed and sustained.

Patna College did have supportive companions like the Khuda Bakh Oriental Public Library and the Anugrah Narayan Sinha Institute of Social Studies (A. N. Sinha Institute). They were living institutions; you could get 'expensive' journals there. But these are the two names that people from outside Bihar are familiar with. One must mention that the *Gai Ghat Putsakalaya* or small mohalla libraries which even small temples used to run allowed some of my friends like

Nasiruddin to read Premchand and Amar Chitra Katha comics. The British Library was where 'elites' were supposed to go, but Patna felt proud to house it. Deepak Goswami, its librarian, was a Bangla poet himself. While you could get only British publications in the library, Deepak in his own modest way turned it into a kind of literary and cultural centre where writers of Hindi and Urdu could converge. Not very far from the British Library was the Sinha Library, which was still a reference point for curious scholars. You had to cross only one street to reach Patna Museum, at the back of which was the famous Kashi Prasad Jaiswal Research Institute where rare Buddhist texts in Pali, brought to India from Tibet by Rahul Sankrityayan, are stored. Bihar Rashtrabhasha Parishad was yet another institution established and nurtured by the great writer and editor Shiv Pujan Sahai, which published books in Hindi in all areas of knowledge. It did not work with a regional, Bihar-centric vision, but became a platform for the best in Hindi.

Patna had a vibrant intellectual and cultural life. Stalwarts of the world of music and dance from all over India made it a point to not miss the annual Durga Puja musical soirees. It would be difficult for a Patna boy or girl born or raised after the 1980s to even imagine the crazy all-night music and dance extravaganza on the narrow streets of Langar Toli and Govind Mitra Road, which would be thronged by the old and the young, men and women, Hindus and Muslims, sitting, standing, awake all night, on the *Ashtamies*, *Navamies* and *Dashamies* to experience the wonders that Birju Maharaj or Sitara Devi or Bismilla Khan wove for them. Talk to those who lived through those years and are still around, and they'll share with you their fond memories of those Puja nights. It was remarkable that, unlike cities like Delhi where classical and popular spaces are clearly divided and rarely meet, classical in Patna was part of street culture.

An active and thriving cine-society through which the Patna youth remained connected to the best of non-Bollywood Indian and world cinema regularly screened its shows at the Indian Medical Association Hall. Regular cinema halls still had slots for 'art cinema'. You could go for the morning or noon shows on Sundays to watch Satyajit Ray, Mrinal Sen, Ritwik Ghatak, Shyam Benegal, Adoor Gopalakrishnan or M. S. Sathyu.

Students of Patna College or from other colleges of the university were familiar with cultural groups like Chetna Samiti and theatre groups like Kala Sangam, Anagat, or Patna IPTA (Indian People's Theatre Association), which used to recruit actors from the campus. Patna theatre was largely amateur, but it operated in a professional manner. It was sustained by students from different colleges of Patna. There were groups that regularly produced and performed Bangla and English plays. Narendra Nath Pandey, a teacher of Physics at the B. N. College, was the driving force behind Anagat, and Shankar Ashish Dutt of Patna College and Muniba Sami of Patna Women's College were part of the small but active English theatre world. A single theatre group could produce three to four full-length plays a year, which is unthinkable now. The mid-1970s witnessed the emergence of street theatre in Patna, and college campuses turned into open theatre spaces. I have seen students who started as curious onlookers turning into active and passionate theatre activists. Some of the finest actors and ablest directors have emerged from these open spaces.

I have talked at length about the cultural life of Patna, which in my view served both as a source of nourishment and a protective ozone layer for collegiate life. There was a lively and healthy interaction between city life and the campus. The well-being of college life depended to a large degree on how the city was doing. It worked both ways—the city felt proud to be the house of the college, and the college could claim its place in the life of the city.

Patna, though not a metro, could still claim to possess a cosmopolitan mind. The tumultuous 1960s introduced it to the worldwide youth unrest and made it part of the great Vietnam solidarity movement. At the same time, through poets like Moloy Rai Chaudhary and Rajkamal Chaudhary, it developed a kinship with the beat generation, which was making waves and shaking the established aesthetic citadels in America under the leadership of Allen Ginsberg and Jack Kerouac. 'Mukti Prasang', a long poem in Hindi by Rajkamal and 'Zakhm' in Bangla by Moloy Rai Chaudhary are Indian equivalents of Allen Ginsberg's legendary 'Howl'.

The India Coffee House had not yet made way for a shopping complex, and you could walk into it to get a glimpse of legendary writers like Nagarjuna or Phanishwar Nath Renu. Patna experimented with styles, literary and cultural, and was decades away from being turned into a cultural colony or satellite of Dilli. Its ambitions and benchmarks, in all spheres, were truly global.

Rajkamal Chaudhary, like Nagarajuna, could write with ease in Maithili and Hindi. The medium of instruction was still Hindi, but the desire to learn languages other than Hindi, mainly English, was strong. You did not need Rapidex English speaking courses or guidebooks to learn English. The leisurely pace of the English classrooms introduced you to the beauty of the language and kindled a desire to master it. This was not a superficial, utilitarian relationship with the language. One toiled to make it one's own. One can recall that all secondary schools in Bihar since colonial times had to be English-medium schools. That is how we got names like the Victoria Memorial High English School or Sarraf High English School. One should also remember that *Khadi boli Hindi*, which we now assume to be the mother tongue of all Biharis, was a very new language. For a Maithili or Bhojpuri speaker, it was still a school language, which had to be acquired and learnt.

Learning languages was an essential prerequisite for a school or college student and was not resented. That happened only with the advent of the politics of Ram Manohar Lohia in the 1960s and Karpuri Thakur who, after taking over as chief minister of Bihar, declared that it was not necessary to pass in English in the matriculation examinations. Students passing their matriculation examination without English were popularly known as members of the 'Karpuri Division'. Kedar Nath Pandey, General Secretary of the Bihar Secondary Teachers' Association, himself a teacher of Hindi, had this to say about this move: 'Karpuri Thakur, by removing English from the secondary education derailed it (*Angrezi ko madhyamik shiksha se hataa kar use patari se utar diya*).' A teacher of long standing and the headmaster of several schools, Pandeyji said that students used to go to schools mainly for two subjects, English and Mathematics. Once the compulsion to learn English was gone, attendance in schools fell sharply, adversely affecting the ethos of the classroom. Karpuri Thakur claimed that the children of Dhanuks and Kurmis failed because of English. Pandeyji agreed that this was true to a large extent. English was a constraint, not only for students from the Backward Classes, but for upper-caste people as well. Ram Dhari Singh 'Dinkar', a legendary poet from Bihar, reminiscing about his student days, wrote that had he been allowed to have Hindi as the medium of instruction, he would have grown much faster. Pandeyji agreed, but felt that Karpuri Thakur had found an easy, rather lazy solution by removing English altogether as a requirement. He stated that in popular imagination, modern education has somehow remained entwined with English.

Teachers were generally polyglots. It was not unusual to find a Nalin Vilochan Sharma in Hindi who could claim equal mastery over Sanskrit and English, or a Kalimuddin Ahmed who was a professor of English, but practised criticism in Urdu. Teachers well versed in at least three languages were not rare on the campus. Students took pride in the fact that they were taught by people whose writings were essential reference points for classes in Delhi University or in Calcutta University. Teachers were recognised as scholars in other parts as well. Nalin Vilochan Sharma was a respected voice in the literary world. It was he who drew the attention of the reading public to a new literary event, the publication of *Maila Anchal* by Phanishwar Nath Renu, a trendsetter in Hindi fiction writing.

Interdisciplinarity was yet to enter the lexicon of college education. It was not unusual, however, to see teachers and students of literature or the sciences crowding the lectures of historian Professor Ram Sharan Sharma, who was very strict about not moving beyond the ancient period in even his popular lectures. Similarly, we would notice our teachers and friends from the departments of History, Political Science or Sociology enjoying literary evenings on the campus and outside. Apart from Professor Ram Sharan Sharma, you had scholars like Syed Hasan Askari and Professor R. N. Nandi at the department of History; the latter, despite his failing eyesight, continued to write. (It is an irony of sorts that the last of this lot, a bright young historian named Papiya Ghosh, was murdered at her Patna home a few years ago.) Then there were teachers like R. K. Sinha or Kapil Muni Tiwari at the department of English; while they did not write much, they were scholars par excellence and revered teachers. For people like Ram Sharan Sharma, scholarship was not an individualistic pursuit. I have heard stories from my teachers about how Professor Sharma used to check the log-in register of the department library and confront his colleagues if their names were found missing.

It is difficult to pinpoint the exact moment when all this started to wane. What we know for sure is that Patna and its college started dying together. The mid-1980s saw the end of the Puja festivities. The British Library closed down in the late 1990s. A. N. Sinha Institute Library could make no new addition to its stock of books. The government started denying aid to the A. N. Sinha Institute, and for years together its affairs were conducted from the state government secretariat as it did not have a regular director. The Kala Sangam, a pioneer in the modern theatre movement, slowed down and IPTA declined dramatically. Amateur groups soon found it difficult to get young actors. Some actors did come, but with the limited aim of using these groups as a training platform to gain entry into the fledgling but expanding world of television serials. Theatre was not their passion. Those who came to Patna after the 1980s were not even aware of an entity called the Cine Society. The light was going out and it seemed impossible to postpone the end anymore.

Sujit had described the changes taking place in the internal academic life of the college which led to its downfall. The separation of postgraduate from undergraduate studies proved disastrous. The college began to be treated as a subsidiary to the postgraduate departments. The hierarchy created by this separation placed the faculty of the colleges on a lower pedestal. The postgraduate departments became the intellectual gurus and all the college had to do was follow their diktat. Academic life started shrinking in the college. Patna College was not an exception in this regard. Older teachers were retiring and there were no fresh appointments in their place. There were few people left to carry forward the story of Patna College.

Along with this shrinking academic life, not only at Patna College but also elsewhere, there was a revival and assertion of the old identities that educational institutions were supposed to moderate or neutralise. Such identities were reinforced through hostels and lodges, which were clearly divided in the name of castes. There was a cluster of hostels in the Saidpur area, traditionally demarcated as Rajput or Bhumihar hostels. It was impossible for somebody outside the fold of a particular caste to set foot in the hostel 'designated' for that caste. Similarly, the 'famous' Patel Chhatrawaas was the abode of students from the 'backward classes' and was situated outside the

Saidpur campus. The 'seniors' ensured that their 'people' did not go astray. Once admitted to the university, they were promptly initiated into their caste 'associations'. It is impossible for a resident of the localities around Ashok Rajpath to erase the memory of the Saraswati Puja procession taken out by the boarders of Patel Chhatrawaas, which had less to do with their devotion to the goddess of *Vidya* (Knowledge) and more to do with demonstrating the might of their caste. The air trembled with fear when the processionists hit the road, armed with hockey sticks and 'fuse'-mercury tubes. The 'professional' colleges were not free of these influences either.

There were selfless caste workers too. I was told by a friend who was my senior, and who is now teaching at Patna College, that he was once offered notes by a 'senior' caste fellow after the latter had found out from his 'sources' that my friend, a brilliant boy from his own caste, had had to miss a good number of classes because of illness. He took the trouble of arranging 'notes' for my friend to save his 'division'. This selfless deed created a lifelong bond between the two. The do-gooder went on to become a senior bank officer, but continues to maintain a directory of students from his caste. This is a multipurpose directory and is used by his community across the world on different occasions for diverse ends.

The above description seems to contradict what André Béteille said about the role of universities in a society like ours:

> .... the universities were among the first open and secular institutions in a society that was governed largely by the rules of kinship, caste and religion. In that sense they were islands of modernity in a world bound largely by tradition. Right until the time of independence, the universities were few and far between. Their influence did not reach very far or penetrate very deeply into a society that was steeped in poverty, illiteracy and inequality. But the influence, no matter how restricted, was progressive, both intellectually and institutionally, and this progressive influence appeared to be spreading gradually, though very slowly (Béteille 2007: 442).

It appears that even these 'islands of modernity' were not left untouched by 'the rules of kinship and caste'. The majority of students joining Patna College or even Science College came from villages where life is organised along caste lines. While it would not be wrong to say that it is simplistic to view every aspect of education through the lens of caste, the perpetual tension between caste and the modernising mission of education defines the character of educational enterprise in India. Bihar is no exception.

Colleges like Patna College were largely the result of efforts of the colonial government, with some help from 'native gentlemen'; other colleges, though, were essentially community initiatives (here, community is to be described strictly in terms of caste). In such a manner was created the Bhumihar-Brahmin College (1899) in Muzaffarpur, another major urban centre of Bihar. It was renamed the Langat Singh College (L. S. College), after its founder Langat Singh, in 1949–50. Bhumihars established another Science College (renamed later as Mahesh Prasad Sinha Science College after Mahesh Prasad Sinha, a stalwart of Bhumihars) and Rajputs opened their own Rameshwar Prasad Singh College (RPS College) in Muzaffarpur. Brahmins established the Tirhut Mahavidyalaya; after the assassination of Lalit Narayan Mishra, who was considered a leader of the Brahmins, this institution was renamed the Lalit Narayan Tirhut College (L. N. T. College). In 1968, the 'backward' classes opened their own college, called the Ram Manohar Lohia Smarak College (R. M. L. S. College).

Did the opening of these colleges reflect the educational aspiration of various caste groups? One is not very sure how to define it. What it did was very interesting. It made the use of unfair means in examinations competitive. Students belonging to the Bhumihar community would fill in their examination forms from the MPS College and Rajput students would appear from their own RPS College. The norm was to get oneself admitted to a college with a good academic reputation, but appear as an examinee from a college belonging to one's own caste. The examination results, therefore, could not be treated as a true measure of the real academic strength of the student.

There were exceptions in Bihar. Patna College was, of course, one such till the 1970s or early 1980s. But as explained earlier, it belonged to a different category. It was largely a state-led initiative. It is true that Bihar cannot boast of a Banaras Hindu University (popularly known as BHU). But there were different versions of Madan Mohan Malaviya (founder of the BHU) here and there (for example, Darhi Baba) who could not find a place in the grand nationalist narrative, but remain part of the local histories. In 1883, a philanthropist named Roy Bahadur Tej Narayan founded in Bhagalpur what is one of the oldest colleges of Bihar, originally known as the Tej Narayan Jubilee College. In 1959, it was renamed as the Tej Narayan Banaili College (TNB College) after an endowment was received from the Banaili estate ('B' replaced 'J' in the name of the college to acknowledge this generosity). It did not draw strength or legitimacy from any particular caste group and had on its teaching staff scholars from all over India. You could find Jawaharlal Wakhloo, a Kashmiri, Neel Mani Acharya, a Bengali, and Ram Swaroop Singh from western Uttar Pradesh, considered the pioneer of biology studies in Bihar. They brought with them diverse educational and cultural experiences. They were competent teachers and good scholars, but displayed no scholarly ambition. Rarely did any teacher want to go in for a Ph.D. But as far as their students were concerned, they were sincere teachers and unconcerned with the caste affiliations of their colleagues or students. My father remembers his teachers as voracious readers who remained immersed in the world of books. Despite facing much rough weather, TNB College, Bhagalpur managed to hold itself together. Does this have to do with its founding cultural principle, the fact that its genesis did not lie in any caste or regional aspiration?

Another such example is the Dayanand Anglo Vedic (DAV) College, Siwan. The name suggests that it was an initiative of the Arya Samaj, a powerful religio-cultural movement. But the people of Siwan do not associate it with any sectoral movement. It was known as the baby of *Darhi Baba*, as Baidyanath Prasad was popularly known. Baidyanath Prasad, a Sunar (goldsmith) by caste, was a local leader of the Arya Samaj; he was, however, primarily a teacher. He was the headmaster of Victoria Memorial High English School (VMHE School) in Siwan in the 1920s, and earlier had been the headmaster of Victoria Memorial Middle School. When it became difficult to accommodate the increasing number of students in the existing building, he erected huts in the Central Maidan of the town, which is now known as Gandhi Maidan. Later, he acquired 50 bighas of land for the school. But here again, caste realities intervened.

Siwan is known for its physical proximity to Jiradei, home to Dr Rajendra Prasad, the first president of independent India. He belonged to the Kayastha community, as had Brijkishore Prasad, another powerful Congress leader. Kayasthas were a powerful presence in Siwan. One also needs to remember that Bengalis dominated nearly every field in Bihar. Till 1911, Bihar had been a part of Bengal and Bengalis were ahead of people from other states in almost all areas of life, education being the most prominent. Kayasthas were the next most educated community. This gave them additional leverage in social manoeuvring. They started interfering in the affairs of VMHE School, and Darhi Baba had to withdraw from the school.

Institution builder that he was, Darhi Baba did not sit still. He immediately founded the Dayanand Anglo Vedic (DAV) Middle School, and after that the DAV High School for boys and Arya Kanya Uccha Vidyalaya for girls. Siwan was a small town and Darhi Baba had keen eyes and sharp ears. The Arya Samaj was not particularly kind to Muslims, but Darhi Baba did not let himself be imprisoned in this religio-political ideology. Ajmat Ali, now 89, remembers his childhood days. As a student of Class VIII, he once fell seriously ill. Darhi Baba came visiting to inquire after his health and gave him medicine, as he also practised Homeopathy. Ajmat was surprised as he was not a student at Darhi Baba's school. This was the beginning of a lifelong bond between the two. This was not an exception, says Ajmat Ali: 'Anwar Husain, one year senior to me, came from an extremely poor family. Darhi Baba ensured free-ship for him and helped him continue with his studies.'

After spending nearly a decade stabilising the newly established schools, Darhi Baba started working towards a college in Siwan. Establishing a college was no mean task then. Siwan was primarily a town of traders. After Banias, Muslims formed the largest group in Siwan. Darhi Baba mobilised the Banias, Brahmins and Muslims, and formed a governing body consisting of representatives from these communities. The local Arya Partinidhi Sabha showed no interest. His long association with educational activity and social reform in Siwan won Darhi Baba the support of all the communities, and he managed to secure some land and a pond for the college. Later, he also convinced the local municipality to give over the factory land of Khuddi Mian to the college. This factory had to be closed because of non-payment of taxes, and the municipal authorities had decided to auction the land to recover the dues. It needs to be noted that in the following years, there was hardly any addition of resources to what had been mobilised in the very first phase of the establishment of the college. This fact needs to be kept in mind as it tells us a lot about the relationship of the institution with the community.

The DAV College was founded in 1941. Darhi Baba, true to his principles, went hunting for faculty and brought in Dr Jhamman Lal Sharma, a D.Sc., as the first principal. This was a rare academic achievement for those times, especially for a small town like Siwan. Darhi Baba managed to attract people with good academic credentials to his college. However, Dr Sharma had to leave very soon. According to some old students, he was made to leave by Darhi Baba, so as to make way for his blue-eyed boy, Banke Bihari Mishra (known as Banke Babu). There are anecdotes involving Banke Bihari Mishra and Darhi Baba, but unfortunately I could not find any written record by Darhi Baba himself, which could have thrown light on his vision of the college.

Darhi Baba kept track of intelligent students. He took under his wing the poor, needy and intelligent students. This was how he came to provide shelter to Banke Bihari Mishra, a rebel Brahmin boy, who was thrown out of his caste by Brahmins for having shared food with 'Harijans'. He remained the eternal patron of Banke Babu who, after abandoning his engineering college, went on to study history with support from Darhi Baba. Banke Babu was made the headmaster of DAV middle school. According to Mahendra Prasad, who was among the first batch of students at the college, DAV College was created with Banke Babu in mind. Banke Babu was not the founding principal, though.

Banke Babu, a historian of repute who went on to become the head of the department of history at the University of Delhi, remained the principal of the college for more than three decades. He went on periodic leave in between to serve at other universities and institutions, both in India and abroad. Munishwarananad Giri, a Sanskrit scholar, worked as officiating principal in his absence. Banke Babu, however, does not come across as an academic visionary. He emerges as a disciplinarian in all the accounts of students and teachers who served under him. Giriji, in sharp contrast, is lovingly remembered as an administrator who had great regard for his colleagues and who never tried to impose himself on them.

Darhi Baba lobbied hard to get affiliation for the courses run by the college from Patna University, which was at that time the only university for the entire region of Bihar and Orissa. In colonial times, it was not permitted to open colleges beyond district towns. DAV College and R. K. College in Madhubani had defied this stricture, and were therefore denied affiliation by Patna University to run undergraduate courses for nearly a decade. In the mid-1950s the college was allowed to start undergraduate courses in science. This was also when higher education expanded in Bihar. Shyam Nandan Sahay was the first Vice-Chancellor of Bihar University, which was carved out from Patna University in 1952, but had its headquarters in Patna. Sahay said that it was high time that conditions set by the colonial masters regarding the opening and maintenance of a college were done away with, and declared that he would strive to open colleges in all the villages of Bihar. Things did take the route suggested by Sinha in the following decades. Colleges located in one or two-room buildings became a normal sight in Bihar. They held out the promise of jobs for hundreds of unemployed postgraduates, who paid hefty sums to the managers of these colleges to be appointed as lecturers. The promise was that the government would absorb all of these postgraduates. The government remained a mute spectator to this farce. This led to the mushrooming of third-rate colleges all over Bihar. Colleges like DAV College had barely stabilised themselves after securing the constituent status when they found themselves surrounded by these spurious colleges.

The 1950s can still be treated as an age of innocence for higher education. The government and the political class were not particularly interested in colleges. But from the early years of the 1960s, when Krishna Kant Singh, a Bhumihar leader of the Congress Party, took over as State Minister of Education, caste as a political mobilising force began asserting itself in the field of education. Bhumihars took to education with great zeal, and it was now their turn to replace Kayasthas from their position of dominance in the field of education. It is difficult to resist the temptation to share an anecdote related to Krishna Kant Singh, which is etched in the memories of nearly everyone I met and talked to, who were young at that time. In the districts, the officer responsible for educational administration was known as the District Education Officer (DEO).

At a particular point in time, there were seventeen Bhumihars serving as DEOs in the districts of Bihar. The total number of districts was eighteen. When this issue was raised in the assembly, Singh is said to have defiantly replied that he could not appoint eighteen Bhumihars as DEOs as he was unable to find the eighteenth qualified Bhumihar. Most colleges in Bihar fell victim to K. K. Singh's brand of politics. Darhi Baba continued to resist, and the college had to pay for this. It was made to starve.

Appointments to teaching and non-teaching posts were the sole prerogative of the governing bodies of colleges, and merit was not always the most important criterion. Satyendra Prasad Singh, Chief Minister of Bihar in the early 1960s, tried to halt this trend when he constituted the University Service Commission (USC) to make selections for teaching posts in all colleges in Bihar centrally. The fortunes of the commission, however, kept fluctuating, with successive governments periodically dissolving and then reconstituting it. Governments have not been sure about a policy concerning the appointment of teachers. There also came a time when all demonstrators, basically laboratory technicians, were automatically promoted to lecturers once they secured a postgraduate degree. Science departments were filled with such promoted teachers. This did a great disservice to the study of sciences across colleges and universities in Bihar. The issue of the appointment of teachers and their service conditions requires a deeper probe.

The USC opened the way for teachers like my father to return to Bihar, his homeland. He had had to leave Bihar as the chances of getting a job in a college were rather dim with the governing bodies (GBs) relying on extra-academic criteria for selections. They tended to patronise their own caste men, leaving little space for people like my father, who had no contacts whatsoever. With the establishment of the USC, the power of the GBs over selection was taken away and the chances of the right kind of people getting teaching jobs brightened. The USC had members who came from academic backgrounds, and did not suffer from political interference. The commission did the selections and assigned colleges to selected teachers, depending on the vacancies there.

My father was asked to join the DAV College, Siwan. This was in 1962. He had come from Silchar College, Assam, which was a very respectable college in the Cachhar region. He was shaken by the shabby appearance of the structure that claimed to be DAV College. The buildings were in bad shape and salaries were infrequent. The only redeeming feature of this college was its neutrality with regard to caste. While talking to Anil Kumar, my Physics teacher at DAV College, I gathered that this was one of the factors that had encouraged him to join DAV College in 1977 (the college had attained the status of a Constituent College in 1975). The fact that only Brahmins had occupied the chair of principal for nearly five decades encouraged some to call it a Brahmin college, but it did not stick. Even today, no caste label can be placed on it.

The political scene became turbulent in the 1960s. With the rise of anti-Congress forces, there emerged leaders like Mahamaya Prasad who were rabble rousers and who saw colleges as recruitment grounds for their parties. Asking students to leave their classes, to go on strikes and then demand a relaxation in examinations became the hallmark of all opposition politics. Teaching was becoming irrelevant. The year 1967 saw the emergence of a new version of left politics that drew inspiration from the armed rebellion in a village of Bengal called Naxalbari. The Naxal movement impacted the campus in a very peculiar manner. Idealistic youth were drawn to it, and many brilliant students left colleges and universities to join this movement. Pursuing an academic career, either as a student or a teacher, was denounced as careerism. Left organisations did form their own student organisations, but their aim was solely to recruit cadre for the party.

Kedar Pandey, who took over as the chief minister in 1972, tried to stem the rot. One of his initiatives was to stop the use of unfair means in examinations. The matriculation results crashed. Parents and students who had become used to this culture resented this move. It became such a grave threat that Pandey had to be removed from his post. The relationship between this resentment and the student movement of the early 1970s against the Congress government of the state and centre, which chose Jai Prakash Narayan (popularly known as JP) as its leader, remains to be probed. We also need to study the impact of the JP agitation on academic life in Bihar. Jai Prakash Narayan (JP), a veteran of the Indian freedom struggle, chose the strategies of the anti-colonial movement. Again, students were asked to boycott examinations and withdraw from the campus. Students did stop attending classes but sat for the examinations as the Congress government, in desperation, had allowed the use of unfair means to combat JP's move. After the JP agitation, the pro- and anti-reservation stir made colleges and universities its theatre. It is very interesting to note that the post-colonial political movements, be they socialist or communist, have repeatedly used the same strategy of campus boycott that was used by Gandhi in his anti-colonial struggle, and that had been criticised by his friend and admirer Tagore. The relationship of the political class with the campus has been extremely utilitarian.

The service condition of college and university teachers improved after they fought a long and bitter struggle with the government in the late 1960s and early 1970s. I remember my father spending nearly a month in the jails of Bihar in 1971. The uncertainty regarding salary and other security eased. But the teachers' movement always acted in a trade-union mode. It demanded the takeover of all types of colleges, the absorption of all types of teachers, and a time-bound promotion policy for them without any qualifier. My father recalls his conversation with Ajamat Ali, a leader of the teachers' movement, in the course of which he told my father that their job was to make demands for teachers, while it was the task of the government to enforce duty on them.

The teachers' movement of Bihar was once considered the strongest in India. It struggled and forced the governments to make the service condition of college and university teachers dignified. It, however, never discussed any academic issue in its entire course. It always acted like a political party or a trade union, eager to increase its membership and bargaining power, and therefore did not mind the entry of teachers in the system through the back doors, using money and political connections. Genuine, honest teachers were lost in this crowd. They thus lost esteem in the eyes of the people, who saw dubious characters entering the profession in hordes. Regular appointments to teaching posts became infrequent and then stopped altogether in the early 1980s, thereby stagnating campus life further.

Anil Kumar, who to us was Anil Babu, had not come through the University Service Commission route. He was a VC appointee in DAV College. Vice-Chancellors had the power to appoint teachers in temporary positions. Although he, like some others, was absorbed as a regular, permanent lecturer in 1981, successive governments have refused to recognise their first date of joining, thereby adversely affecting seniority and pay. He had moved the court to get things right. But this constant battle had not diminished his youthful desire and hope to do something for his students and college, which had struck me as a student when I participated in the Einstein Centenary Celebrations organised by him at DAV College. He was the second person with a Ph.D. to join as lecturer in the history of DAV College. He had studied Physics at Bihar University and was a CSIR fellow. His teacher, Professor B. N. Roy, had encouraged him to go for research.

Research and Ph.D.s were never popular with teachers in Bihar. In fact, those opting for them were mocked by the general teaching community. My father recounts his student days at the TNB College where one of the teachers went to Germany for his Ph.D. and was derided by his colleagues for having brought a suitcase full of books back with him. He was also not allowed space to install his equipment or the instruments he had brought along. He was mocked and harassed and finally decided to move back to Germany. The educational journey of a college teacher ended once he joined his job. Moreover, there was no incentive for it. Things had, however, changed since my father's days. Anil Babu had seen seven or eight of his teachers going to England on state fellowships. They received some sustenance allowance along with their full salary. It is difficult to explain when and why this practice stopped. Anil Babu remembers these teachers bubbling with excitement and energy to do something new upon their return, which started diminishing when they could not find students willing to pursue research with them. 'A teacher is as good as his students,' he says, and laments that he himself could not get research students after his return from France and the United States. Some lecturers did come to him just after his return, but they never came back once they discovered that research involved real, hard work. 'Now, at the fag end of my teaching career, two students have come to me whom I have sent to the Inter-University Accelerator Centre at Delhi for training. I also would join them at some point to learn some practical physics,' he said, smiling wryly.

Despite this lack of an educational culture, Anil Babu cherishes the memories of his days spent at a mofussil place like the DAV College.

He was welcomed into the fold by his senior teachers and did not feel the need to look for his caste fellows. He found his colleagues sincere and dedicated to their students. Lack of electricity or other facilities did not form excuses for not working or missing practicals. He still remembers his daily four-hour darkroom work without fans or light, preparing spectrum with the help of a sodium flame in candlelight.

Teachers did have different political views and affiliations, but there were no adversarial groups based on these. Anil Babu recalls his contest with R. S. Pandey, a Communist Party man, for the post of president of the college teachers' association,

> I defeated Pandeyji, but our relations remained as cordial as before. Teachers avoided participating in the election campaigns of political parties. The Member of Parliament from Siwan was a Jan Sangh (later BJP) man, but no teacher ideologically close to the party ever canvassed for him. Teachers did not want or allow extraneous factors to pollute or dent their identity as teachers.

Siwan had life. It was small and did not have basic civic amenities, but it still felt connected to the world outside. College teachers, doctors and lawyers still sent their children to the local, common schools. It did have an educated class, its own elite, comprising lawyers, doctors, and school and college teachers. Their associations and friendships cut across ideological and professional affiliations. They used to meet formally and informally. My father, a botany teacher of broad left leaning and a Nehruvian, had Mahendra Prasad, a senior RSS functionary and headmaster of a high school, as one of his close friends. This was not an exception. I remember the friendship between Mahendra Prasad and Faizul Hasan, a school teacher. Siwan had a sizeable Muslim population, but as mentioned earlier, it remained untouched by the sentiments of the Hindu-Muslim divide. My father had taken a house in Sheikh Mohalla, a Muslim locality, when he came to Siwan. Our first landlord was Hashim Saheb, a genial gentleman, headmaster of the Islamia High School. My elder brother studied there. My father says that he chose it because it was supposed to be the best school in Siwan. I went to the more 'upmarket' DAV High School. Hashim Saheb was very upset when he learnt this.

Things started changing in 1977–78 with the announcement of 27 per cent reservation in educational institutes for students from 'Backward' communities. The 'forward' caste students and teachers felt threatened and began boycotting classes. The government wanted classes to be held at any cost. The violence with which the 'forwards' reacted to this move towards affirmative action in the field of education created bitterness among 'backward' students and teachers. The rift between the two communities has been growing since then. Anil Babu remembers his student days, when there was hardly any student from the depressed classes, or women—except in the humanities stream—on campus. That teachers, even from the left, never questioned this state of affairs baffles him. This political move, however, was not backed by any effort to augment the resources in the colleges. No addition was made to the infrastructure of the colleges. An increase in the number of students was never matched with additional funds for laboratories or libraries.

The teacher was the only resource. 'But he was the one who kept getting setback after setback in successive generations,' rues Anil Babu. The political classes felt that teachers were demeaning themselves by demanding a raise in their pay scales. They were treated with respect, but were not supposed to be given enough to live respectfully. Anil Babu does not remember a government or an education secretary who did not reopen the files of the pay fixation of teachers. Teachers have always lived in a perpetual state of uncertainty regarding their pay scales, increments, their parity with colleagues at other universities, their seniority, and pensions. This permanent anxiety in the teaching community killed all possible academic aspiration within them. From the first day of joining till the day of retirement, the teacher had to fight a battle at every step, from pay fixation to securing increments, to ensuring that the pension was fixed and released on time. For teachers, courts of law have now become a place more frequented than classrooms.

'We have been forced to this condition,' says Bharat Prasad, a teacher of Economics and colleague of Anil Babu at DAV College, who has now developed an expertise in these mundane matters. 'There are nearly 10,000 cases pending in the courts, all filed by teachers pleading that the government be asked to honour the directives of the courts. These are cases against the government for its contempt of the Court orders,' he explains. I am talking to him in his rented house, which throws me back to my childhood days when we, the children of a college teacher, lived crammed together in a small two-room house. An electric bulb hanging over Bharat Prasad's head spreads a sickly light through the room. He has taken a connection from a generator for a bulb and a fan, as electricity supply is not dependable. In places like Siwan, L still stands for 'Lalten' (Lantern) in children's alphabet books. The voltage keeps fluctuating. He sits there, his vest rolled up his chest, already wet with sweat, sifting through his papers to explain the intricacies of the legal issues he is dealing with. I can count the blades on the ceiling fan.

'Towns like Siwan are devoid of oxygen,' says Anil Babu. It takes courage to live in these places, as you suffocate from the absence of any cultural air. I recall my days at the DAV College when societies like Rajendra Parishad and Sahitya Sabha (literary society) were very active. The birthday celebrations of the poet Tulsidas used to be a month-long affair, with all schools, including the Islamia High School, organising debates and speech, essay and recitation competitions. *Kavi Sammelans* were also an integral part of the month-long event. The DAV School used to host the annual Kavi Sammelans. *Mushairas* were an annual feature, organised at the initiative of the Urdu Department of DAV College. It was therefore an opportunity for the town people to visit the school and college spaces.

The Wheeler bookstall at Siwan railway station was an attraction for a growing child like me, as the beginning of the month signalled the arrival of a new lot of pocketbooks from Gyan Bharati. I used to rush to the bookstall and newspaper stand for the new issues of children's magazines like *Nandan, Parag, Champak* and *Chanda Mama* on the first of the month. My father had friends like Achyut Ghosh, a practising Homeopath, who had a rich collection of neatly kept Bangla books. My father used to take great care in keeping them in shape so that Dr Ghosh would continue to lend his precious books to him. *Kanaihya Lal Pustakalaya* was a storehouse of old and new books. This was the library where we read our first Sarat Chandra and Premchand. Gradually, however, these centres shrivelled. I was given my first lessons in modern rationality through the 'adventures' of Khattar Kaka, the protagonist of brilliant satires by Harimohan Jha in Maithili, read out to us by my father.

'There is no promise left in these towns now, be it Siwan or Chhapra or Muzaffarpur,' feels Anil Babu. There is no electricity and life looks dark and gloomy here. New people do not want to live in these places. They leave their families in Patna and commute daily from Patna to their workplaces. While they work here, they do not belong, either to the town or the college. You would hardly find a woman teacher here. 'Nearly 25–30 [women teachers] had joined the colleges in Siwan and Chapra in 1996, but now all of them have moved to either Patna or places close by,' Anil Babu informed me.

After his research stint, Anil Babu returned to DAV College in 1990 to find most older colleagues retired, or on the verge of retirement. No fresh appointments were made for more than a decade and a half. There were some unfamiliar faces. These were lecturers from the new mushrooming affiliated colleges. These were insecure positions because they were not sanctioned by the government, which therefore was not responsible for maintaining them either. Through political connections and money, the lecturers had themselves transferred to constituent colleges and slowly entrenched themselves there. It created a peculiar situation as colleges now had teachers who had never been selected through a legally tenable process, but had imposed themselves on the colleges. Their academic insecurity made them hostile to the pre-existing members. Since their extra-academic loyalties had brought them here, they spent their time consolidating those, for they held the promise of even better opportunities. While transfers were permitted between colleges of the universities—barring Patna University—they used to be very rare, but became rampant in the 1980s. A good number of them are now heading departments at the postgraduate level at the university, having elbowed out the really deserving ones. Most have never taught classes above the intermediate level, which is practically the final stage of school.

When the separation of the intermediate level (earlier known as Higher Secondary) from colleges was initiated, major colleges like DAV College were left out of the scheme. 'It turned college teachers into school teachers. Even worse, the government refuses to count the hours spent on these classes,' says Bharat Prasad. It is a crafty way of concealing the workload of the colleges to justify the non-sanctioning of fresh posts to such colleges, he explains. It also places them on a lower pedestal than colleges like Patna College, demoralising teachers even more. Is college education finished in Bihar, I wonder. 'With all science teachers except those of Patna University teaching only intermediate classes for years together, what advancement do you expect in the field of knowledge? Staff Training College programmes or refresher programmes have been practically dead for more than two decades,' Anil Babu says.

All this made college a strange place for teachers like Anil Babu. In 1990 Bihar University, of which DAV College was a constituent unit, was bifurcated into two universities—Bihar University (renamed as Bheem Rao Ambedkar University in 1992) and Jai Prakash Vishwavidyalay. The college now became part of the freshly created entity called Jai Prakash University. The university wanted to create postgraduate departments. Applications were invited from college teachers. Anil Babu was selected through this process. Rajendra College, Chhapra, in the absence of sanctioned posts, doubled as the PG centre of the new university. Anil Babu moved to Rajendra College, hoping for an opportunity to work at the postgraduate centre of the university. He did get that opportunity, but was moved back to Rajendra College after a while, elbowed out by people who had clout with the Vice-Chancellor.

The political class in Bihar, represented by successive governments, has continued to create an illusion of expansion in college and university education. In the mid-1980s, DAV College was elevated to a Postgraduate College. Postgraduate classes were added, but no new teaching positions were created. No additional funds for the laboratory or the library, which were already decaying, were sanctioned. Teachers who had never before touched a journal pertaining to their discipline, or who had been out of touch with developments in their subject area for decades together, were suddenly asked to teach postgraduate classes. 'I came to Delhi and went to the Jawaharlal Nehru University to see my nephew, who was a research scholar at the centre of life science there. Here, students were working with instruments we had seen only in books. And it was the last phase of my career,' my father recalls. Naturally, the teachers felt diffident when faced with the task of teaching PG classes, although they did make a valiant effort.

This illusory expansion was not new in higher education in Bihar. Earlier, Bihar had witnessed the opening of *kagazi* colleges (college on paper). Opened by local political leaders catering to the aspirations of different caste groups and operating from single or double-room apartments, they held out the promise of jobs for unemployed youth.

They also enrolled students who could appear as private candidates from the regular colleges. Colleges which were deemed to be 'easy centres' were chosen. It was a less painful way to get a degree. The owners of these colleges took money from the job-aspirants and gave them phony appointments. Thus, the parents of these youth could claim their children were 'engaged' and demand dowry (in the case of men) or treat this 'job' as an additional qualification (in the case of women). Once 'engaged', these teachers had their jobs cut out for them. Now the burden to regularise the college fell upon them. It became a never-ending race or investment as they kept collecting money to pay the decision-makers. Led to believe that they were lecturers, it was now their duty to turn this fantasy into reality. They did succeed, though. In stages, such spurious colleges were taken over by the state. Now the struggle reached a new level with these 'teachers' finding ways to enter constituent colleges so as to further secure their positions. Luck did smile on many of them; they were transferred from 'non-sanctioned' to 'sanctioned' posts. From there, they moved to the university departments. 'Teachers who have never taught an undergraduate class in their lives are now heading PG departments. This is the final equalising blow to the system of higher education in Bihar,' sighs Anil Babu.

One such college is Raja Singh College, Siwan, which has now been selected by none less than the University Grants Commission as the coveted Centre of Potential for Excellence (at the expense of DAV College), and whose second principal rose to become the Vice-Chancellor of BR Ambedkar University. A 360-degree turn has taken place, with the bad coin finally kicking out the good one.

Educational weeds like Raja Singh College have grown faster and have choked the growth of genuine institutions like DAV College. In earlier days, institutions like Rajendra College, Chhapra, or Langat Singh College, Muzaffarpur, or even a distant college like TNB College, Bhagalpur, used to be reference points for DAV College. Now, it is RJS College. Before RJS, Islamia College had been established in Siwan. These were also individual initiatives. It is important to remember the difference between them and people like Darhi Baba. Darhi Baba had no extra-academic agenda to pursue through the college—neither the propagation of his Arya Samaj ideology, nor the patronisation of a community.

Darhi Baba was no exception; my father told me the story of the birth of Deoghar College in Deoghar (now in Jharkhand). Vinodanand Jha, an active Congressman who later became the chief minister of Bihar, belonged to the powerful Panda (Brahmin) community of Deoghar. But he chose Krishna Vallabh Sahaya, a Kayastha, as the first principal and gave him complete autonomy. Sahaya was a man of many parts—he was an authority on Hindi poetry, a master of English literature and an archaeologist. Jha used his power to resist attempts by the community or other forces to interfere in college affairs. On the other hand, Sahaya, like Banke Bihari Mishra, drew strength from his scholarship and not from his proximity to the chief of the Governing Body. In turn, he chose his teachers on the basis of their academic credentials. The new individual initiatives came from an entirely different universe. Using the shield of communitarian aspirations, these initiatives were used to further the political or commercial interest of that particular individual. With the growth of an increasing number of such colleges and the clamour to regularise them to bring them on par with colleges like DAV College, it became difficult for the latter to maintain their distinct identity. It was also no longer possible for the town to identify with a single educational entity. The college, too, lost its community and identity.

The legacy, however, takes time to die. DAV College has been notorious for conducting fair examinations. As the centre for examinations, DAV College is a nightmare for examinees. This has created a peculiar situation. Since examinations for undergraduates are conducted within the college itself, the enrolment in undergraduate classes is very poor as students choose to take admission in other, 'easy' colleges. However, the postgraduate courses are always full, not because of the quality of teaching, but because of the fact that PG examinations are held at other centres and not in the DAV College.

Fair examination or assessment has always been resented by parents or the society. The image of hordes of 'helpers' outside examination halls being chased away by the police has never left me. Ramdhari Singh Dinakar recalls that when he went to join Bhagalpur University as Vice-Chancellor in 1964, he came across instances of loudspeakers installed outside examination centres, announcing answers for the benefit of the students. This starts from the school level and then continues. Attempts by college and university authorities or governments to stop it have always been resisted violently by the people. Parents have fought pitched battles on the streets with the police and the administration, demanding the right to use unfair means.

'Society seems to be confused about the meaning of education,' Surendra Prasad, who taught us English in college, reflects.

> It is investing a lot more in education now, but is not very clear about its substance. Or perhaps I am wrong. It knows what is to be expected from where. Moreover, quality was never an issue even for the teachers' unions. We fought for everything but quality. Curriculum reforms never entered the lexicon of [the] teachers' movement. What are we despairing for, then? Since degrees are the prerogative of these state-approved institutions and they still hold some prestige, parents enrol their wards there. But they also know that colleges do not have anything substantial to offer other than the degrees, they prefer to be safe with the students joining useful coaching centres.

Young boys and girls still come to Surendra Babu to learn English. 'It is becoming more and more difficult to teach language now. Undergraduate students cannot form a meaningful sentence even in Hindi.' There is a tinge of sadness in his voice. I remember him gently teaching me, a young higher-secondary student then, that directness in poetry is not always a virtue. It was becoming impossible for colleges to keep pace with the expectations of the market and parents. Markets were impatient. As the economy outside changed, new types of jobs appeared on the scene and the universities or colleges were caught unawares. New disciplines were forged to save departments. Something called Functional English became the mainstay for the English departments. But there were faster options for Functional English. Coaching institutes popped up and surrounded colleges and universities. It is quite ironical that nowadays the walls of Patna University colleges are full of advertisements for institutes offering crash courses in English. There was something leisurely about learning in a collegiate way. Colleges started suffocating. That they are still alive has something to do with this strange obsession with the graduate degree. Once the compulsion for a graduate degree goes, colleges will perish in the hundreds and there will be no Sujit Mukherji to write elegies for them.

'Rise of the coaching industry for various professional courses meant further downslide for college education. There are nearly 115 admissions in the department of Physics. But hardly two or three students come. The rest are busy with some more important "technical" or "professional courses",' Anil Babu says. College education is now a 'side activity'. The most famous and celebrated academic personality from Bihar is no university don, but Anand Kumar, who has been running a successful coaching centre preparing students for admission to the IITs (Indian Institutes of Technology). He is feted as a mathematician. Big hoardings greet you when you pass through the road taking you to Patna airport, boldly announcing '*Patna ko doosra Kota banana hai*' ('We have to turn Patna into another Kota'). Kota is a town in Rajasthan, famous for its coaching centres that prepare students for the IITs and other professional courses.

However, I also need to tell you about the underbelly of higher education in Bihar. About how a lab technician-turned-demonstrator of the Science College became the czar of higher education in Bihar under the regime of Lalu Prasad Yadav in the 1990s. How our revered teachers started crawling before him for Vice-Chancellorships or other positions. And they came from all castes. How the teachers' movement cracked. The one-and-a-half-decade-long rule of this man, who enjoyed the power no chancellor would ever dream of, is very crucial to understanding the psychological makeover that the academic life of Bihar has undergone. This man, who was once a confidante of Lalu Prasad, is now a respected Member of Parliament from the party Nitish Kumar—the successor of the Lalu regime and the present chief minister of Bihar—belongs to.

The time when I saw my teachers in Patna protracting before this man was also the period when my good old DAV College suffered a grievous blow from the flag bearers of the politics of social justice in Bihar. I can never forget the morning of 25 September 1991. I had come from Patna to Siwan to spend time with my parents. My father left for college in the morning, as had been his practice for nearly three decades. I started arranging the bookshelf. Suddenly, I found my father standing before me, blood dripping from his head, his kurta drenched in blood. Did he fall on the way? No! He said, very calmly, that he had been assaulted by the goons of the Member of Parliament of the ruling party (Rashtriya Janata Dal) from Siwan.

Called out of his department, surrounded by gun-toting young men, hit on the head with the butt of a revolver. They could have killed him. They did not want to. They wanted to send a plain message to all members of the teaching community, to fall in line. To surrender. MP saheb, who was till recently a student at the same college, wanted it served on his plate. My father returned home alone. There was no teacher to accompany an injured colleague. He was not the first. One after another, three teachers had been assaulted. No reporter had the guts to report it. Silence fell on the college. On the town, rather.

The college remained closed for more than a month after this incident. People started speaking in whispers. Divisions appeared—Hindu teachers, Muslim teachers, backward teachers, forward teachers, secular teachers, communal teachers. For the sake of the larger cause of secularism, the powerful federation of college and university teachers, led by communists, decided not to protest. Until recently, Bihar was known for its powerful teachers' organisation. It developed cracks after the advent of the politics of social justice under the leadership of Lalu Prasad Yadav. His party created its own teachers' units, which further weakened the teachers' unions.

The reign of terror continued. The MP enjoyed having his *darbar* (court) on the college campus. 'I came to college every day, my eyes lowered to the ground, fearing a call from his goons. I was terrified. The reign of terror lasted for more than a decade. Retirement was a great relief,' Surendra Babu, one of the most respected and ablest teachers of the college, said.

The MP became an educationist. He built new academic blocks from his funds for the college—an auditorium, an indoor stadium, a new administrative block, and a guest house. He established an engineering college in Siwan and donated generously to all the educational institutions. His imprint is everywhere, on the college and on the landscape of Siwan.

I am in the college. It wears a forlorn look. I want to see the botanical garden. There are only weeds there. Wild grasses have blocked the path to the practical block. A sign board of IGNOU (Indira Gandhi National Open University) adorns the central building, which serves as its study centre. These days, colleges clamour to get these study centres as they bring them money; for teachers, this means extra money.

The regime in Bihar has changed. The MP is in jail now. This means, however, that there is no benefactor to give money to the DAV College to clear the grass that seems to devour it. My teacher, Surendra Prasad, lives near Daha, a small tributary of the river Sarayu. I am sitting with him in the darkening humid evening. The waters of Daha are still, a thick layer of moss covering its blackness. Why do I not get the stink of this stagnated water, I wonder. My mind wanders to Sujit. He is not there. Patna College still beckons the Ganga. Distracted it flows.

Note

1. I would like to remember with gratitude Shri Ajmat Ali, Shri Surendra Prasad, Shri Indra Bali Shukla, Shri Tripathi Siya Raman, Dr Kare Prasad Verma, Shri Ravindra Nath Tripathi, Shri Bharat Prasad, and Dr Anil Kumar, all colleagues of my father and my teachers. Conversations with Shri Mahendraa Kumar and Shri Kedar Nath Pandey, headmasters of high schools in Siwan, were also useful.

References

Béteille, André, 'Universities at the Crossroads', *Current Science* 92 (4), 2007, pp. 441–49.

Clark, Burton R., *The Distinctive College: Antioch, Reeds and Swarthmore* (Chicago: Aldine Publishing Co., 1970).

______, 'The Organizational Saga in Higher Education', *Administrative Science Quarterly* 17 (1), 1972, pp. 178–84.

Mukherjee, Sujit, 'The College by a River: Patna College', in M. Hasan (ed.), *Knowledge, Power and Politics: Educational Institutions in India* (New Delhi: Roli Books, 1998), 239–57.

— three —

What is the Point of Multidisciplinary Research Universities in India?

Lessons from International Experience

Sachi Hatakenaka

Introduction

There has been a sea change in the way policymakers around the world view the economic role of universities over the past 30 years. With the rise of the idea of knowledge economy, universities are today regarded as potential engines of growth, capable of contributing to the creation of both individual companies and new industries. Central to this international debate has been the need for entrepreneurial multidisciplinary research universities. Today, in the Organisation for Economic Cooperation and Development (OECD) and developing countries alike, most governments have clear strategies to develop such a special category of multidisciplinary research universities.

In India, there have been repeated calls for multidisciplinary research universities by leading scientists, most recently by the committee led by Professor Yash Pal (GoI 2009). No action has been taken by the government to date, even though some recognition has been given to the need for the sciences for national economic development. There is no sense of this being a policy priority, either within the higher education sector or as part of economic development policy.

This is perhaps not surprising. For one thing, it is not easy to develop and sustain a sense of urgency on a matter as 'waffly' as multidisciplinary research universities. Indeed, it is easy to see the questions that could be asked. Exactly why and how important are they? What are the pitfalls, and what are the different approaches possible? And how urgent is the need to get action in place? Can it not wait, given that India is far from being a 'knowledge economy'? The problem is that these are 'system-level' questions, which cannot be answered simply by looking at the Indian scenario alone. To explore the answers to these questions and to come up with options, it is essential to undertake a system-level analysis, not just by comparing India's performance data against those of 'other similar systems' (which often generate nationalistic and simplistic reactions), but by examining the historical experience of system development and their performance in other countries. It is also essential to gain insight into how certain capabilities can be developed over time.

The objective of this chapter is to fill this gap and provide a qualitative analysis of the Indian higher education system as a system, to explore what it might be missing, what the consequences could be, and what options there are for further development, based on insight gained through system-level comparisons with other national systems.

To do so, this chapter will begin with an overview of the Indian higher education context, highlighting key issues as commonly articulated today. The chapter will then turn to system-level analysis using international experience to explore four key questions; (*a*) What are the critical systemic needs related to rapid expansion; (*b*) What kind of multidisciplinarity is desirable, and why; (*c*) Must multidisciplinary research reside in universities; and (*d*) Is the structure and content of Ph.D. training appropriate?

THE INDIAN CONTEXT

India's higher education system is at a crossroads. Today, it is the third largest higher education system in the world, with almost 30 million students. It has a small number of highly selective institutions, well-established in their reputation for producing high-quality graduates. The resulting rich human resource base has enabled India to leapfrog into the modern Information Technology (IT) industry—something that few had predicted. The ensuing economic boom for India comprised not only conventional foreign direct investors coming for cheap labour, but also a number of foreign corporate Research and Development (R&D) laboratories, which came to India for its brains.

Notwithstanding such past successes, the road ahead does not look simple. India's higher education system is already one of the most complex higher education systems in the world (Agarwal 2009),[1] with over 700 universities and more than 36,000 colleges, many of which are private and/or affiliated to universities (GoI 2014). Institutional arrangements are extremely diverse, with interlocking responsibilities and accountabilities at the central as well as state levels.

The complexity unfortunately masks a variable quality in the graduates produced. While the best of the higher education institutions are well-respected nationally and internationally, with their graduates highly sought after in the world's best postgraduate programmes, a large number of institutions are reported to be delivering poor-quality education. In 2013, the government tightened the regulatory framework for quality by making accreditation mandatory, a step forward from the past voluntary accreditation system that had been in place since the 1990s. The main remaining issue is the lack of qualified personnel, for both academic and administrative staff.

Fuelling the concern is the ongoing and expected expansion of the higher education sector. India's higher education enrolment ratio reached 21 per cent in 2011–12, rising sharply from 15 per cent reported as recently as 2009–10. The system has been stretched thin through decades of expansion. The annual growth has risen from 5 per cent in 1990–95, to 11 per cent in 2000–05, to over 14 per cent in 2005–10. Only recently have there been signs of slowdown, with 6 per cent reported between 2010–11. The number of students increased by more than a million annually throughout the 2000s. In 2010 alone, which marked the peak of this spurt of expansion, more than 7,000 institutions were newly established.

If the past and ongoing expansion has strained the system, today's acute shortage of high-level skills in the economy are crippling it. Even elite institutions such as the Indian Institutes of Technology (IITs) have found it difficult to recruit staff, with some institutions reporting vacancies in as many as a third of their staff positions (Bagla 2011). Staff shortages are expected to worsen in the future, if the expansion is to meet the government's continuously ambitious target of enrolling 30 per cent of the age cohort of students by 2030, revised upwards from 20 per cent by 2020.

India's Ph.D. output remains small, at 10,000–13,000 Ph.D. graduates in 2008–09.[2] A study had projected that even to meet the government's previous ambitious expansion target of 20 per cent by 2020, about a million new teaching staff would have to be recruited into the sector, which could have taken 50 years at the rate of Ph.D. production at that time (Winkler, et al. 2011)—assuming that they all would have to have doctoral degrees. Given the ambitious target,[3] expansion of Ph.D. training continues to be a high-priority agenda in the minds of many concerned.

A weak research culture in universities has also been a source of concern, particularly amongst the leading scientists, as they see it as the principal cause of poor quality in higher education (Bhattacharya 2011). In India, universities were slow to develop research capacity because of the historical division of labour between national research institutions, which have played the leading role in research, and universities which were developed principally for education. Even the IITs did not develop significant research capacity (Indiresan 2007). Indeed, there is concern that they rarely appear in global university rankings, because of the rankings' bias towards research performance. The Indian Institute of Science, Bangalore, and Punjab University were the best listed amongst Indian institutions in the Times Higher Education rankings in 2014, appearing between the 275th and 300th place; this is to be contrasted with two Chinese higher education institutions listed within the top 100.

The weak research in higher education institutions reflects this historical division of labour—as has also happened in many other countries. Over the years, India developed a large national research sector comprising many specialised research institutes, large and small, including both applied and basic sciences, falling under some 12 major scientific agencies. The division of labour between universities with poor facilities and teaching responsibilities, and elite research institutions with no teaching responsibilities, created unhealthy tension, termed 'a two-box disease' by a prominent Indian scientist.[4] There have been repeated recommendations and initiatives for better integration of research with education, or for improved linkages between the two sectors. However, little change has been accomplished and the two sectors appear to have become 'set in their separation' over time (Bhattacharya 2011; Udagaonkar 1993).

Statistics endorse the dominance of the national research institutes. While India's national investment in R&D is small by OECD standards (averaging 0.9 per cent of the Gross Domestic Product [GDP] in recent years), the central government research sector has the largest share (over 50 per cent), whereas higher education's share has been less than 5 per cent (GoI 2015). Of the total R&D manpower, about 30 per cent were working for major scientific agencies and their institutes, with less than half the number in the academic sector.

This is not to say that there are no signs of better integration of research and education. On the one hand, the Indian Institutes of Science, Education and Research (IISER) have been introduced as new institutional models, with education as well as research as an explicit part of their institutional mandate. On the other hand, leading national research institutes have initiated visible steps to take on greater Ph.D. training roles by officially adopting 'deemed university' status.[5] Although government funding of research is by no means stable yet—as witnessed by the bonanza years in the late 2000s, followed by the 'austerity' years starting in 2012 (Jayaraman 2009, 2012, 2014; Nayar 2011; Padma 2015)—the general thrust has been towards increasing 'extramural R&D support', which has been largely competitively provided, with higher education institutions taking the lion's share of such support.[6]

The portrayal of India's systemic issues, as above, is based on many assumptions. The first step must be to examine the validity of such assumptions in light of the international system experience. For instance, should there be a systemic basis for establishing expansion targets? Should research capacity be an aim for all higher education institutions? Will having enough Ph.D. graduates really solve quality issues for the entire higher education system? Even the simple sums that show that Ph.D.s cannot be produced fast enough to support the expansion seem disingenuous, given that many higher education teaching staff did not have Ph.D.s before the expansion. It may be easy to say that research capacity would be good to have for the future, but given India's complex development needs, can we be sure that it is a priority for today?

FRAMEWORK FOR INSTITUTIONAL ANALYSIS

To address these issues, it is important to establish a framework for analysing higher education institutions. Here, the proposed framework is to use two dimensions that distinguish institutional characteristics: responsiveness or application orientation, and basic science orientation. Responsiveness refers to the institutions' ability and inclination to respond to changing practical and industrial needs. Basic science orientation measures the level of commitment to fundamental science.

FIGURE 3.1: Institutional Characteristics: Responsiveness and Basic Science Orientation

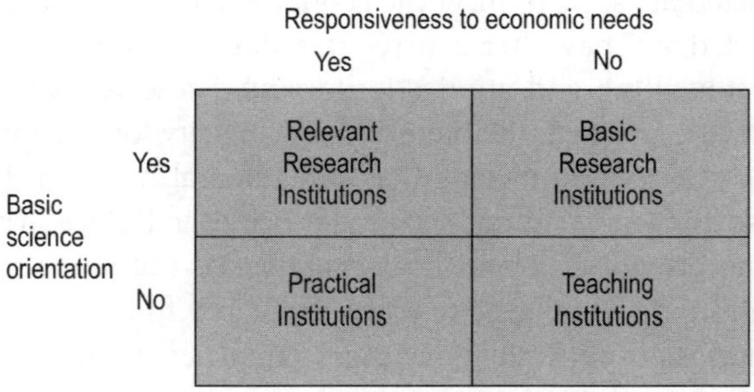

Source: Hatakenaka (2010), as adapted from Stokes (1997).

The top left-hand cell is occupied by Relevant Research Universities, which conduct fundamental research, but with an eye to its relevance to society. These institutions are committed to fundamental science but are also concerned about being useful, and they strive to remain responsive to socio–economic needs. Surprisingly, not many institutions fit this category. A primary example is a group of American research universities that, in their development, embraced the value of relevance (Geiger 2004; Mazzoleni and Nelson 2007; Rosenberg and Nelson 1994). When these universities became the envy of the world because of their contributions to high-tech industry such as biotechnology and ICT, the world initially looked to all American universities as if they were all the same. Over time, it became clear that even within the American system there were different types of universities, and that only certain research universities were proactive in industrial innovation.

The top right-hand cell is occupied by Basic Research Universities, which are driven principally by the core values of fundamental science, with little interest in or capacity for responding to external needs. This is where the classic ivory-tower universities with well-developed research capabilities belong; indeed, the great majority of research universities in the world have belonged to this cell—at least until recently, when economic relevance became a global catchphrase. These institutions value cutting-edge science, reward scientific discoveries, and encourage their academics to define actively the direction of scientific research. Until the 1990s, this cell represented what most higher education institutions aspired to be.

The bottom left-hand cell contains Practically Oriented Institutions that aspire to meet the economy's need for practical skills and knowledge. They offer courses relevant to employers and often conduct consulting and application-oriented research with and for employers. They have little interest in, or capacity for, the furtherance of generic scientific knowledge or fundamental research. Examples are diverse; they range from the Grandes Ecoles in France, which were designed to provide elite professional education (although some have now begun to develop basic research capacity), to many polytechnic schools and their equivalents in other countries. Similarly, the IITs, before they started developing research capacity, fit this cell.

The bottom right-hand cell is occupied by Teaching-focused Institutions, which are neither practically oriented in their teaching nor research-oriented. The US liberal arts colleges are good examples because they are committed to offering broad curricula, with an emphasis on generic skills rather than vocational or professional content. They define their identity in terms of their commitment to teaching and conduct hardly any research. Most universities in developing countries fall into the teaching-focused category by default, simply because they do not have the resources to be active in research.

WHAT ARE THE CRITICAL SYSTEMIC NEEDS RELATED TO RAPID EXPANSION?

The ongoing expansion is bringing India to a new level in its higher education system development. Higher education experts would argue that Indian higher education has entered the phase of 'massification', with its gross enrolment ratio well above 15 per cent—regarded as the point at which higher education becomes accessible to the broader 'mass' population and is no longer limited to an 'elite' (Trow 1974). Observations of early massification, particularly in the United States, have led experts to conclude that during such a phase, there is a system-level need for institutional diversity, or differentiation—the most well-articulated version of which is the Californian higher education system.[7] It is not adequate simply to have traditional research universities; it is increasingly necessary to have much larger numbers of teaching-focused institutions and practically oriented institutions, as described in the previous section.

This is because incoming students have become increasingly diverse, with variable academic preparation from secondary schools, with diverse preferences and interests. As one OECD review of the Californian system noted: 'For post-secondary institutions to serve as a hospitable environment for those without a tradition of participation in academic life, special efforts are needed to improve the quality of instruction and services for an increasingly diverse student body. It means teaching students through very different learning styles' (OECD 1990). For many students, the kind of teaching that Ph.D.-qualified staff can offer is simply inadequate. Employer demands for skills also change rapidly, diversifying and becoming unpredictable, particularly as the economy goes through a rapid development phase.

Diversification requirements subtly change the rationale and urgency for research universities or for Ph.D. expansion. First, research universities represent a critical facet of such a differentiated system at its apex, essential for setting the overall quality of the sector. It is the ultimate provider of higher education for those who are well-suited academically. In this sense, it is essential that a small group of high quality institutions should develop, which can have commanding systemic influence. It is interesting that even in Germany, policies to develop a small group of 'apex' research universities have become the norm since the mid-2000s, in striking contrast to the past when the majority of German academics were of the rock solid belief that all universities must be equal and with significant research capacity. The number of such apex institutions can only be small, because today's research is too expensive to duplicate facilities. In the US, students enrolled in research universities remained roughly the same, at about 3 per cent, throughout the 1970s, when the gross enrolment was approaching 40 per cent (OECD 1990).

In what sense should the 'apex research universities' ensure the quality of the system? In the US, community colleges, which are arguably the 'lowest' tier institutions, offering open entry to secondary school graduates, provide a combination of short-cycle education programmes covering: (*a*) remedial education for poorly prepared students; (*b*) vocational education for those needing to enter the labour market without completing Bachelor's degrees; and (*c*) liberal arts education for those who aspire to transfer to other higher education institutions for their Bachelor's degrees. Articulation agreements between the 'apex' research universities and community colleges ensure that there are commonly held quality standards. 'Apex' institutions are the ultimate destination for all academically inclined students who aspire to transfer from community colleges. This transfer mechanism has been a powerful route for those academically able students who are poorly prepared at the time of secondary graduation. It is also welcomed by research universities as it provides them with excellent candidates from diverse backgrounds—helping to avoid the assertion that they serve only the established 'elite'. About 30 per cent of the graduates from the University of California system (including the University of California, Berkeley and the University of California, Los Angeles) and nearly 60 per cent of those from the California State University system transferred from California community colleges.[8]

The second diversification requirement is that an expansion through teaching-focused institutions can reduce concerns about Ph.D. shortages. This is because many of the teaching institutions in massification will not need staff to have Ph.D.s. In professional education institutions, practitioners can dominate the staffing requirements, as has been the case in the Grandes Ecoles in France, which are well-known for producing France's elite in government and industry.[9] It is highly unlikely that Ph.D.s make the best teachers for remedial education—which may well be what is needed in many of these institutions, given the poor quality of secondary graduates. In the US, one of the earliest massifying countries, there are many colleges and universities whose focus is exclusively on Bachelor's degrees, where they do not expect their staff to undertake research, and which have been staffed by non-Ph.D.s. The fact that many such teaching institutions in the US now do have Ph.D.s in part reflects an overproduction of Ph.D.s, rather than the needs of the job. In many US elite research universities, undergraduate students are increasingly taught by postgraduate students, who are much cheaper—a source of controversy in its own right (Hacker and Dreifus 2010).

Today, new institutional models are emerging which, if replicated, could further ease Ph.D. shortages during massification. The Monterrey Institute of Technology in Mexico provides a model of innovation for scaling up teaching through new ways of delivering education, using technology and developing new roles and preparation for teachers. Although for-profit models such as the University of Phoenix continue to be controversial, they provide less Ph.D. intensive education models as well.

International experience illuminates a path for massification in which a massive expansion of Ph.D. is neither required nor recommended, although there is still a real need for there to be a small group of leading research-oriented institutions.

WHAT KIND OF MULTIDISCIPLINARITY IS NEEDED AND WHY?

There is an increasingly articulate desire for India to have not just any research capacity, but one that contributes to meeting India's challenges (Science Advisory Council to the Prime Minister of India 2010). India is not alone in expecting tangible benefits for economic and social development from research.

This is where the distinction between Basic Research Universities and Relevant Research Universities becomes critical. While the literature has consistently highlighted a group of US research universities as the global institutional models for offering research that leads to innovation, not all US research universities excel in the same way. Rather, it is a small group of institutions with an ethos of practical relevance, many created with an explicit mission to serve society's needs (Rosenberg and Nelson 1994). Well-established examples include the Massachusetts Institute of Technology (MIT) and the University of Stanford, whose roles in regional innovation around Boston and Silicon Valley have become legendary.

In the UK, after more than a decade of pioneering efforts to recreate innovation systems around its higher education institutions, including the high-profile Cambridge–MIT partnership, which was largely paid for by the UK government, an analytical report by civil servants remarked that 'few UK institutions appear to match the depth and breadth of engagement seen in the leading institutions' (Department of Innovation, Universities and Science 2008).

So, what kind of multidisciplinarity do these institutions have? There appear to be several distinct factors providing a definition of the needed 'multidisciplinarity'.

First, they all have a good breadth of disciplinary coverage, always spanning basic and applied sciences, but also usually including engineering and medicine, as well as a full range of social sciences, all of which are consciously managed to ensure their overall relevance. MIT is a good example of one that started with a narrower base, as it was established as a technical engineering school before the turn of the twentieth century, albeit with an unusual emphasis on basic sciences (Etzkowitz 2002). However, it made a strategic decision to develop research capacity early in the twentieth century and changed its disciplinary shape, first to include social sciences and humanities after World War II, and then to strengthen biological research capacity dramatically in the 1980s. It is not good enough for an institution to have broad coverage at a given time; it must be able to make continuous strategic decisions to expand or modify its disciplinary coverage to maintain relevance.

Second, as MIT academics would argue, there is no point in having many disciplines unless the academics from different disciplines respect each other. Academics are disciplinary communities and disciplinary boundaries are surprisingly powerful; for them to 'bother' to work across disciplines, they must feel confident that their partners are at least as good as they are in their respective fields (Hatakenaka 2004).[10] World-class engineers would not work with second-class business school academics.[11]

Third, having a good range of disciplines would have made no difference if there was no organisational mechanism to enable academics to work across campus. Many US research universities developed a system of flexible interdisciplinary research centres, an unusual mechanism at the time, to bring together an interdisciplinary community of scholars whose home departments existed elsewhere. While many universities around the world have established 'research centres', these have tended to be permanent interdisciplinary institutions with permanent staff. The innovation in the Relevant Research Universities was to have an organisational model which could scale up and down as the needs rose and declined (Geiger 2004; Hatakenaka 2004).

High flyers such as Stanford and MIT have since developed far more sophisticated mechanisms to support the development of interdisciplinary work on their campus. Stanford's 'Bio–X' represents a more recent organisational innovation, which helped step up interdisciplinary research around biology to an unprecedented level, allowing ever greater flexibility in the use of space and other resources in the 2000s.

Finally, Relevant Research Universities have a culture of working closely with industry, which has constantly pushed the frontiers of their work, leading them to develop specialisations/fields and disciplines to help with industry's research needs (Mowery, et al. 2004). Active academics in Relevant Research Universities recognise the need to work with industry to 'keep current'. MIT's early relationships with the oil industry in the twentieth century defined the content of chemical engineering. In Relevant Research Universities, research that is rooted in the practical interests of user communities can co-evolve with industrial research.

Such 'requirements' for multidisciplinarity makes it clear that not many Indian institutions have such a capacity. Some central universities may have the breadth (although often with weak engineering or medicine), but most of them do not have the organisational governance structures or autonomy to allow them to evolve strategically in this flexible way. In addition, some research institutions may have the research capacity in basic and applied sciences, but lack the breadth or ability to venture into new fields. Of course, it is possible for universities or research institutes to evolve to develop the right multidisciplinarity. But the next question then is: Does it matter whether this is done in research institutes or in universities?

Must Multidisciplinary Research Reside in Universities?

The new paradigms of the 'knowledge economy' and 'innovation' tend to favour research universities over specialised research institutions in innovation and economic development. Part of that is historical chance—US universities, which developed the powerful model for 'relevant research', happened to adopt the role in basic science, starting with Johns Hopkins, the first research university in the US, in the nineteenth century.

Nonetheless, there is a certain logic to why universities provide a better 'fit' for 'relevant research', which encompass both fundamental science and application orientation. For instance, universities, given their education mandate, need a certain breadth in their disciplinarity, which in turn gives them much greater flexibility in developing new fields of research, including interdisciplinary ones. Their educational mandate also means that they are exposed to a constant flow of young talent, ready to move into cutting-edge fields of science as well as science-driven businesses. These bright students also exert 'market pressures'—unless disciplinary communities maintain their 'relevance' to the world, good students are unlikely to keep joining them.

Through education, universities create one of the most critical inputs for the knowledge economy: a highly skilled labour force trained to fit the needs of the emerging industry. The fact that universities *can* play such critical roles in innovation and entrepreneurship does not mean that all universities should do so. Indeed, developing research universities to become better players in innovation ecosystems has been one of the principal preoccupations of many governments—with many failures. In one comparative analysis, several Japanese scholars compared curricular change in electronics in Stanford to that in the Tokyo Institute of Technology (TIT), one of the best engineering schools in Japan. They concluded that there is a fundamental difference, in that Stanford renovated its curriculum through continuous change, which often included seeds for fundamental changes, whereas TIT conducted curricular revision through non-continuous, periodic reviews (Hoshino, et al. 2003). Further, they observed that curricular changes in Stanford were part of their institutional 'responsiveness', in which strategic research agenda were constantly identified in the light of changing industrial contexts; this 'institutional responsiveness' in itself was a critical characteristic that Stanford and other US institutions developed to remain competitive in the highly competitive system of higher education.

In contrast, research institutions tend to have well-defined domains of excellence, usually set up to meet specific needs of the country. However, they can be structurally susceptible to stagnation as a result of their narrowness or uniqueness. Over time, when their original rationale diminishes, when the original field becomes obsolete, or when industry and universities develop capabilities in similar fields, it is not easy for the research institute to evolve into new fields to meet new needs, precisely because of their narrowness. Also, there is usually no equivalent to 'institutional competition' that can push them constantly for renewal.

As a former MIT president observed, 'The problem with independent research institutes is that they tend to dry up after a few years because of the lack of inflow of younger staff and students.'[12] Conversely, one prominent Indian scientist who had significant experience in US and Indian national research institutes observed that US universities can be incredibly nimble and change rapidly in response to the changing environment.[13]

In the past several decades, there has been a pronounced international trend in national efforts to strengthen and revamp university research. Emphasising competition for research resources, concentrating large facilities and resources to create centres of excellence, building innovation ecosystems around selected universities, and encouraging interdisciplinary research in strategic areas have all been common policies adopted by governments to promote university research.

There have been parallel efforts to reform or revamp national research institutions in a number of countries. The rising costs of research undoubtedly made the elimination of duplication and fragmentation a high-priority fiscal issue. Some national research sectors have been dramatically 'reconfigured'. In the UK, a significant number of research institutions were abolished, privatised or diminished when institutional reviews indicated that they could no longer justify their existence (Boden, et al. 2004). In Denmark (as well as in countries such as Estonia and Albania), the bulk of the national research institutes were merged with universities when their isolation from university science was seen to be leading to fragmentation and duplication (Government of Denmark 2009).

The Chinese experience of S&T reforms is perhaps extreme, given their original need to reverse the ills of the cultural revolution. However, they demonstrated graphically how they needed to work with both sectors to rebuild university research from the ground up and to readjust the role of their research institutions, in order to solve their version of the 'two box disease'. Starting in 1978, the Open Policy, which marked China's transition to a market economy, led to massive reforms in both sectors (International Development Research Centre and State Science and Technology Commission 1997). Research institutes were subjected to serious restructuring to create 'technology markets', and their dedicated budgets were duly cut, sometimes by as much as 70 per cent. More than a decade later, the President of the Chinese Academy of Sciences (CAS) was still describing the status of its 123 research institutes as 'overstaffed, weakened by serious inbreeding, closed to outsiders, and far less dynamic in both personnel and research than similar institutions abroad'. In the ensuing process of reforms, they 'made the institutions more open to university professors, increased mobility into and from the institutes, introduced a system of peer review and competition, enhanced international collaboration, and gave more opportunities to a younger generation of scientists' (Guangzhao 1995).

By the mid-1990s, the CAS funding base had been transformed from one of simple central government support to one that comprised 20 per cent central government funding; 30 per cent central government contracts; 30 per cent from contracts with enterprises; and 20 per cent from state and municipal governments (International Development Research Centre and State Science and Technology Commission 1997). Their roles to serve the need of the high-technology industry were enhanced at the same time; a CAS physicist was China's first to establish a 'spin-off' company based on his basic research, with a number of other companies following suit.

China has consistently taken what appear to be exemplary steps to establish a research base within higher education. Starting in 1978,

Chinese universities have undergone thorough reforms. From the beginning, emphasis was given to identifying and developing elite institutions under the name of key universities and key laboratories (Ma 2007). Funding cuts in the 1980s marked a powerful starting point for competition and institutional innovation, with competitive funding for research being established as early as 1986.[14] Collaborative arrangements that CAS developed with universities, together with a transfer of key basic research functions from CAS to universities, provided helpful starting points for universities to build their research base. Subsequently, massive investments have been given to the best universities to improve physical and human infrastructure for research, resulting in the emergence of a group of elite research universities. The government has been highly selective in granting rights to institutions to award doctoral degrees; only a limited number of institutions have been given the go ahead. Since the 1990s, special programmes have been in place to bring back talented Chinese scientists from abroad to join CAS and 'national' universities. Chinese universities have been competing amongst themselves to improve their research capacity, particularly to attain international standards. It is no accident that the global university ranking was started by one such competitive Chinese university, Shanghai Jiao Tong.

Even with such top-down and systematic reform efforts, implemented consistently over a period of time, building research capacity in universities was not easy. Indeed, Western observers continually discerned a 'considerable fragility' within the system. The IRDC review of China's S&T reforms in 1997 pointed out that, rhetoric aside, much variability in implementation was still observable across the vast country (International Development Research Centre and State Science and Technology Commission 1997). A decade later, *Nature* reported that the massive expansion of higher education and an insatiable demand for ever higher degrees have led to too rapid an expansion of doctoral programmes, which are beginning to be sharply criticised for the variability in quality (Nayar 2011).

Germany is arguably the only country where national research institutions have been defined to undertake interdisciplinary research in ways that complement and enrich their universities. One could argue that this is because they were developed almost specifically to complement university research, when universities were too rigid to cope with the emerging national research needs, starting in the nineteenth century (Clark 1995). Indeed, in Germany, it has been the universities rather than national research institutions which have been under attack for their need for reform. At the end of the 1990s, having coped with the integration of East German higher education institutions (a process which raised the level of the academia's understanding about systemic quality issues), a scholar of higher education reflected that the mood was now much more open to addressing the reform needs of German universities more broadly (Kehm 1999).

What is interesting is that in Germany, certain organisational features are built into research institutions to avoid obsolescence and to enforce competitiveness. On the basic science end, the Max Planck Society defined its role in fundamental research in the emerging interdisciplinary fields of importance, something universities are known not to undertake well. Individual institutes are established through an elaborate process of scientific scoping and global recruiting to ensure excellence, competitiveness and impact. The 'life' of an individual institution is limited to that of the appointed director in order to avoid obsolescence over time.[15] On the applied science end, the Fraunhoffer Society specialises in interdisciplinary work in application-oriented research. These institutes are set income generating expectations (currently about 70 per cent), which ensure that they remain competitive, with their scale kept at an appropriate level, given the societal needs. Both sets of institutions have extensive implicit and explicit connections with universities, with many of their key scientists holding professorial positions in universities. While the system has served Germany well, some prominent German scientists argue that the existence of Max Planck as separate institutions is inimical to developing excellence in universities (Vogel 2008). It is possible that if and when German universities develop their institutional capacity to be strategic and 'nimble' as fully as their US peers, their relationships with national research institutes may need to be revised once again.

The US research universities, in contrast, have long been established as the main forum for basic research. Some US research universities developed an entrepreneurial organisational capacity to engage in interdisciplinary research, as discussed above. They have also developed the capacity to translate cutting-edge science into practical applications. The government has various laboratories, including national laboratories, to serve its own purposes, but has tended to see universities as the best places for basic research, and has therefore set up some of their own laboratories in ways that complement universities. Indeed, some national laboratories whose research profile comes closest to that of universities are 'managed' by universities. National laboratories remain well-respected institutions, with sufficient organisational flexibility and size to be able to adapt continuously to changing needs, in competition with each other and with universities (Westwick 2003).

International experience indicates that universities have a competitive edge in conducting 'relevant research', which blends basic research with application potential. Such research can be powerful, as it complements the more narrow and application-oriented research that industry tends to take on its own. Universities are also multifaceted players, in that they also provide important 'labour inputs' in an innovation system through not only graduate, but also undergraduate education.

However, international experience also shows that different configurations are possible and sustainable for basic and applied multidisciplinary research, in either higher education research and/or national research institutions. But for the system to be sustainable, it is important for there to be (*a*) a clear sense of complementarity, and (*b*) mechanisms to maintain both higher education as well as national research institutions as competitive.

Is the Structure and Content of Ph.D. Training Appropriate?

In Indian institutions, the traditional mode of Ph.D. training has been one of individual apprenticeship with mentors—a tradition that has been widely practised across many countries, not least in Europe. The normal route to a Ph.D. in India has been through Master's programmes, where requisite coursework is to be taken. Recently, more institutions are introducing structured coursework into the Ph.D. programme itself, with some having the first year dedicated to Ph.D.-specific coursework to provide the requisite knowledge in broader relevant fields (Clarke and Lunt 2014).

Such changes are consistent with the 'silent revolution' that has been going on in doctoral training in Europe (Kottmann 2011). Although many people in Europe attribute the change to the ongoing Bologna process (an effort to integrate European higher education markets), the initial changes started much further back.

In Germany, there has been an early recognition that traditional Ph.D. training took too long and was often ineffective. In the early 1990s, the German Science Council called for the creation of structured Ph.D. programmes (Kehm 2009) and funded selected research units to create such programmes. Today, there are over 250 such programmes, many of them offering training in English.

In Germany, universities are not the only ones contributing to reforms in Ph.D. education. The Max Planck Institutes—Germany's highly respected non-university research institutes—also started establishing elite Ph.D. programmes together with the Association of Universities and Other Education Institutions in Germany in 1999, with an emphasis on interdisciplinary basic research (Burkhardt and Neher 2008). The resulting International Max Planck Research Schools (IMPRS) offer especially gifted students from Germany and abroad the possibility of working towards their Ph.D. in a structured interdisciplinary programme, with access to the research staff and facilities of Max Planck Institutes. The idea was to open the manpower and resources of the Max Planck Society to scientific education and to join forces with universities to create world-class research training, particularly in interdisciplinary subjects.

Europe is not alone in such a trend. In China, the prestigious Chinese Academy of Sciences (CAS) has played a pivotal role in the development of graduate education in the aftermath of the cultural revolution, by establishing China's first graduate school in 1978. The subsequent 30 years have seen significant restructuring, both of its own research institutes and the research training in them. By 1995, CAS was clearly articulating the training of next-generation scientists as one of its three institutional objectives (Guangzhao 1995). In 2001, unified quality standards were established across 100 research institutes by means of clearer central roles in student admission, curricula, degree conferral and courses offered in three dedicated campuses. Today, all CAS first-year postgraduates go through coursework in their central campuses before proceeding to undertake research in one of its 100 research institutes all over China (see english.cas.cn). Currently, there are over 40,000 students, with half of them pursuing Ph.D. training.

In such reforms, responding to industrial demand for research training has been a key challenge, leading to significant change in the content of Ph.D. training. In Germany, there has been a significant increase in the number of doctoral students, many of whom end up working not in academia, but in government and industrial research laboratories. In the UK, there has been a clear trend among many universities to offer doctorate programmes with greater taught elements, particularly for those intending to work in industry. The number of students in such professional doctorate programmes rose by some 70 per cent between 2000 and 2005 (Denicolo, et al. 2010).

In this respect, Japan's experience provides a powerful reminder of the pitfalls of expanding Ph.D. programmes without meeting industry needs. When Japanese companies became research-active in the 1980s, they tended to develop their own internal doctoral training—an unusual phenomenon in which Ph.D. training was 'transferred' to industry, as noted by a world renowned higher education expert at the time (Clark 1995). To the extent that the companies worked closely with universities in research in the 1980s, they tended to do so with universities in the US and the UK, much to the dismay of Japanese universities.[16] The problem appeared to be that Japanese universities were not equipped to offer relevant research opportunities to industrial staff. An important opportunity was missed for universities and industry to grow together in science.

Japanese universities took a decisive step to expand their Ph.D. programmes in the 1990s, motivated by the policy target to propel Japan into a knowledge-based economy and prompted by the low level of Ph.D. production as compared with other developed countries. The quality standards of university research in Japan were already well established, and so the Ph.D. expansion took place mainly through an expansion of programmes in well-established universities. The result was still problematic—a 'Ph.D. glut', which soon turned into a fully-fledged 'Post Doc' glut. Industry recruiting never took off on the scale that universities expected. The industry-side argument was that university-trained Ph.D.s were not sufficiently equipped to work in industry, either in terms of their fields of expertise or in their attitudes to work: there was a significant skills mismatch (Cyranoski, et al. 2011; Hatakenaka 2010b). This was the price for Japanese universities not working closely with industry to develop their research capacity, facilities or Ph.D. programmes at the time of the industrial takeoff—or thereafter.

Whether higher education institutions are able to produce Ph.D.s to meet the growing needs of industry is itself a critical issue. If they can, then universities and industry can co-evolve as industry becomes increasingly research-oriented. There will be a positive spiral in the sense that the capacity of industry to work with universities on research will in turn improve with the injection of Ph.D.s. MIT's early experience in developing Ph.D. programmes while working closely with industries such as DuPont and Bell Labs, where their own graduates already held key positions (Kaiser 2011), illustrates the power of such co-evolution. Similarly, a group of US research universities co-evolved with government research agencies as well as with industry in the post-war period (Leslie 1993), thereby establishing the US Ph.D. as a degree not only for academia, but also for government and industry. Such institutional capacity to produce Ph.D.s relevant to the needs of industry was critical to the later production of Ph.D.s in new disciplines such as computer science or biotechnology—which in turn enabled a rapid expansion of science-based industries in the US. The types of research skills cultivated by universities were deemed useful by industry.

Today, another powerful trend is developing rapidly: more and more interdisciplinary Ph.D. training is on offer. In the US, one study showed that 28 per cent of all Ph.D.s were already reported to be interdisciplinary, with MIT at a much higher level of 43 per cent in 2010. The record is likely to be far higher today.

The international experience shows that restructuring doctoral training is important not only to improve the 'academic' quality, with interdisciplinarity as an increasingly necessary feature, but also to broaden the content and make it relevant to emerging national and industrial needs. Indian companies are already showing signs of going alone—IT companies such as Infosys, as well as pharmaceutical companies such as Dr Reddy's Laboratories, now provide internal research training, albeit at a level lower than Ph.D.—but in a style similar to Japanese companies in the 1970s. In due course, they will begin to need higher-level human resources, and if universities can provide relevant training to supply them, industries and universities could develop even deeper relationships in the future. Unless universities become responsive and engage with industries *now*, the two sectors could evolve separately. If that happens, India is unlikely to see the emergence of any truly science-based, high-tech industry.

One further complication for India is that there has been a long tradition of bright graduates from India going overseas to earn Ph.D.s. On the positive side, this has contributed to the formation of invaluable human capital, from which India can gain through repatriation in the future. On the negative side, this has generated a formidable challenge for domestic institutions to compete for the best brains for their Ph.D. programmes. If Indian higher education institutions can develop Ph.D. programmes in close contact with India's evolving industry, the dynamism of which is the envy of the world, such economic dynamism may also be a powerful tool to attract good students.

CONCLUSION

What are the implications for India? If international experience is any guide, the ongoing massification in India calls for rapid diversification in higher education institutions. The most urgent need may be for a small number of elite research institutions, which can set quality standards for the whole higher education system.

There is also a strong case for building genuine multidisciplinary universities in order to meet India's needs in knowledge creation and in education—with the requisite breadth of disciplinary coverage spanning basic sciences, social sciences, humanities to professional disciplines; for instance, including engineering and medicine.

International experience posts a strong warning against the rapid expansion of Ph.D. programmes. If China found it hard to expand Ph.D. education, having made massive investments to re-establish its elite research universities and institutions, India's research system would seem far too fragile to cope with a rapid expansion of Ph.D. production. If pushed too far, it could result in meaningless 'credentialism' and the escalation of fraudulent practices (Fang, et al. 2012).[17]

A slower pace of expansion for Ph.D. programmes also makes sense, given the global climate of qualitative reform in Ph.D. education. One key reform agenda for Ph.D. programmes that requires urgent attention is the need for universities to work with industry so that their emerging skills and research needs are fully captured in the new Ph.D. programmes. India, on the verge of economic takeoff, is at a critical juncture to establish 'Relevant Research Institutions', which can co-evolve with industry. Failing such timing, the two spheres could begin to evolve separately, making it much harder for industry to maintain a competitive edge—or for universities to re-engage with industry later.

Given India's tradition of having separate institutions for research and for education, what should be done to develop research-oriented universities? International experience shows that the pressure to separate research from education is endemic, and that the only sustainable solution may lie in developing 'responsive' institutions on *both* sides. Indeed, it can take multiple reforms on both sides to reach a final and viable institutional configuration—and this will probably be the case for India too.

The hard reality is that very few of the existing institutions currently display the organisational characteristics needed for developing into multidisciplinary research universities of the type discussed in this chapter. However, there are many candidates which could develop in that direction. For example, with appropriate governance and management reforms, some of the existing universities could develop into such institutions. Some of the elite specialist institutions, such as the IITs or IISTs or the newly created IISERs, could develop a wider disciplinary coverage to become multidisciplinary research universities. Similarly, some existing government research institutes could evolve into such institutions by developing a clearly articulated institutional commitment to education and extending their disciplinary coverage to create sufficient breadth and size to foster a vibrant postgraduate community. Alternatively, or in addition, universities could forge dynamic partnerships with research institutes to evolve into research-oriented education institutions. A third option, as a wild card, could be that some of the more vocationally oriented engineering colleges with strong linkages with industry could develop into research universities over time, as did MIT. However, for each of these types of development, the road would be a long one, for a variety of reasons. Above all, it is not easy to change existing institutions, especially if they have existed for decades without strategic governance to enable nimble organisational changes.

Any shifts in this direction would require a policy context that actively encourages such growth and development. At the minimum, the goal should be to create an environment in which researchers are keen to engage with the real problems of India, working with industry, with the government and with communities. Over time, this environment would create a culture amongst scientists that could push scientific frontiers in a novel way. A key ingredient would be funding arrangements in which government agencies (as well as industrial support and other philanthropies) supported research that was relevant to India, but in a creative way. For example, India has a range of Science and Technology Departments in the government with various mandates and interests in science; these could become critical clients for research and partners in their respective areas, and could invest in upgrading research and training capabilities in universities. In this way, these universities would belong to the nation rather than to specific departments, and their full potential would be developed collectively by all government agencies, central and state. This may also be the most productive long-term solution to solving jurisdictional problems.

There is a further potential lever for change. The government has already indicated its intention to invest in a set of new institutions; these could be a critical catalyst for the future. If the new institutions simply replicated existing ones, this would endorse the roles and functions of universities as they are today—with all the shortcomings noted above. What India needs in its expansion is *not* more of the same, but more diversity and breadth, along the lines set out in this chapter, to support a diversified growth of the economy.

One critical issue in creating such new institutions has to do with governance and management structures and the role of their leadership. If a higher education institution is to become strategic and nimble in the way described in this chapter, it must be able to make organisational decisions about its respective missions, to develop strategies, to make changes, and to use its resources autonomously to such ends.

Making a bold experiment with a new class of institutions with different governance and management structures is an option open to India (but not available to most other countries). This needs a timed action plan with adequate resources and with a strong leadership to implement it. Few countries have the wealth and internationally competitive brainpower to set up multiple world-class institutions quickly; further, most struggle with governance reforms in a system which has no room for a group of new institutions. India also has the historical track record of being able to create groups of institutions of excellence—such as the IITs, IIMs, National Law Schools, etc. It will help that the intention is to establish a whole group of new institutions, rather than just one or two, as they are then more likely to become a force that influences the attitudes of existing ones. Once developed as a group, they could provide institutional models to underpin quality and excellence in established institutions, and could influence the direction of their development for the future.

All of this explains why Indian higher education is at a crossroads. Many options are still open and India has distinct advantages over many other countries. India is extremely fortunate in having highly motivated students, corporate leaders who are willing to invest in higher education, and entrepreneurial talents willing to try. India is also endowed with unusually rich human resources, inside and outside the country, to the envy of many other nations. In this respect, India's problem can be seen as one of building the right institutions with the right organisational and management models to harness the full potential of its rich human resources. Having a nationwide sense of crisis is surely a good first step towards the solution.

NOTES

1. For a comprehensive and detailed overview of the sector, see Agarwal 2009.

2. The number of Ph.D.s in engineering and technology at just over 1,000 was one-eighth of that of the United States or China. To put this in perspective, the OECD average Ph.D. production per 1,000 population was 175, while that of India was 16; China 24, Brazil 55, and Turkey 53.

3. The official targets were 15 per cent by 2012 and 21 per cent by 2017, as described in Government of India 2010.

4. Jayant Narlikar, as quoted in Parthasarathi 2005.

5. For instance, since the early 2000s, the Atomic Energy and Space Department has been active in getting its laboratories the status of deemed universities. The Indian Space Research Organisation (ISRO) established the Indian Institute of Space Science and Technology (IIST) in 2007 to offer both undergraduate and postgraduate programmes, including research-based ones. In July 2011, the Academy for Scientific and Innovative Research (AcSIR) Bill was introduced in Parliament to permit the Centre for Scientific and Industrial Research (CSIR) to develop a fully-fledged deemed university which should more than double its Ph.D. outputs. One of CSIR's flagship laboratories, the National Chemical Laboratory (NCL), has as many as 400 Ph.D. students on site, undertaking research with 200 researchers who have Ph.D.s.

6. The reported share of higher education was 64 per cent in 2009–10.

7. For specific commentary on India's lack of differentiation, see Altbach (2009). More generally, see Trow 1988, 2005.

8. California Community Colleges, Scholarship Endowment, 2011.

9. Although some of them have begun to build research capacity recently, apparently in response to global competition around ranking. There have also been French efforts to create ranking that reflect their strengths in creating an industrial elite. See Deer 2009.

10. Based on a personal conversation with a former Provost of MIT, dated 7 September 2001.

11. It made a conscious decision not to develop its own medical school, but instead developed strong ties with Harvard Medical School as well as with nearby hospitals for clinical work. Personal interview with Charles Vest, former President of MIT, dated 28 August 2000.

12. Personal interview with Paul Gray, former President of MIT, dated 9 January 2001.

13. Personal interview (under condition of anonymity), dated 2 April 2010.

14. This was extremely early, given that China had only opened up in the beginning of the decade with scientific reforms starting in the mid-1980s, and when countries such as Korea, which were far more advanced in economic development, were just establishing their own research foundations (the Korean Research Foundation was established in 1981).

15. Personal interview with a former director of a Max Planck Institute (under condition of anonymity), dated 1 March 2010.

16. Personal interview with Akito Arima, former President of Tokyo University, dated 14 March 2001.

17. This has been already happening. Reported cases of plagiarism and duplicate publications are already disproportionately large for both China and India.

REFERENCES

Agarwal, Pawan, *Indian Higher Education: Envisioning the Future* (New Delhi: Sage Publications, 2009).

Altbach, Philip, 'The Giants Awake: Higher Education Systems in India and China', *Economic and Political Weekly* 44 (23), 2009, pp. 39–51.

Bagla, Pallava, 'Faculties Wither as Higher Education System Rapidly Expands', *Science* 332 (6029), 2011, p. 524.

Bhattacharya, Sabyasachi, 'Indian Science Today: An Indigenously Crafted Crisis', *Social Research* 78 (1), 2011, pp. 255–80.

Boden, R., D. Cox, M. Nedeva, and K. Barker, *Scrutinising Science: The Changing UK Government of Science* (London: Palgrave MacMillan, 2004).

Burkhardt, Steffen and Erwin Neher, 'The International Max Planck Research Schools for Molecular Biology and Neurosciences in Gottingen (Germany) as Examples for Joint Doctoral Training by a German University and its Non-University Partners', *Higher Education in Europe* 33 (1), 2008, pp. 27–34.

Clark, Burton, *Places of Inquiry: Research and Advanced Education in Modern Universities* (Berkeley: University of California Press, 1995).

Clarke, Gillian and Ingrid Lunt, 'International Comparisons in Postgraduate Education: Quality, Access and Employment Outcomes', Report to the Higher Education Funding Council of England, 2014. Available at www.ukcge.ac.uk.

Cyranoski, David, Natasha Gilbert, Heidi Ledford, Anjali Nayar, and Mohammed Yahia, 'The Ph.D. Factory: The World is Producing More Ph.D.s than Ever Before. Is it Time to Stop?', *Nature* 472 (7343), 2011, pp. 276–79.

Deer, Cecile, 'Elite Higher Education in France', in David Palfreyman and Ted Taper (eds), *Structuring Mass Higher Education: The Role of Elite Institutions* (New York: Routledge, 2009), 219–36.

Denicolo, Pam, Michael Fuller, Dianne Berry, and Carolyn Raven, 'A Review of Graduate Schools in the UK', UK Council for Graduate Education, 2010. Available at www2.le.ac.uk.

Department of Innovation, Universities and Science, *Innovation Nation: Background Analysis of Strengths and Weaknesses of the UK Innovation System* (United Kingdom: Department of Innovation, Universities and Science, 2008).

Etzkowitz, Henry, *MIT and the Rise of Entrepreneurial Science* (New York: Routledge, 2002).

Fang, Ferric C., R. Grant Steen and Arturo Casadevali, 'Misconduct accounts for the majority of retracted scientific publications', *Proceedings of the National Academy of Sciences* 109 (42), 2012, pp. 17028–33.

Geiger, Roger, *American Research Universities since World War II: Research and Relevant Knowledge* (New Brunswick: Transaction Publishers, 2004).

Government of Denmark, 'The University Evaluation Report, 2009' (Denmark: Ministry of Science, Technology and Innovation, 2009). Available at www.ubst.dk.

Government of India (GoI), 'The Report of the Committee to Advise on Renovation and Rejuvenation of Higher Education in India chaired by Professor Yash Pal', 2009. Available at www.academics-india.com.

_____, 'Report to the People on Education', 2010. Available at www.mhrd.gov.in.

_____, 'Educational Statistics at a Glance, 2014', 2014. Available at www.mhrd.gov.in.

_____, 'Research and Development Statistics at a Glance 2011–12', 2015. Available at www.nstmis-dst.org.

Guangzhao, Zhou, 'The Course of Reform at the Chinese Academy of Sciences'. *Science* 279 (5239), 1995, p. 1153.

Hacker, Andrew and Claudia Dreifus, *Higher Education? How Colleges are Wasting Our Money and Failing Our Kids—and What We Can Do About It* (New York: St. Martin's Griffin, 2010).

Hatakenaka, Sachi, *University-Industry Partnerships in MIT, Cambridge and Tokyo* (New York: Routledge, 2004).

_____, 'The Role of Higher Education in High-Technology Industrial Development: What Can International Experience Tell Us?', Annual World Bank Conference on Development Economics, Washington, D.C., 2010a.

_____, 'What's the Point of Universities? The Economic Role of Universities in Japan', *Japan Forum* 22 (1–2), 2010b, pp. 89–119.

Hoshino, Yu, Yuko Harayama and Shigeo Hatatani, 'Daigaku no gaibu henka heno taio sei [Responsiveness of Universities to External Change (trans.)]', in Yuko Harayama (ed.), *Sangaku Renkei* (Tokyo: Toyo Keizai Shinposha, 2003).

Indiresan, P. V., 'Prospect for World-Class Research Universities in India', in Philip G. Altbach and Jorge Balán (eds), *World Class Worldwide: Transforming Research Universities in Asia and Latin America*. (Baltimore: Johns Hopkins University Press, 2007), 95–121.

International Development Research Centre and State Science and Technology Commission, *A Decade of Reform: Science and Technology Policy in China* (China, 1997).

Jayaraman, K. S., 'India Hikes Science Budget Despite Slowdown', *Nature News* 8 July 2009.

———, 'Indian budget disappoints', *Nature India* 483 (7390), 2012, p. 384.

———, 'First Modi budget spells austerity for Indian science', *Nature News* 11 July 2014.

Kaiser, David, *Becoming MIT: Moments of Decisions* (Cambridge, MA: MIT Press, 2011).

Kehm, Barbara, 'Higher Education in Germany: Developments, Problems and Perspectives', Institute for Higher Education Research and UNESCO CEPES, 1999. Available at www.unesdoc.unesco.org.

———, 'Current Trends in Doctoral Education in Germany', International Forum on Research and the University, Bogotá, 2009. Available at www.colombiaaprende.edu.co.

Kottmann, Andrea, 'Reform of Doctoral Training in Europe', in J. Enders, H. F. de Boer and D. F. Westerheijden (eds), *Reform of Higher Education in Europe* (Rotterdam: Sense Publishers, 2011), 29–43.

Leslie, Stuart W., *The Cold War and American Science: The Military–Industrial–Academic Complex at MIT and Stanford* (New York: Columbia University Press, 1993).

Ma, Wanhua, 'The Flagship University and China's Economic Reform', in Philip G. Altbach and Jorge Balán (eds), *World Class Worldwide: Transforming Research Universities in Asia and Latin America* (Baltimore: Johns Hopkins University Press, 2007), 31–53.

Mazzoleni, Roberto and Richard R. Nelson, 'Public Research Institutions and Economic Catch Up', *Research Policy* 36, 2007, pp. 1512–28.

Mowery, David C., Richard R. Nelson, Bhavan N. Sampat, and Arvids Ziedonis, *Ivory Tower and Industrial Innovation* (Stanford: Stanford University Press, 2004).

Nayar, Anjali, 'Educating India', *Nature* 472, 2011, pp. 24–26.

Padma, T. V., 'India's budget disappoints scientists', *Nature News* 2 March 2015.

Parthasarathi, A., 'Opinion: Fusion to improve higher education', *The Hindu* 19 October 2005.

Organization for Economic Cooperation and Development (OECD), *Reviews of National Policies for Education: Higher Education in California* (Paris: OECD, 1990).

Rosenberg, Nathan and Richard R. Nelson, 'American Universities and Technical Advance in Industry', *Research Policy* 23, 1994, pp. 323–48.

Science Advisory Council to the Prime Minister of India, 'India as a Global Leader in Science', 2010. Available at www.dst.gov.in.

Stokes, Donald E., *Stokes Pasteur's Quadrant: Basic Science and Technological Innovation* (Washington D.C.: Brookings Institution Press, 1997).

Trow, Martin, 'Problems in the Transition from Elite to Mass Higher Education, in Policies for Higher Education', OECD Conference on Future Structures of Post-Secondary Education, Paris, 1974. Available at www.eric.ed.gov.

______, 'Comparative perspectives of higher education policy in the US and the UK', *Oxford Review of Education* 14 (1), 1988, pp. 81–96.

______, 'Reflections on the Transition from Elite to Mass to Universal Access: Forms and Phases of Higher Education in Modern Societies since WWII', in James F. Forest and Philip Altbach (eds), *International Handbook of Higher Education: Part I* (Dordrecht: Springer, 2005), 243–80.

Udagaonkar, B. M., 'Scientific Research: Autonomous Research Institutions and Universities', in Suma Chitnis and Philip Altbach (eds), *Higher Education Reform in India* (New Delhi: Sage Publications, 1993).

Vogel, Gretchen, 'Max Planck Accused of Hobbling Universities', *Science* 319 (5862), 2008, p. 396.

Westwick, Peter J., *The National Labs: Science in an American System 1917–1974* (Cambridge, MA: Harvard University Press, 2003).

Winkler, Anne-Laure, B. Venkatesh Kumar, David L. Finegold, and Vikas Argod, 'Will They Return? The Willingness of Potential Faculty to Return to India and the Key Factors Affecting Their Decisions', Joint Report by Tata Institute of Social Sciences, Rutgers University and Penn State University, 2011. Available at www.indiabioscience.org.

— *four* —

The Case for Vocationalising Higher Education

Manish Sabharwal and *Srinivasan Kannan*

The Changing World of Higher Education

College is not what it used to be; we estimate that 31 per cent of retail sales clerks in the US, 60 per cent of taxi drivers in Korea, and 15 per cent of high-end security guards in India now have a college degree. A college degree continues to have high social signalling, while many parents tend to view vocational training as something very desirable and important 'for other people's children, not my children'.

India's quest for a higher gross enrolment ratio in higher education will probably not be achieved through traditional colleges; the massification of higher education requires the vocationalisation of higher education. Vocational or Skill Universities are different from normal universities in three ways; they pray to the one god of employers, a very small proportion of their students are on campus (most are in apprenticeships and study through distance education), and a very small proportion of their students are taking degree courses (most are doing certificate and diploma courses, but have the ability to complete degree courses modularly over time). It is time to consider having two different regulatory regimes: one for small research universities (whose objective is global university rankings) and the other for large vocational universities (whose objectives are scale, employability, and strong employer connectivity).

Vocational universities will meet the increased demand for greater accessibility to higher education in a society where tertiary studies have traditionally been available exclusively to the middle class and the affluent. For India's rural and underprivileged populations, the lack of relevant and affordable higher education—or any higher education at all—and the consequent inability to meet employer requirements results in unemployment, or in employment with very limited scope for upward mobility. Vocational universities can provide the necessary support; today, we estimate that India has 20 million students in higher education physical classrooms, 5 million students in distance education, and 400,000 apprentices. Over the next decade, vocational universities could change this configuration considerably, with distance education and apprenticeships reaching 10 million students each.

GER-BASED CLASSIFICATION AND FEATURES OF HIGHER EDUCATION SYSTEMS

The gross enrolment ratio (GER)[1] of a country is among the indicators used in denoting its development status. Its higher educational system is classified, according to Trow (2000), as elite (0–15 per cent GER), mass (15–50 per cent GER), or universal (50–100 per cent GER). The Government of India plans to attain a 30 per cent GER by 2020 (MHRD-CII 2014), thus transitioning to a mass system of higher education. Trow posits that new forms of education must be created through appropriate structural changes during a transitional period of this sort, and points to the American system as a model that could be adapted for the needs of developing countries; this applies to India as well. He asserts that the American system was well-prepared, in the post-World War II surge in student enrolment, to make higher education widely accessible via community colleges, through curricular innovations like the introduction of electives, credit assignment for courses and transfer options, and by raising funds from local sources and through the institutional adoption of a market relevant approach. India, in its efforts to achieve a similarly inclusive system of higher education and to bring about a higher GER, could draw from certain measures in the American system, including additional modes of delivery (such as distance education), the provision of exit-level flexibility (through curricular modularisation and a broad range of programme tenure), allowing entry-level flexibility for older students, permitting flexible instruction times for employed students, introducing new curricular approaches such as work-related learning, and establishing new types of institutions (such as vocational universities).

By the end of the previous century, around 90 countries (Raby 2009) established a new category of tertiary educational institutions in order to fulfil vocational skill needs and community education requirements. Geo-political changes, the switch to a market economy, technological advances, and globalised competition to offer quality materials at low cost compelled industries worldwide to create new types of jobs requiring multiple skills, frequent upgrades and market sensitivity. The establishment of vocational universities and community colleges was a response to these new demands. The Community College Movement started in India (Alphonse and Valeau 2009) in 1995 with the establishment of the Pondicherry University Community College. It was followed by the founding of the Madras Community College in August 1996 (Madras Centre for Research and Development of Community Education 2003), and the establishment in September 1998 by the Manonmaniam Sundaranar University of five community colleges. JMJ Community College was founded in Tenali, Andhra Pradesh, in July 1999, and institutions were subsequently set up in the states of Gujarat, Maharashtra, Kerala, Karnataka, and Uttaranchal. These institutions were offering job-oriented, skill-based and life skills programmes, but not leading to Degree Programmes. The National Knowledge Commission Reports, 2006–09 (GoI 2009a) and Eleventh Five-Year Plan document on 'Education' (GoI 2008) visualised community colleges as a means to increase access to higher education. Still, a firm regulatory approval mechanism from the University Grants Commission (UGC) or from 14 professional councils operating under different ministries of the Government of India did not come through for the establishment of community colleges, which created a structural challenge for the growth of the community college system and for the offer of degree programmes. The community college movement received a stimulus thanks to a scheme brought in 2009 by the Indira Gandhi National Open University (IGNOU), New Delhi, to offer Associate Degree programmes through institutions registered under it as community colleges. The initiative of IGNOU, which is the managing body for one of the professional councils, Distance Education Council, provided legitimacy to the offer of Associate Degree and Degree programmes through community colleges. It has grown to include 504 community colleges as of July 2011. IGNOU, amidst its statutory structure, has formed three central bodies dedicated to the governance of community colleges operating under its ambit. As a first government-supported initiative, a decision was taken at the Conference of State and Union Territory Education Ministers held on 22 February 2012 in New Delhi to start 100 community colleges on a pilot basis in 2012–13 and scale it up gradually (GoI 2012).

Globally, community colleges and vocational universities carry out multiple missions; these institutions offer industry relevant academic programmes, provide developmental education to the local community, help in industry recruitment, host small business incubators, provide entrepreneurship development training, and meld coursework with industry apprenticeships. These institutions serve the unorganised sector, the micro, small and medium enterprises, and the local community, apart from offering credential-based academic programmes. The vision is inclusive access. A vocational university, with its university status, has an in-built degree granting status and offers programmes at all levels (certificate, diploma, associate degree, degree, and doctoral degree). A community college is a unique form of post-secondary institution that offers two-year Associate Degree Programmes and their lower modules to post-secondary students. To grant an associate degree, community colleges need statutory scaffolding by being a constituent or affiliated college of a university, or through approval granted by a national accreditation body. Due to the flexibility of the curriculum followed in community colleges and vocational universities, a candidate can register for short-tenure Certificate and Diploma Programmes and then progress to Associate Degree and Degree Programmes after a hiatus, if needed, on financial, family or occupational grounds. After studying for an Associate Degree in a community college, a student can complete a Degree Programme through the parent university (if the community college is a constituent or affiliated college) or by transfer to other universities with which articulation arrangements have been made by the community college. The parent universities can also provide academic support and project guidance to community colleges as well as facilities for postgraduate programmes.

In the Indian context, an 'on and off the ramp' arrangement of study with a break has significant advantages; it is seen that as the number of years of study increases, GER and the number of credentials awarded decrease. The reasons are financial, cultural, social, or access-based. Two instances are cited:

(*i*) The GERs along three stages of education in India exhibit a conical pattern, narrowing steeply from elementary, through secondary to higher education. As per Selected Educational Statistics 2004–05, the GERs for classes I–VIII, classes IX–XII and higher education were 93.54 per cent, 39.91 per cent and 9.97 per cent, respectively (as on 30 September 2004) (GoI 2007). In other words, only one out of four 12th standard pass-outs joins Degree Programmes. Vocational universities provide flexible options to those left out to access higher education at various phases in their lives.

(*ii*) Regarding the declining number of credentials at higher levels, IGNOU provides statistical evidence with its huge student strength of three million at present. Out of the seven lakh qualifications awarded by IGNOU during 2006–11, 65 per cent were Certificates and Diplomas and 35 per cent were graduates and above (requiring a longer study period). Community college thus has a dual purpose—to provide students with an education that is an end in itself and equips them to seek employment, and to provide students with a remedial course of study that brings them up to the standard of a university student seeking baccalaureate recognition. The case for vocational universities, then, lies in their flexibility and their educational structure, which makes further education through universities accessible to students who would previously have been unqualified as applicants.

The institutional leadership of community colleges and vocational universities needs to adopt a variety of strategies and competencies in order to accomplish multiple missions (Ding 2003; US Department of Education 2004). Institutional policies should provide respectable status to the outreach and extension education wing on par with teaching departments in relation to resource allocation, career progression and professional development. The institutional culture needs to reflect sensitivity to labour market changes and local community requirements. The information system must be built around developmental schemes, national policies and international approaches. The leadership has to assume responsibility for raising resources through multifarious and optimum use of institutional facilities, and encourage the faculty to explore avenues for funded projects. The leadership needs to be adept at building public-private/community-institution/industry-institution partnerships, as these are demanding situations requiring negotiation and team-building skills, apart from abilities to overcome impediments in execution. But why should the government support collaboration with community colleges and vocational universities? The Government of India has formulated a National Policy on Skill Development for mass skill inculcation of around 400 million till 2022 (GoI 2015). Since the Eleventh Five-Year Plan (2007–12), many government departments have initiated funded schemes as part of the agenda for skill inculcation. As the government alone cannot accomplish this task, a call has been given to educational and training institutions to utilise the schemes under various ministries for skill/competency building. It requires a proactive approach on the part of institutional management to come up with suitable proposals and strategies and carry out follow-up actions as part of the national skill-building initiative. Appropriate evaluation is to be carried out to gauge the effectiveness of partnerships in the suggested initiatives.

Community colleges and vocational universities can contribute significantly to the GER of a country: 40 per cent in Canada, 42 per cent in the US, 58 per cent in Israel, and 26 per cent in Japan (Raby 2009). These educational systems are most successful in countries where (*i*) market forces create a need for post-secondary institutions, whose skilled technicians are in demand to support technological, vocational and industrial development; (*ii*) adult and continuing education is legitimised as post-secondary education; and (*iii*) post-secondary education is equated with social and economic mobility.

UNORGANISED-SECTOR TRAINING THROUGH VOCATIONAL UNIVERSITIES

Around 92 per cent of India's workforce is unorganised in nature and prone to economic distress, as it lacks social security measures and any guarantee of employment. For the most part, the higher education sector in India has remained unconnected to the progress of the unorganised workforce. Vocational universities have the potential to create significant social change through positive intervention methods focused on the unorganised labour demographic. In order to create a sustained approach to training this sector, vocational universities can seek avenues for funded projects and collaborative work with various departments of the central and state governments. A number of ministries have established funded initiatives to inculcate skills and meet the social welfare needs of the unorganised sector through a range of training projects. A comprehensive list of these programmes is provided in Appendix 4.1.

VOCATIONAL UNIVERSITIES IN SUPPORT OF MICRO, SMALL AND MEDIUM ENTERPRISES

Micro, small and medium enterprises (MSMEs)[2] have been accepted globally as the engine of economic growth and for promoting equitable development. But of India's 63 million enterprises, 12 million do not have an office or address, 12 million work from home, only 8 million have some kind of tax registration, only 1.3 million comply with mandatory employer pension and healthcare obligations, and there are only 1 million companies. Of these 1 million companies, only 14,500 have a paid-up capital of more than Rs 10 crore. MSMEs that have a significant presence in the agriculture, horticulture and forestry sectors allow for entrepreneurship and self-employment, but need big help in productivity, which vocational universities can provide. A Task Force on MSMEs constituted under the directive of former Prime Minister of India, Manmohan Singh, suggested that MSMEs need support in the following areas: credit, marketing, labour rehabilitation, exit policy, infrastructure, technology, skill development, taxation, and legal matters (GoI 2010). A vocational university or a cluster of community colleges and the relevant curriculum could be capable of mapping the needs of MSMEs, and could provide them with the consultancy and technical support required during and after inception. Due to the MSME sector's favourable labour-to-capital ratio, as compared to large-scale industry, it has higher employment potential than large enterprises. In recent years, the MSME sector has consistently registered a higher growth rate compared to the overall industrial sector, despite the recent economic downturn and recession. As per the available statistics (fourth All-India Census of MSMEs), the MSME sector employs an estimated 60 million persons spread over 26 million enterprises. It is estimated that the MSME sector accounts for about 45 per cent of the manufacturing output, around 40 per cent of the total export of the country, and 8 per cent of GDP (GoI 2010). Community colleges can contact specific industry associations and identify their unique requirements, business environments and pertinent government policies. Vocational universities could provide support to MSMEs by investigating potentially viable government education and training programmes, such as those offered by the MSME ministry. A comprehensive list of the ministry's units that lend themselves to collaborative projects for the offer of education and training programmes is provided in Appendix 4.2. The mutual advantage of such partnerships is that MSMEs receive consultancy, opportunities for employee education and skill development, and technical support, while community college students are given on-job training and placement opportunities. The suggestion regarding possibilities of partnerships is a derivative of the mass skill inculcation scheme under the National Policy on Skill Development; its effectiveness needs to be judged through evaluative procedures.

Vocational Universities—A Supportive Mechanism for Work-related Learning and Apprenticeships

A compelling case for vocational universities and their collaboration with industrial and government enterprises is made by the need to increase the social and practical relevance of higher education, and to draw students whose backgrounds and circumstances demand a pragmatic and employment-focused approach. Work-related learning (WRL) emerges from the partnership between a university and an enterprise or a community organisation. Work-related learning can (*i*) facilitate learning from workplace practices (that is, work experience); (*ii*) aid in learning and managing the self in varied situations (metacognition); and (*iii*) help to bring about an awareness of the efforts needed to produce the desired level of performance (self-efficacy) (Moreland 2005). Six types of WRL structures are vendor certification, company training, apprenticeships, bespoke programmes, workplace delivery, and the transdisciplinary model or Mode 2 approach.

Among the WRL types mentioned, vendor certification refers to competency-based certification, for which curriculum is designed with a problem-solving approach in a vendor specific product. The vendors directly conduct the assessment for certification. Employers value such certification, despite it being from a non-university source. Microsoft Operating System and Applications, CISCO Networking Technologies, SAP (Systems Applications and Products in Data Processing) in Enterprise Resource Planning (ERP) domain, etc., are a few valued vendor products. Vendor certification is not of particular relevance to community colleges as such. In case the vendor curriculum is adopted by a university as part of academic credential, it becomes an example for the transdisciplinary model; such an arrangement can lead to dual certification—one by the vendor and the other by the university.

Company training is an essential aspect of vocational universities, since it paves the way for offering non-credit training programmes to employees of MSMEs through the optimal use of institutional resources. It can lead to a multiplier effect, as acceptable results achieved by community colleges in one enterprise can be replicated in similar enterprises of the same sector. Community colleges need to liaison with industry associations of particular segments of MSMEs, as these units may not have established training wings like the large industrial units. If company training is conducted by an institution as a credit programme towards a university credential, it becomes a bespoke programme.

An explanatory write-up is given on the features of apprenticeship programmes implemented in India, along with a few suggestions for their effective execution through the involvement of community colleges; we make use of the clauses of the Apprentices Act, 1961, and the Planning Commission Sub-Committee Report on Re-modeling India's Apprenticeship Regime (GoI 2009c). The Planning Commission of India appointed a sub-committee to examine the administrative, regulatory, financial, and other issues related to the scheme, and suggest remedial measures. The sub-committee offered detailed recommendations for re-modelling the apprenticeship programmes. The apprenticeships carry stipends, but not a job guarantee. As per sub-sections (1) and (2) of Section 22 of the Apprentices Act, it shall not be obligatory on the part of the employer to offer employment to an apprentice after completion of the apprenticeship training, unless the contract of apprenticeship has a condition for the provision of employment. Two ministries are entrusted with the responsibility of implementing the apprenticeship programmes in collaboration with industry in the public or private sector (as per pages 2 and 10–16 of the Sub-Committee Report).

- The Ministry of Labour and Employment controls aspects related to trade apprentices belonging to the Craftsman Training Scheme (CTS) and the Apprentice Training Scheme (ATS). The CTS apprentices join the industry after completing their training and certification at Industrial Training Institutes or Industrial Training Centres. The ATS apprentices are inducted into the scheme directly after completing the eighth or 10th or 12th standards. For ATS apprentices, the tenure of training varies from six months to four years, depending on the trades; also, the industries have to provide basic training and shop floor training apart from on-job training, which the industries consider a burden. The tenure is less for CTS apprentices, as they are exempt from basic and shop floor training in view of prior technical studies.
- The Ministry of Human Resource Development administers the apprenticeship programmes for graduate apprentices (holding a Bachelor's Degree in Engineering), technician apprentices (holding a Diploma in Engineering), and technician (vocational) apprentices (those who have passed the 12th standard through the vocational stream); the tenure is one year.

- The All India Council for Technical Education (AICTE) has issued guidelines for the National Employability Enhancement Mission (NEEM), which is creating the space for educational institutions and employers to construct and innovate on-job training programmes.

Many countries across the world use the apprenticeship route for getting work-ready candidates for jobs in the industry. The German scheme is quoted as a role model with a combination of formal education (in a classroom and online) and on-job experience at a workplace, which ensures a skill match between training and industry requirements. In the Indian context, the apprenticeship scheme is not popular. The course curricula are obsolete and not in tune with industry requirements. Further, it is seen that the ATS is open for 188 trades, which do not represent many skills required in the manufacturing sector and misses out the services sector almost completely. Employers, especially in the private sector, are averse to taking apprentices under ATS. The candidates are not enthusiastic about joining as apprentices. There are issues in getting approvals from multiple agencies working under the two ministries. Four of the sub-committee recommendations suggested in relation to tenure, basic and shop floor training, cost to industry, and curricular relevance (pages 27, 29 and 30 of the Sub-Committee Report) provide a ground for suggesting a supporting role for community colleges to popularise ATS among both employers and candidates. As an enabling measure, the Apprentices Act, 1961 needs to be modified through amendments; we focus on two of the modifications suggested by the sub-committee and include the third to make the scheme more inclusive.

(*i*) The apprentice programmes should be integrated with the courses designed for the inculcation of modular employable skills (MES) under the Skill Development Initiative Scheme (SDIS) of the Ministry of Labour and Employment.

(*ii*) The outsourcing of basic and shop floor training needs to be facilitated in educational institutions operating under universities and statutory bodies. The services of Vocational Training Providers, who conduct training for SDIS, can also be used.

(*iii*) The scheme should also be open for candidates who have passed Standard V to ensure an inclusive approach and maintain parity with MES courses.

The parity of the apprenticeship curriculum with MES courses ensures the industrial relevance and inclusion of 1,406 trades (as on July 2012) in 70 sectors in four graded levels, with a fair spread over the Services, Manufacture and Natural Resources sectors. These aspects can enhance compatibility with the needs and capabilities of a wide section of candidates, who are willing to spend a shorter time on apprenticeship before getting a job at a particular level in a sector. The outsourcing of basic and shop floor training to educational institutions results in cost-saving for the industries in terms of infrastructure and faculty, as these are not required in their routine production activities. Further, the industries save by paying a stipend for only the period of on-job training. Community colleges have become eligible to provide basic and shop floor training as outsourcing institutions under ATS in the amended apprentice scheme. These colleges need to take the initiative in providing consultancy and training facilities to the industry and its employees, which will prepare the necessary ground for participation as an outsourcing institution. Community colleges also need a mechanism to contact prospective candidates from the local community (especially school dropouts) for recruitment as apprentices.

Bespoke programmes are tailored to specific staff development needs of organisations and industry associations. Universities can provide an academic programme format for the functional training of the staff, serving the twin needs of preparing the staff for organisational work and university credentials. Community colleges and vocational universities can establish tie-ups with industry associations, and design and offer academic programmes that have a thematic compatibility with the functions of a particular sector. For such an offer, needs analysis is a critical pre-requisite to ensure viability. As community colleges (with the facility to offer an Associate Degree and further study) were established in the Indian context in July 2009, efforts are yet to be taken to offer bespoke programmes. Recent examples of Indian bespoke programmes (although from non-community college sources) are Manipal University's Postgraduate

Diploma in Banking and its MBA in Banking and Finance, designed to prepare new entrants of ICICI Bank to become effective business managers.

Another form of work-related learning is programme delivery at the workplace, which provides part or the whole of the academic curriculum in the workplace. Internships and on-job training (OJT) are offered to students in medicine, engineering, law, nursing, and hospitality. Shortly, we will discuss the requirements for the effective implementation of OJT. Another version of workplace delivery permits an employee of an organisation enrolled in an academic programme on her/his initiative to carry out part of the study in the workplace to save on time and travel. The Indira Gandhi National Open University, New Delhi, offers distance education for this purpose through its B.Ed. and Certificate Program in Laboratory Techniques, among other programmes.

The last among the work-related learning types is called 'Mode 2' or the transdisciplinary model; this term was introduced by Gibbons, et al. (1994). 'Mode 1' knowledge is produced using the established practices of particular disciplines in educational institutions and universities. The discipline experts hold autonomy in the creation of Mode 1 knowledge. The process of knowledge creation followed in almost all universities pertains to the Mode 1 type. In contrast, 'Mode 2' knowledge arises out of the collective inquiry of experts drawn from diverse fields into socially relevant or industrial application-oriented issues, using a problem-solving approach (Nowotny, et al. 2003). An integrated approach facilitates the holistic investigation of relevant issues. Following Gibbons, Mode 2 knowledge creation is used in developed countries in the areas of health, medicine, environmental protection, and risk analysis; it should be applicable for socio-economic development in developing countries as well (Gibbons 1998). The main attributes of Mode 2 knowledge are (Gibbons 2000):

(*i*) Mode 2 knowledge is created in an application context (whereas in Mode 1, applied usage is not a precondition for its creation and may follow subsequently, as happens in Basic Sciences). Mode 2 knowledge is produced with the purpose of solving specific issues related to the industry or society.

(*ii*) Mode 2 knowledge requires a transdisciplinary approach (while Mode 1 requires a discipline-based approach). Depending on the complexity of the issues to be addressed during Mode 2 knowledge creation, the methodology crosses the frontiers of established disciplines. The principles that evolve out of Mode 2 knowledge cannot be fragmented into component disciplines. Mode 2 knowledge gives rise to its own theoretical structures, research methods and practices, and may undergo further progression into new problem contexts. The results are communicated by the practitioners using formal and informal means, but not necessarily through professional journals and conferences. Mode 2 knowledge generated in one context may be suitably adapted, utilised and refined to fit another. In other words, transdiciplinarity allows for a dynamic problem-solving capability. Gibbons illustrates transdisciplinarity through the example of the creation of next generation computer architecture by experts drawn from computer science, software engineering, solid state physics, linguistics, psychology, and philosophy.

(*iii*) Mode 2 knowledge creation may require heterogeneous players in the form of specialists and users drawn from various disciplines of universities, research centres, consultancies, government agencies, professional bodies, industries, and community establishments. The Mode 2 knowledge producing group is less firmly institutionalised and is constituted into temporary teams to solve specific issues (whereas Mode 1 knowledge is derived from a homogeneous source of disciplines, which are institutionalised as departments of universities). A diversified organisational approach is required to produce Mode 2 knowledge. Flexibility of approach and sensitivity to response time are the key factors.

(*iv*) Social accountability and reflexivity are quite significant in Mode 2 knowledge creation. Accountability is decided in terms of the audience for whom the issues are addressed through Mode 2 knowledge. The incorporation of reflexivity signifies that due consideration is to be given to the accommodation of the values and preferences of the different individuals and groups involved in knowledge creation and usage. (In Mode

1 knowledge, social accountability and reflexivity are not the main issues, as it is generated in a context-free environment or, in some cases, is even devoid of specific applications to start with).

(*v*) Quality control in Mode 2 incorporates a diverse range of criteria, which pertains to intellectual, social, economic, and political interests (whereas in Mode 1 knowledge, the peer group decides the quality parameters).

Some implications of Mode 2 knowledge generation on university management as listed by Gibbons (1998) are: Universities need to go in for partnerships and alliances, which will lead to changes in the organisational structure and quality assurance procedures. The universities need to find ways to commercialise research, which can also bring in the concept of contractual employment. Virtual universities may spring up, offering life-long learning opportunities for workers in various organisations. The positive and negative aspects of these features are reflected in publications focusing on the South African context (Musson 2006; National Commission on Higher Education 1996; Subotzky 2000). Some of the main concerns expressed in these publications are: the linkage between Mode 1 and Mode 2 is not clearly expressed, as both have relevant applications and one is not to replace the other completely. While commercialisation of research through Mode 2 is recommended, the mechanism and requisite 'safety net' are not clearly explained to ensure the protection of discipline-based basic research and socially relevant research for community welfare. The possible effect of commercial research on the quality of teaching functions is not discussed. Policy implications in relation to an altered organisational structure and functions of a university are also critical issues to be addressed. There is a fear expressed that Mode 2 knowledge growth may erode university autonomy, academic freedom and peer review mechanisms.

As a counter, the advantages of adopting Mode 2 knowledge creation as part of university culture are: As Mode 2 knowledge is application-driven towards social and industrial causes, it has the potential to contribute to socio-economic development and poverty alleviation. It can encourage participatory mechanisms for decision-making among stakeholders drawn from divergent fields. Although

Gibbons referred to Mode 2 in the context of knowledge created through collaborative research, it can just as well be applied to teaching-learning processes. In the context of an industry-institution partnership, it could pave the way for experiential learning of the workers, which, through the National Qualifications Framework (of South Africa), can eventually support the massification of higher education.

Many of the Mode 2 knowledge outcomes discussed in the South African context are appropriate for India as well. The implied application of Mode 2 learning for the unorganised sector is included as part of the National Policy on Skill Development. The document discusses a mechanism for the testing and certification of skills acquired in non-formal and informal arrangements, which is known as prior learning accreditation. It is considered for the integration of credentials into higher education programmes through the National Vocational Qualifications Framework.

Another version of Mode 2 knowledge accumulation is through a negotiated learning agreement between an employee/learner, the employer and an academic (Brennan and Little 1996). The agreement specifies the learning objectives, learning processes and activities, outcomes, assessment criteria, support by the university, and the role of the employer. It may include prior learning, but emphasises the planning and execution of future learning activities. Both prior learning accreditation and negotiated learning are yet to be adopted in the Indian system.

Gibbons, while discussing the role of Mode 2 knowledge in providing relevant higher education, quoted Walshok (1995) and recommended that institutions facilitate basic, applied and collaborative research, interaction with civil society, and the provision of a number of direct services apart from the offer of academic programmes, continuing education programmes and consultancy (Gibbons 1998). Collaborative functions with industrial units, government bodies, community organisations, and other educational institutions need to be seen as opportunities for the provision of services, revenue generation and participation in socio-economic development. Community colleges and vocational universities are better positioned for Mode 2 knowledge generation and for the associated functions. As community colleges and vocational universities are in a formative stage in India, adequate attention needs to be paid to the formulation of a compatible institutional vision and mission, statutory and administrative provisions, recruitment and professional development criteria, curricular design and implementation pattern, and research and extension services areas.

REQUIREMENTS FOR EFFECTIVE IMPLEMENTATION OF WORK-RELATED LEARNING THROUGH VOCATIONAL UNIVERSITIES

We intend to discuss the prerequisites for executing work-related learning effectively through vocational universities in the Indian environment, using the on-job training context. The efficacy of the on-job training component depends on institution-industry interaction. According to Soares, the integration of vocation and employability in academic programmes has been termed the 'new vocationalism movement', which demands active institution-industry interaction (Soares 2010). Effective management of institution-industry interaction is one of the factors behind the success of community colleges in the US, which is evident from their enrolment figures of 12 million students in credit and non-credit programmes, and a GER contribution nearly equal to that of four-year institutions. In order to implement work-related learning with equal success in the Indian community college system, it is important to understand the particular challenges that it faces in India (see Box 4.1).

DESIGNING CURRICULAR COMPONENTS FOR ON-JOB TRAINING

Learning theories that may be employed in the effective implementation of on-job training and in optimising its outcomes are constructivism (Ally 2008; Driscoll 2000), situated cognition (Driscoll 2000) and social constructivism (Driscoll 2000; Vygotsky 1978). A short write-up on each theory is given to act as a background for application to the on-job training context. These theories include the learning

Box 4.1

Challenges Facing Work-related Learning in India

1. A lack of commitment to on-job training from the top-level management of an institution can work against partnership with the industry and internship gains (Moran and Rumble 2004).
2. Enterprise-institution partnership is not part of institutional planning, but is driven only by the individual initiatives of a few academics.
3. Workplace learning is not integrated appropriately into the curriculum. Neither academics nor workplace mentors are adequately trained to handle OJT. There is a dichotomy between institution and enterprise, which is detrimental to the learner (Martin 2000).
4. Academics in universities are overly concerned with teaching theoretical concepts, leaving learners without sufficient workshop/laboratory/hands-on skills required for application aspects (Bansal, et al. 2010).
5. The mushrooming of institutions has increased the demand for internships in enterprises, but an organised approach is lacking. Some enterprises focus overly on providing completion certificates rather than offering effective training (Bansal 2004).
6. Mechanisms for appropriate assessment are not in place (Bansal 2004).
7. Although providing stipends increases motivation (Adkoli, et al. 2010), very few enterprises currently offer them.
8. Monitoring mechanisms and corrective actions for quality improvement have not been designed (Bansal, et al. 2010).
9. The tenure of most internships is too short to be effective (Bansal, et al. 2010).
10. There is often no mentoring or academic support from universities (Martin 2000).
11. Workload adjustment is an issue with an increase in the allotment of students.
12. Only a few Indian enterprises support research projects within universities. Most of the collaboration is in the form of small-scale consultancies. Indian universities are not fully aware of the importance of intellectual property rights (IPRs), and there is a dearth of resources to manage them, contributing to the lack of interest on the part of industry for collaborations with universities (Nezu 2005).

environment and collaboration as critical features, but differ in their emphasis on the focal aspects of teaching-learning processes.

- Constructivism focuses on the importance of an individual's active approach to the learning process, rather than being a passive recipient of information. It emphasises that a learner constructs knowledge through interaction with the environment, which could also be an individual's earlier experiences. The learner receives, interprets and processes information, and then creates knowledge. The teacher assumes the role of facilitator and does not transfer knowledge directly, but provides an environment, knowing the previous attainments of the learner. The teacher presents new opportunities for learning in a sequential and structured manner. The constructivist approach facilitates a learner in attaining problem-solving skills (by working out problems by identifying the stages), critical thinking (by analysing peer work or a case study), reflective use of knowledge (by answering chapter-wise exercises, or presenting a topic before peers, or publication of one's work), self-regulation (by maintaining and analysing learning journals or record of activities), and self-awareness (the ability to understand multiple perspectives, choosing a particular line of thought and defending it against criticism). The methods of instruction under the constructivist approach can be face to face, print mode, video, web-based, role play, debates and collaborative learning. Collaboration is used to understand others' viewpoints and challenge one's own views. Web-based learning offers opportunities in terms of providing a rich information source and an authentic learning environment for interpreting concepts and solving ill-defined problems. The efficacy of computer-mediated collaborative learning on the solving of ill-defined problems has been reported (Uribe, et al. 2003), as collaborative functioning provides greater access to problem-related information.
- Situated cognition focuses on the application of concepts and tools amidst a community of practice, such as a workplace or an industry or a hospital. Collaboration among the workforce provides an authentic context for the learning. In situated cognition, learning is inseparable from the environment in

which it is situated. The workplace forms the environment, with its social, cultural and economic context facilitating the attainment of workplace-related skills. An expert or a master trainer in the place of work provides a situation for active learning, makes learners apply the concepts to a practical situation (or in a simulated job environment), and provides interpretation. The exercises enable a learner to move from peripheral involvement in a community of practice to legitimate participation through graded progress. The materials and activities in a workplace or a DVD loaded with workplace-related information supported by a video anchor can serve as inputs. The learner can participate in person as an apprentice or intern (as happens in medical or technical domains), or take up anchored instruction using a DVD and carry out the suggested activities. For effective execution, the training programme should be well-planned, optimally timed and monitored with a provision of support (by two mentors, one from the institution and the other from the workplace), and with emphasis on the multifarious situations of the workplace. Such an approach has been suggested by TeamLease in its Labour Report through a conceptual framework model (TeamLease 2012), which needs to be tested for validity. The details of this model are discussed a little later.

- Social constructivism focuses on the collaborative activities of a group as the source of learning. According to Vygotsky, who developed social constructivism, learning is a social process. The social constructivist view of the environment relates to interaction with other group members; this is in contrast to the constructivist view, which visualises the environment in terms of the individual's earlier experience. Language and culture play a crucial role in intellectual development. The role of a teacher is to provide multiple opportunities and sources of information for group interactions. The teacher or collaborative peers need to provide guidance along the lines of scaffolding, facilitating the learner to reach the desired level of problem solving. Once a learner is capable of solving problems by her/himself at a particular level, support should be withdrawn, allowing for individual initiatives. There should be recognition of the zone of proximal development of an individual, while planning the level of teaching support or social interactions for learning. The zone of proximal development is the gap between the existing level of development and the potential development level that a learner can achieve through guidance or from more capable peers. To ensure effectiveness, learners should possess team skills; the relationship among partners should be inter-subjective; and the group should be compatible. Inter-subjectivity requires a spirit of co-construction of knowledge, with shared power and authority and without domination. The application of Social Constructivism can be seen in the facilities provided by Moodle for online content creation and collaboration. It enables various social and communication tools that support teacher-student, student-student and teacher-teacher interactions (Kok 2008).

During the execution of on-job training, an institution needs to apply aspects drawn from the above approaches, depending on the available facilities.

DESIGNING OPERATIONAL ASPECTS FOR ON-JOB TRAINING

In order to visualise the factors required for effective implementation of OJT, a working hypothesis can be formulated as a conceptual framework, consisting of a triad comprising enterprise aspect, learner aspect and institution aspect. The purpose behind its formulation is to facilitate further inquiry, which may ultimately give rise to an acceptable theory, regardless of whether the working hypothesis itself is proved or disproved. The conceptual framework here is depicted through a Venn diagram of three intersecting circles, allowing for the exploration of the relationships between any two members of the triad, or among all three. It has been designed using the framework model adopted by Koole (2009) to explain learning through a triad, comprising learner aspect, mobile device aspect and social aspect. The conceptual framework model considers organisational and operational aspects of the enterprise, as well as the social and personal aspects of learners. The model makes use of situated cognition, constructivism, and Vygotsky's social constructivism, and operates in the context of workplace skills. The interactions among components of the triad decide the extent to which the on-job training implementation is effective. Figure 4.1 provides a pictorial representation of the conceptual framework used to inculcate workplace skills through on-job training.

FIGURE 4.1: On-job Training: Conceptual Framework Representation

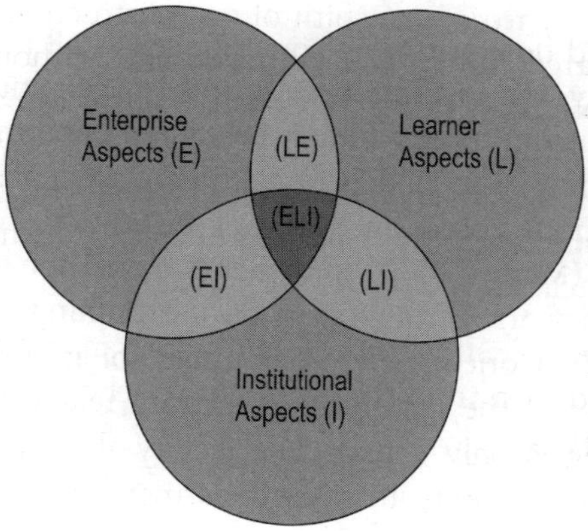

Learner aspects (L), institutional aspects (I) and enterprise aspects (E) are represented as circles. The attributes of partnership intersection (EI) and enterprise accessibility intersection (LE) signify the affordances of the enterprise environment. The intersectional area (EI) denotes the extent to which the enterprise environment is accessible for partnership with the institution, and (LE) represents the degree to which the enterprise allows the learner to use its facilities. The intersection (LI) denotes institutional learning, and is governed by all the instructional and learning theories. The area of overlap of all three circles (ELI) is the primary intersection. All three aspects converge at the primary intersection, symbolising the cultivation of workplace skills through on-job training.

Learner Aspects (L)

Learner aspects (L) refer to the subject's present competencies and skills, including prior knowledge, facility of memory, emotional balance, and willingness to learn, predicated by the assumption that the learner has a required minimum of prerequisite knowledge and mental disposition, allowing for confident interactions with academics and a peer group in the institution, and with mentors and other employees at the enterprise.

Institutional Aspects (I)

In building and demonstrating commitment to all aspects of work-related learning, the institution and top management must develop a process document, policy framework and a department dedicated to on-job training. The UNESCO document, 'Managing University-Industry Relations based on Study of Institutional Practices from 12 Countries' (Martin 2000), provides a model for the preparation of policy framework pertaining to on-job training. The institution needs to conduct orientation programmes for its faculty regarding various aspects of the institution-enterprise relationship, of which on-job training is only a part. The faculty should be encouraged through service benefits to secure partnerships with enterprises for work-related learning. The orientation programme should have components on collaborative R&D with the industry. Faculty orientation programmes need to include features of the funding schemes available for R&D from central government departments/agencies. The faculty could be deputed to training programmes conducted by the Consultancy Development Centre, functioning under the Department of Scientific and Industrial Research, Government of India. In addition to the establishment of the on-job training curriculum discussed previously, institutional infrastructure should be made available for related activities. The facilitation of institutional mentor-workplace interaction, learner-mentor interaction, and learner-learner interaction is crucial.

Enterprise Aspects (E)

A broad definition of the term 'enterprise'—which can be an individual industry, whether micro, small, medium or large, an industry group, a Chamber of Commerce, or a community organisation such as a non-governmental organisation (Soares 2010)—allows for a wide range of opportunities for on-job training-focused collaboration between organisations and community colleges. The willingness of the enterprise to offer its facilities may be motivated by a sense of its corporate social responsibility, tax benefits, or the support system that the institution offers to the enterprise. We have already discussed the support that vocational universities and community colleges can offer MSME units.

Martin (2000) states that the efficacy of the EI partnership depends on the existence of a research and teaching capacity within the institution, and R&D activity and staff development in the industry, which are stimulated by government-sponsored financial incentives. Also required are an entrepreneurial culture within the institution, an academic reward system, and incentives for staff to collaborate in programmes with industry. A system of dual mentoring should be introduced, with a mentor provided from both the faculty and the enterprise. There is a general tendency among learners to avoid small enterprises for on-job training, and institutions must identify the unique characteristics of enterprises to facilitate OJT attachment, irrespective of size. Around six months of training has been indicated as the desirable tenure. The curriculum should be relevant to enterprise needs and the theory-to-practice ratio should be adequate for skill-based programmes (Bansal, et al. 2010). Enterprises should be involved in curriculum design and implementation wherever possible. Assessment patterns should be evolved and implemented jointly by both the mentors. McLellan (1993) recommends a three-part assessment model: diagnosis (analysing journal entries), summary statistics (computer-based and personal interactions) and portfolio.

For the learner, the advantages of successful on-job training implementation include attainment of workplace knowledge, increase in confidence level, and gainful employment. An educational institution is afforded an increased retention rate, enrolment and employer satisfaction, as well as the possibility of resource generation through consultancy and continuing education of the host industries. The advantages for an enterprise include pre-evaluation of potential employees, reduced entry-level turnover, and a lower rate of employee attrition.

Success Stories of On-Job Training and Work-related Learning Implementation

A number of institutions provide models for the successful implementation of OJT and WRL. The Practice School of BITS, Pilani, while not a community college, is a useful example. It assigns on-job training based on industry-relevant projects, which are overseen by the resident faculty stationed at the industry. The resulting success propelled it to establish itself as a leader in continuing education for the corporate world through the distance mode as early as 1988 (Martin 2000).

The Jefferson Community and Technical College (JCTC), Louisville, United Parcel Service (UPS), Kentucky's largest employer, and the University of Louisville formed a partnership for the purpose of offering work-related learning to the employees of UPS (Soares 2010). Its effectiveness is indicated by the reduced attrition rate among UPS' employees, and in their receiving post-secondary credentials. In addition, JCTC has seen an increased retention rate of students.

Community colleges in India have great potential to increase the employability of the unorganised and underprivileged sectors, as well as afford students the opportunity to transfer to degree-granting universities, while contributing to India's goal of a 30 per cent GER by 2030. The avenues for mutually beneficial collaborations between colleges and private or public organisations allow students to receive practical training and employment opportunities through work-related learning and on-job training, while companies benefit from the consultancy, support, and employee certification provided by educational institutions. A well-organised community college system and a focused effort to make higher education socially relevant and accessible on a mass level would benefit students and industry alike.

Conclusion

Vocational universities are new entrants to the higher education system in India. It becomes imperative to showcase their potential advantages to the stakeholders. Students can choose from a wide variety of disciplines, ranging from vocational to science and technology, depending on their aptitude. Students from underprivileged sections can benefit economically from programmes of a suitable tenure, as employability is integrated into the curriculum. Facilities will be provided for the continuation of studies up to graduation and above, even after taking up jobs. In a globalised competition, community colleges have the potential to provide MSMEs with a level playing ground, in terms of enhancing the skills of employees in ICT and domain areas. In vocational universities, the government will find a support system for enhancing access and equity in higher education, as it has set the goal of achieving 30 per cent GER by 2030. Vocational universities can participate in capacity-building initiatives to enhance the income levels of unorganised labour and provide non-formal education for community welfare; these are, generally, beyond the goals of the contemporary university system. This chapter encourages community colleges to augment their resources through the offer of innovative programmes for a wide clientele, provision of services to MSMEs, and involvement in government-funded schemes for unorganised labour and community education.

There could be initial scepticism regarding the efficacy of this approach, as vocational universities have a wide ambit in relation to clientele, curriculum and functions. Any antagonistic reactions have to be met with continued performance and quality of service, keeping in view the evolution of similar systems at the global level. Vocational universities have the responsibility to proceed with a planned strategy in order to gain the confidence of stakeholders. The National Knowledge Commission and Eleventh Five-Year Plan have recommended the establishment of community colleges to expedite socio-economic development. In conformity with this spirit, the central and state governments can assist vocational universities through infrastructure and fiscal support, recruitment openings for graduates and popularisation through the media. Vocational universities need to set up appropriate measures for teaching-learning processes. Steps need to be taken to train the academics and support staff to ensure the execution of multiple functions. For vocational universities, the establishment of an acceptable environment for the students, agencies in the government, the private sector, and the neighbouring community is quite challenging, but is nevertheless a requirement to achieve its ambitious goals.

APPENDIX 4.1

TABLE A4.1: Government-funded Initiatives for Unorganised-sector Training

Ministry/Agency	*Programmes/Purpose*
Ministry of Rural Development	• Diksha scheme • Swarnjayanti Gram Swarojgar Yojana • National Rural Livelihoods Mission
Council for Advancement of People's Action and Rural Technology (CAPART)	A nodal agency for catalysing and coordinating partnership between voluntary organisations and the government for the promotion of sustainable development of rural areas
Ministry of Labour and Employment	• V. V. Giri National Labour Institute • Central Board of Worker Education • Skills Development Initiative Scheme (SDIS)
Ministry of Tourism	• National Council for Hotel Management and Catering Technology • 29 Institutes of Hotel Management run by central and state governments, and five Food Craft Institutes • Ashok Institute of Hospitality and Tourism Management, New Delhi • Indian Institute of Tourism and Travel Management (IITTM) • Capacity Building for Service Providers (CBSP) Scheme
Ministry of Textiles	• National Institutes of Fashion Technology (NIFTs) • Apparel Training and Design Centres (ATDCs); 25 Community Colleges (in partnership with Indira Gandhi National Open University) • Integrated Skill Development Scheme

APPENDIX 4.2

Education and training programmes offered by the Micro, Small and Medium Enterprises Ministry through the following:

- National Institute of Micro, Small and Medium Enterprises (NIMSME), Hyderabad
- Indian Institute of Entrepreneurship (IIE), Guwahati
- Khadi and Village Industries Commission (KVIC)

- Coir Board
- Mahatma Gandhi Institute for Rural Industrialisation
- Trade Related Entrepreneurship Assistance and Development Scheme for Women
- Prime Minister's Employment Generation Programme for Women
- Mahila Coir Yojana

NOTES

1. The term gross enrolment ratio (GER) is used to denote the amount of enrolment in higher education institutions in relation to the population in the 18–23 age group.

GER = Students enrolled in post-higher secondary classes × 100 / Total population in 18–23 age group.

2. Micro, small and medium enterprises are defined as per the Micro, Small and Medium Enterprises Development Act, 2006, based on their investment in plant and machinery (for manufacturing enterprise) and on equipment (for enterprises providing or rendering services).

Classification	*Manufacturing enterprises**	*Service enterprises***
Micro	Rupees 25 lakh	Rupees 10 lakh
Small	Rupees 5 crore	Rupees 2 crore
Medium	Rupees 10 crore	Rupees 5 crore

Note: * Investment limit in Plant & Machinery; ** Investment limit in equipment.

REFERENCES

Adkoli, B. V., A. Goel, A. Kumar, R. Sood, and R. Venkat, 'Structured Internship Orientation Programme for Undergraduate Students: Easy Transition to Clinical Work', *The National Medical Journal of India* 23 (3), 2010, pp. 160–62. Available at http://nmji.in/archives/Volume-23/Issue-3/PDF-volume-23-issue-3/Medical-Education.pdf.

Ally, M., 'Foundations of educational theory for online learning', in Terry Anderson (ed.), *The Theory and Practice of Online Learning*, (Edmonton, AB: Athabasca University Press, 2008), 15–44.

Alphonse, X. and E. Valeau, 'Indian Community College System: Democratic Response to Globalization', in R. L. Raby and R. Valeau (eds), *Community College Models. Globalization and Higher Education Reform* (Springer, 2009), 79–89.

Anning, D., 'China's Vocational Universities', *ERIC Digest* ED 467848, 2003. Available at http://www.ericdigests.org/2003-2/china.html.

Bansal, R. K., 'Need for Strengthening of Internship (Rotatory Housemanship) Training in India', *Education for Health* 17, 2004, pp. 332–38.

Bansal, V. K., S. Grover and A. Kumar, 'Feedback on Students Industrial Training for Enhancing Engineering Education Quality: A Survey Based Analysis', *International Journal of Engineering Science and Technology* 2 (9), 2010, pp. 4807–16.

Brennan, J. and B. Little, 'Designing and Realising Work Based Learning', in *A Review of Work Based Learning in Higher Education* (Quality Support Centre [A Centre for Higher Education Research and Information], Department for Education and Employment, The Open University, 1996), 63–76. Available at https://www.open.ac.uk/cheri/documents/Areviewofworkbasedlearninginhighereducation.pdf.

Driscoll, M. P., *Psychology of Learning for Instruction* (Boston: Pearson Education, Inc., 2000).

Gibbons, M., 'Higher Education Relevance in the 21st Century', in *World Conference on Higher Education. Higher Education in the Twenty-first Century—Vision and Action*, Volume III: Commissions, Part II: Commission Reports and Papers (Paris: UNESCO, 1998). Available at http://unesdoc.unesco.org/images/0011/001164/116429m.pdf.

______, 'Appendix: Some attributes of knowledge production in mode 2', in A. Kraak (ed.), *Changing Modes: New Knowledge Production and its Implications for Higher Education in South Africa* (HSRC Press, 2000), 133–40. Available at http://www.hsrcpress.ac.za/product.php?productid=1938&freedownload=1.

Gibbons, M., C. Limoges, H. Nowotny, S. Schwartzman, P. Scott, and M. Trow, *The New Production of Knowledge: The Dynamics of Science and Research in Contemporary Societies* (London: Sage Publications, 1994).

Government of India (GoI), *Selected Educational Statistics 2004–2005* (New Delhi: Ministry of Human Resources Development, 2007).

______, *Eleventh Five Year Plan 2007–12: Education, Volume II: Social Sector* (New Delhi: Planning Commission of India, 2008).

______, *Report to the Nation 2006–2009* (New Delhi: National Knowledge Commission, 2009a).

______, *National Policy on Skill Development* (New Delhi: Ministry of Labour and Employment, 2009b).

______, *Report and Recommendations of Planning Commission Sub-Committee on Re-modeling India's Apprenticeship Regime* (New Delhi: Planning Commission, 2009c).

———, *Report of Prime Minister's Task Force on Micro, Small and Medium Enterprises* (New Delhi: Ministry of Micro, Small and Medium Enterprises, 2010).

———, *The Newsletter on Higher Education: Issue 07* (New Delhi: Department of Higher Education, Ministry of Human Resources Development, 2012).

Kok, A., 'An Online Social Constructivist Tool: A Secondary School Experience in the Developing World', *Turkish Online Journal of Distance Education—TOJDE* 9 (3), 2008. Available at http://tojde.anadolu.edu.tr/yonetim/icerik/makaleler/426-published.pdf.

Koole, M. L., 'A Model for Framing Mobile Learning', in Mohamed Ally (ed.), *Mobile Learning: Transforming the Delivery of Education and Training* (Edmonton, AB: Athabasca University Press, 2009), 25–47.

MacAllum, K., K. Yoder., and R. Poliakoff, 'The 21st-Century Community College: A Strategic Guide to Maximizing Labor Market Responsiveness', Vol. 1: Unleashing the Power of the Community College (Washington, DC: Academy for Educational Development [AED], and Westat, Rockville, MD.: Office of Vocational and Adult Education [OVAE], US Department of Education, 2004), 1–30. Available at http://files.eric.ed.gov/fulltext/ED491848.pdf.

Madras Centre for Research and Development of Community Education, 'The Impact and Prospects of the Community College System in India', Research Project submitted to Socio-economic Research Division, Planning Commission, Government of India, 2003.

Martin, M., 'Managing University-Industry Relations: A Study of Institutional Practices from 12 Different Countries', Working Document (Series on Improving the Managerial Effectiveness of Higher Education Institutions), International Institute of Educational Planning/UNESCO, Paris, 2000.

McLellan, H., 'Situated Learning in Focus: Introduction to Special Issue', *Educational Technology* 33 (3), 1993, pp. 5–9.

Ministry of Human Resource Development, Government of India (MHRD)–Confederation of Indian Industry (CII), 'FDI in Indian Higher Education', in *ASHE 2014 Annual Status of Higher Education in States and UTs in India, 2014* (New Delhi: Confederation of Indian Industry, 2014), 15–20. Available at http://www2.deloitte.com/content/dam/Deloitte/in/Documents/IMO/in-imo-annual-status-of-higher-education-2014-noexp.pdf.

Moran, L. M. and G. Rumble, 'Policy Frameworks for Vocational Education and Training in an Electronic Age', in Louise Moran and Greville Rumble (eds), *World Review of Distance Education and Open Learning*, Vol. 5 (New York: Routledge Falmer, 2004), 205–26.

Moreland, N., 'Work-related learning in higher education', in M. Yorke (ed.), *Learning and Employability Series Two* (York: The Higher Education Academy, 2005), 1–33. Available at https://www.heacademy.ac.uk/sites/default/files/id370_work-related_learning_in_higher_education_582.pdf.

Musson, D., 'The Production of Mode 2 Knowledge in Higher Education in South Africa', Ph.D. dissertation, University of South Africa, 2006. Available at http://uir.unisa.ac.za/bitstream/handle/10500/775/thesis.pdf?sequence=1.

National Commission on Higher Education (NCHE), *An Overview of a New Policy Framework for Higher Education Transformation* (Pretoria: NCHE, 1996).

Nezu, R., 'Technology Transfer, Intellectual Property and Effective University-Industry Partnerships: The Experience of China, India, Japan, Philippines, The Republic of Korea, Singapore and Thailand' (Geneva: World Intellectual Property Organization, 2005). Available at http://www.wipo.int/edocs/pubdocs/en/intproperty/928/wipo_pub_928.pdf.

Nowotny, H., P. Scott and M. Gibbons, '"Mode 2" Revisited: The New Production of Knowledge', *Minerva* 41 (3), 2003, pp. 179–94.

Raby, R. L., 'Defining the Community College Model', in R. L. Raby and E. Valeau (eds), *Community College Models. Globalization and Higher Education Reform* (Springer, 2009), 3–19.

Soares, L., *The Power of the Education-Industry Partnership: Fostering Innovation in Collaboration between Community Colleges and Businesses* (Washington, DC: Center for American Progress, 2010), 1–15. Available at https://cdn.americanprogress.org/wp-content/uploads/issues/2010/09/pdf/community_colleges.pdf.

Subotzky, G., 'Complementing the Marketisation of Higher Education: New Modes of Knowledge Production in Community-Higher Education Partnerships', in A. Kraak (ed.), *Changing Modes: New knowledge production and its implications for higher education in South Africa* (HSRC Press, 2000), 65–89. Available at http://www.hsrcpress.ac.za/product.php?productid=1938&freedownload=1.

TeamLease, 'India Labour Report 2012—Massifying Indian Higher Education: The Access and Employability Case for Community Colleges', 2012, 87–108. Available at http://www.teamlease.com/resources/reports/india-labour-report/.

Trow, M., 'From Mass Higher Education to Universal Access: The American Advantage', in *Research and Occasional Paper Series: CSHE.1.00* (Berkeley: Centre for Studies in Higher Education, University of

California, 2000), 1–16. Available at http://www.cshe.berkeley.edu/sites/default/files/shared/publications/docs/PP.Trow.MassHE.1.00.pdf.

Uribe, E. I., J. D. Klein and H. Sullivan, 'The Effect of Computer-Mediated Collaborative Learning on Solving III-Defined Problems', *Educational Technology Research and Development* 51 (1), 2003, pp. 5–19.

Vygotsky, L. S., *Mind in Society* (Cambridge, MA: Harvard University Press, 1978).

Walshok, M. L., *Knowledge without Boundaries: What America's Research Universities Can do for the Economy, the Workplace, and the Community* (San Francisco: Jossy-Bass Publishers, 1995).

— *five* —

Skill Development in India

The Supply Side Story

Megha Agarwal

Introduction[1]

With over 640 million people under the age of 25, and a projected median age of 29 in 2020,[2] India has a very young population—a potential force for her growth story in the next decade. Currently, around 54 per cent of India's population is in the working age group (15–59 years), and the size of this labour force is expected to increase by 32 per cent in the next 20 years.[3] India's 'demographic dividend' can translate into higher growth via improved output, production and consumption. However, this is achievable only if this youth force can be armed with appropriate skill sets that maximise its productivity potential.

During the past decade, India has faced a high unemployment rate, with a large proportion of educated youth unable to find employment. Simultaneously, the organised private sector is struggling to find skilled workers. This paradox clearly points to the need for a skilled workforce.

India has a limited capacity for skill development. Currently, only close to 5 per cent[4] of the total Indian workforce has obtained any vocational skills through formal means, in comparison with 60–96 per cent in industrialised countries.

Looking ahead, at current growth rates, a large number of employment opportunities are expected to be created in the next decade. The National Policy on Skill Development and Entrepreneurship, launched in July 2015, states clearly that India is estimated to generate an incremental requirement for approximately 109.7 million skilled workers across 24 key sectors by 2022.

The construction sector (real estate and infrastructure) has the potential to create as many as 31 million jobs by 2022. In addition, 17.3 million in retail, 11.7 million in transportation and logistics, and 10 million in beauty and wellness are estimated to be created during the same period. The current capacity for training employees in skills is c.7 million annually.[5]

The urgent need to develop a strong system for skill development or vocational education and training (VET), as it has traditionally been known in India,[6] is underscored by the fact that 93 per cent of the entire labour force is currently employed in the unorganised sector. It is critical to develop a system that enables increased participation in the organised sector, as well as to structure skill development opportunities catering to India's large informal economy. If unaddressed, India's much vaunted demographic trend may well become her biggest tragedy—a large number of unemployable young Indians, who are hungry to learn, but who lack the skills needed to participate in the Indian growth story.

In order to better understand the nature of skill development in India, it is useful to look at the demand and supply of skill development. On the demand side, it is important to understand what industry and employers (both in the organised and unorganised sectors) need from their employees.

On the supply side, India has witnessed landmark changes over the past six years. Until fairly recently, India had a weak and fragmented skill development sector, underpinned by a dizzying array of decentralised government programmes, weak and inconsistent delivery mechanisms and poor private-sector participation, with students treating it as an option of last resort. What was once a scattered landscape now appears to be coalescing into a unified effort, starting with the formation of the NSDC in 2009, and lately, with the landmark creation of a centralised Ministry for Skill Development and Entrepreneurship (MSDE) in 2014. Clearly, given the relative youth of the skill development ministry and its allied entities and the fact that several initiatives are still in their early phase, one can anticipate changes over the next few years. That notwithstanding, the recent reforms provide us an optimal opportunity to evaluate the state of skill development in India, and anticipate the extent to which the current policy responds to the critical challenges faced in this sector.

This chapter focuses mainly on government initiatives. Currently, private initiatives are at a nascent stage, and are expected to engage in the space depending on the quality and effectiveness of the public frameworks and incentives that will be rolled out. In particular, the subsequent evaluation of NSDC in this chapter becomes critical to this discussion. The remainder of the chapter is structured as follows.

Section 2 looks at the historical challenges faced in the sector, and the revised framework for skill development. Section 3 maps the different initiatives rolled out by the government against the key challenges outlined. It evaluates five key initiatives, each focusing on a different aspect of the supply side of skill development. Section 4 concludes the chapter by highlighting some important overarching takeaways about the policy environment and the supply side of skill development, and what it means for the future of skill development in India.

INDIA'S NEW SKILL DEVELOPMENT FRAMEWORK

Challenges Faced by the Sector

Despite the recent spate of news and academic literature on the issues plaguing skill development in India, the core challenges faced by the system have been articulated in several forums over the years, and are well-known to decision-making policy bodies.

These challenges range from having a large informal sector impacted by stringent labour laws, to a lack of high-quality institutes with top-notch trainers who are well-connected to industry needs. There is also a serious aspirations mismatch between potential workers and industries that are starved for talent. This can be traced to the absence of mechanisms that provide genuine signals of quality to the employers, thus hindering labour market efficiency. The same inability to signal quality also results in worker populations self-selecting away from the professions that are expected to drive real growth in India. A more detailed examination of the key problems is set out in Table 5.1.

TABLE 5.1: Key Challenges Faced by the Skill Development Sector

Constraint	*Implications*
Limited capacity for VET	Only a very small proportion of the Indian labour force has any formal skill qualifications, thereby leading to a less productive national workforce.
Limited focus on informal economy	93% of the labour force is employed in the informal economy. An absence of formal skills training and clear pathways linking the informal economy to the formal economy leads to reduced productivity.
Lack of clear framework defining quality	The lack of a comprehensive framework makes it difficult for employers and students to gauge the quality of a course, that is, VET fails as a signalling mechanism in the labour market.
Lack of flexibility and mobility within VET space	Lack of vertical mobility within VET and horizontal mobility between VET and higher education contribute to it being perceived as a dead end. Inflexible course delivery makes VET inaccessible to economically disadvantaged students.
Mismatch between courses offered and those required by industry	Leads to poor labour market outcomes. An unemployable labour force accompanied by industry being unable to find suitable employees negatively affects growth and productivity.
Lack of industry involvement in VET	Industry involvement in delivery, management of institutions and curriculum design is critical to ensure a direct connection to the labour market, and to bring about organisational and productive innovations.
Lack of quality trainers	Lack of 'training the trainer' institutes, innovation in hiring and remuneration methods, policy on ensuring quality through regular up-skilling for trainers represent a major supply constraint and affect the quality of training.

Overhaul of Government Architecture

Given the systemic nature of the problem, there has been a longstanding recognition of the need for an integrated and strategic approach to skill development. Prior to the recent reforms, India had a significantly fragmented landscape, which was unable to envision and implement a coordinated and efficient strategic effort required to solve the systemic challenges in the sector. For instance, skills were a joint concern of over 20 ministries at the central level. Vocational education in schools was a concern of the Ministry of Human Resource Development, while ITIs and polytechnics were under the Ministry of Labour and Employment. For specific sectors, such as the aviation industry, relevant central ministries had decision-making authority in setting skills and standards. Livelihood schemes in rural areas, a potentially critical plank for increasing informal engagement in skill development, was (and continues to be) under the aegis of the Ministry of Rural Development. In addition, skill development was (and continues to be) a concurrent centre and state subject, with each state being responsible for the implementation of local schemes, supported by their own machinery for delivery.

In response to the growing awareness around the importance of skill development in India, the new NDA government formed the Ministry of Skill Development and Entrepreneurship (MSDE) in November 2014. The hope is that the MSDE will consolidate and streamline the efforts of discretely operating ministries. While the MHRD, MoLE and MoRD remain integral to government-run skill programmes, the MSDE aims to take control of coordinating/administering/facilitating all skill development programmes.

The MSDE acts as an umbrella organisation, coordinating a wide range of skill development efforts. Its functional arms include the National Skill Development Agency (NSDA), the National Skill Development Corporation (NSDC), the National Skill Development Fund (NSDF), 33 regional Sector Skill Councils (SSCs) and the Directorate General of Training.

Figure 5.1: MSDE Structure

Role of the Ministry of Skill Development and Entrepreneurship

As the apex body, MSDE has been proactive in its role as consolidator of the various scattered strands of skill development. In July 2015, MSDE launched its ambitious National Policy on Skill Development and Entrepreneurship with the aim of providing clarity concerning the government's role in skill development and encouraging a concerted approach to government initiatives. In addition, MSDE is playing an increasingly active role in skill development in areas that traditionally belonged to other ministries, through either direct control of schemes (for instance, the vocationalisation of schools and the DGET are now under the purview of the MSDE) or through a collaborative approach by entering into MOUs with other ministries (for example, MSDE is working with the Ministries of Civil Aviation, Railways and Defence).

Apart from its role as consolidator and coordinator, MSDE engages with different aspects of skill development through four different verticals. While these bodies predate the MSDE, they are themselves relatively new, or have been given material mandates in recent years. These are described briefly below.

The National Skill Development Corporation was set up in October 2009 as a public-private partnership (PPP), with the mandate to create 150 million skilled workers by 2022. The primary mandate assigned to the NSDC is to incentivise private-sector participation in all aspects of the skill development process, that is, developing curriculum, delivery of training, quality assurance, and placement. With the inception of the MSDE, the NSDC has become a functional arm of the ministry and the administering organisation for a variety of MSDE programmes.

The National Skill Development Agency was set up in 2013 with a two-pronged objective of quality assurance and policy research. The NSDA is responsible for conceptualising, operationalising and implementing the National Skills Qualification Framework. This ambitious project aims to enable vertical and horizontal mobility for students and workers by setting up an overarching set of standards that will integrate skill development with the traditional education apparatus.

Sector Skill Councils were set up by the NSDC as autonomous industry bodies for 37 identified sectors to enable an industry-led approach to skill development in India. The SSC works closely with the NSDA and the NSDC to set appropriate skilling standards that meet the needs of the industry.

The Directorate General of Training was transferred to the MSDE from the MoLE in 2015, and is responsible for the delivery of formal skills training through government institutes. In effect, this enables the MSDE control of Industrial Training Institutes, which constitute the largest share of the formal skill development delivery channels in India.

Conclusion

At this stage, while there is still significant consolidation left to be done, the MSDE has made notable strides in providing a systematic integrated approach to skilling. Moreover, it appears that there is clarity and alignment of the roles and mandates of the different bodies run by the MSDE, which are individually focusing on different aspects of the skill development challenge.

Both of these are vital elements to the success of any structural overhaul. The following sections examine the question of execution by evaluating specific schemes implemented by the different bodies, and assess the degree to which they have been able to address the key challenges faced by the sector.

EVALUATION OF KEY INITIATIVES

Introduction

The MSDE, through different bodies, has put in place a range of schemes that aim to tackle the challenges faced by the skill development sector. At the time of writing, most of the key problems have certain initiatives already in progress, although in the early stages. Initiatives currently in place focus on the challenges of capacity, quality frameworks and industry involvement. Initiatives around quality of training and bringing informal economies into the fold are at too early a stage for analysis at this point in time. Table 5.2 maps the initiatives against the challenges faced by the sector.

Table 5.2: MSDE Initiatives to Counter Challenges Faced by the Skill Development Sector

Constraint	*Critical initiatives*
Limited capacity for VET	1. Vocationalisation of schools 2. Upgradation of ITIs 3. Private-sector initiatives funded by NSDC
Lack of clear framework defining quality	4. NSQF framework responsible for creating overarching standards enabling high quality and flexibility.
Lack of flexibility and mobility within VET space	
Mismatch between courses offered and those required by industry	5. The Sector Skill Councils prepare occupational standards that feed into the NSQF framework, and are responsible for industry involvement and representation.
Lack of industry involvement in VET	
Lack of quality trainers	No clearly identified initiative/at an early stage of development. This is currently part of the MSDE and NSDC mandate.
Limited focus on informal economy	Recognition of prior learning through government schemes like the Pradhan Mantri Kaushal Vikas Yojana (PMKVY) scheme set up in 2015. This is enabled by the NSQF. These are at a very early stage of development.

Evaluation of Initiatives

This section examines five of the key initiatives and highlights areas where progress has been made, and what could be done better going forward. At the outset, it should be recognised that most of these initiatives are in the early stages. It is too early to highlight significant successes, but there have been lessons learnt from some early stage failures.

Vocationalisation of Secondary Education: Overview

Vocational education has been offered in schools in Classes XI and XII in India since the 1960s, but due to structural and quality issues has not been very effective in reaching a broad swathe of the student population, or in providing clear employment pathways.

In an effort to improve vocational schooling, a pilot for the introduction of vocational education from Class IX onwards was launched under the National Vocational Education Qualifications Framework (now the NSQF) in September 2012 in Haryana. The pilot, implemented in partnership with the Wadhwani Foundation, covered 40 schools and approximately 4,600 children.[7] The MHRD drew various significant learnings from the pilot, including the need to mainstream vocationalisation by integrating it with general education, the importance of making sure that content is driven by industry, and the importance of providing core employability skills that would be useful across various sectors to give students career flexibility.[8]

Based on these learnings, the MHRD rolled out a full-fledged scheme, called the Centrally Sponsored Scheme of Vocationalisation of Secondary Education, which would offer school students vocational modules in select sectors as an additional or compulsory subject. This is structured as a four-year offering, commencing when the student is in Class IX and ending with a placement initiative just before they complete Class XII.

This scheme has since been taken over by the MSDE. The National Policy for Skill Development and Entrepreneurship aims to integrate skilling within formal education (starting from Class IX) in 25 per cent of schools within five years.[9] The NSDC is responsible for implementing this scheme through its training partners and Sector Skill Councils (SSCs), in partnership with state governments. It is designed to align with the NSQF. As of the 2014–15 academic cycle, the scheme was being extended to 1,439 schools in 10 states.[10]

According to the MSDE website, state governments are responsible for providing physical infrastructure, while NSDC-funded private partners implement all aspects of the training.[11] Importantly, the curriculum utilised aligns with NSQF qualifications, which should make the transition from secondary education to post-secondary institutions seamless. The SSCs are meant to provide assessments and certifications aligned with the NSQF that will facilitate multiple entries and exits at each level (or within a level), with the bundle of credits earned clearly certified.

It is useful to note that government measures, such as the pilot programme described above, are being implemented in partnership with private enterprises. The MSDE and NSDC have entered into a partnership with the Wadhwani Foundation to implement this initiative.

Assessment

This initiative is ambitious and wide-ranging. If executed efficiently, it will go a long way in mainstreaming vocational education in the Indian education system. The idea that it is quality, not scale, that is the long-term binding constraint has been clearly articulated by external researchers over the years. The World Bank strongly recommended that the government first conduct in-depth work to better understand how to use vocational education in schools effectively, before committing vast resources and time to expand capacity.

At first glance, it does seem that the scheme aims to address many of the core issues surrounding vocational schooling; however, it will face significant challenges, particularly due to the vast number and spread of schools which are envisioned to offer vocational courses.

- The success of this scheme depends on the ability to provide high-quality teachers, whilst urgently tackling the perception issues associated with vocational education.
- There is a material mismatch between student aspirations and what the industry needs, which is something that may not have been taken fully into account.[12]
- The success of this scheme relies heavily on the quality of training provided by NSDC training partners. Effective monitoring and ensuring a strict adherence to quality standards for these training organisations is critical to the success of this initiative.

It is also worth noting that although the MHRD launched a seemingly successful pilot project, the scheme is still in a very early stage and would benefit from an extensive (and public) assessment of implementation quality before investing more resources into capacity enhancement. The quantitative assessment of the pilot programme has not been made publicly available, and the presence of public information regarding government measures for vocational programmes in schools is new and its development is thin.

Upgradation of Industrial Training Institutes: Overview

Historically, the government has provided vocational training primarily through a network of Industrial Training Institutes (ITIs) and Private Industrial Training Institutes (PITIs). There are presently around 2,284 ITIs and over 9,680 PITIs under the purview of the Directorate General of Employment and Training (DGET).

The ITIs have previously been under the Ministry of Labour and Employment, and have performed poorly. Several initiatives had been rolled out during the past decade, which were unable to meet expectations. The responsibility to upgrade the quality of ITIs was moved over to the MSDE in April 2015.

The government's 2015 national skill development policy includes ITIs and PITIs as important channels for high-quality, industry relevant skills training. This policy clearly identifies ITIs as a core plank that needs to be fixed and leveraged to meet the capacity needs of the country. Traditionally the primary channel for skills training in India, ITIs continue to account for 24 per cent of all skills training capacity in the country.

This section focuses on outlining the performance of the ITIs and on some of the challenges that the MSDE will face in upgrading the ITIs.

Historically Poor Performance

These institutions follow the curriculum outlined by the National Council for Vocational Training (NCVT) and offer training under two main schemes—the Craftsmen Training Scheme and the Apprenticeship Training Scheme. Together, these two schemes have a total capacity for approximately 16.9 million seats annually,[13] which is equivalent to 24 per cent of the total skilling capacity in India as estimated in 2014.[14] The fact that these institutes account for such a significant proportion of the skilling ecosystem in India means that their ability to provide high-quality, industry-relevant training to enrolled learners is critical to the success of skilling efforts being made in the country.

Over the years, ITIs have unfortunately been associated with poor quality training outcomes. There has been detailed research on these institutions, highlighting several limitations associated with them in the past decade. A World Bank study in 2006 outlined serious gaps in and drawbacks of the quality associated with ITIs and PITIs. In particular, it highlighted the poor labour market outcomes of graduates due to a mismatch between the quality of skills provided and those needed by employers, poor linkages with industry, lack of quality trainers and infrastructure, emphasis on manufacturing/engineering trades (several of which were deemed obsolete by the industry), with inadequate representation of the service industry (World Bank 2006).

Initiatives such as the adoption of ITIs by industry and the adoption of select ITIs by the government to create model centres of excellence, among others, have underperformed. A large proportion of the private sector is apprehensive about adopting ITIs due to fears of corruption in the state government. The big challenge is that even after adoption, private-sector partners face excessive political interference from the state government. Moreover, the centre perceives the quality control mechanism at the state level as a failure.

Limited industry involvement in the arrangement has taken the form of having four members from industry in the Institution Management Committee (IMC). Private partners in such cases have sometimes not been actively invested or involved in the development of the institutions. The quality of trainers also continues to be a big problem. Additionally, although new non-engineering courses have been developed in the past few years, the capacity for such courses is still limited.

On the demand side, in addition to the negative perception associated with VET in general, ITIs and PITIs continue to be a low-priority option for students due to their reputation as being ineffective in providing desirable employment opportunities.

MSDE Initiatives

The 2015 skill development policy highlights several initiatives to upgrade the quality of ITIs. Some of these are: following an outcome-based approach, creating pathways between ITIs and formal education, creating additional courses with curriculum aligned to industry demand, using technology in the design and delivery of curriculum, and creating an additional interface for ITIs with industry to enhance apprenticeship opportunities and create employment pathways for students.

Companies have begun to collaborate with government-run ITIs to help design training programmes in line with industry-specific needs. For example, Maruti Suzuki has helped to set up automobile skill enhancement centres. In 2014, Flipkart, Tata Sons, the Raymond Group and Gujarat Industrial Power Company signed agreements with the Labour Ministry to help design training programmes for ITIs, a huge step forward in terms of connecting ITIs with industry.

However, these institutions have several decades of history behind them, and serious demand and supply side limitations. MSDE will have to work closely with all the different stakeholders to address each of these challenges in an efficient and organised manner, in order to transform ITIs into high-quality, aspirational institutions for skills training.

It must also be noted that stringent and inoptimal labour regulations play a part in this. In general, only very large companies, such as Maruti Suzuki or Honda, pay higher wages to workers trained in ITIs versus high school graduates. At the same time, large factories that employ over 500 regular workers comprise only 2 per cent of India's factories, according to the Labour Bureau (Varma 2015). This implies that at best, MSDE will be able to solve only a part of the problem. This is a critical point which requires addressing. MSDE's ability to integrate the informal economy into the skill development framework will be fundamental to the long-term success of these institutions.

Recent performance indicates that there is still a long way to go. While ITIs have reported an increase of 20 per cent in enrolment in 2014–15, this is still a low utilisation rate. For example, in Gujarat, although there are a large number of ITIs, many of the slots go unfilled. In an attempt to fill the 1.71 lakh seats in 779 ITIs, the

Gujarat government has tried to target the 4.8 lakh students who failed the Class X board exams in 2015. From an effectiveness perspective, a Labour Bureau report in 2014 indicated that among those who received formal training in an institution like an ITI, the unemployment rate was high—at 14.5 per cent—compared to 2.6 per cent overall. In a breakdown by field, the Bureau found that except for trades like leather work, plumbing, motor driving and tour/travel operations, all other categories of skilled persons had double-digit unemployment figures. Further, core fields such as engineering (other than civil and computer) had an unemployment rate of over 25 per cent. In addition, around 17 per cent of those with textile-related training and over 14 per cent with machine operator skills were unemployed.

To conclude, while focusing on the ITIs is a sensible way of leveraging the existing capacity, the challenge lies in the fact that these institutes bring with them serious questions of credibility and effectiveness, from the perspective of both employers and students. Currently, an ITI as provider is the last choice for its participants, and MSDE has to provide material investments in these bodies to upgrade the quality in line with industry requirements.

Private-sector Initiatives Led by NSDC Description

In order to address the fragmented nature of the regulatory landscape and promote private-sector involvement in skill development, the government announced a National Skill Development Mission/Agenda in 2008. The NSDC was set up in October 2009 as a public-private partnership (PPP), with the mandate to create 150 million skilled workers by 2022. Indian industry holds a 51 per cent stake and 49 per cent is held by the government. Industry associations such as the Confederation of Indian Industry (CII), Federation of Indian Chambers of Commerce and Industry (FICCI), Associated Chambers of Commerce and Industry of India (ASSOCHAM) and National Association of Software and Service Companies (NASSCOM) each have 5.1 per cent equity, and are on the board of NSDC. NSDC has been very active and has made significant progress in fostering private-sector involvement in skill development since it started operations. With the inception of the MSDE, the NSDC has become a functional arm of the ministry and the administering organisation for a variety of MSDE programmes.

The primary mandate assigned to the NSDC is to incentivise private-sector participation in all aspects of the skill development process, that is, curriculum development, delivery of training, quality assurance, as well as placements. The NSDC is encouraging industry, NGOs, business associations, social entrepreneurs, as well as existing training and skill development institutions to participate in the skill development process. In many sectors, market mechanisms alone cannot incentivise entry. Thus, the NSDC provides significant capital in the form of grants, equity and loans as incentive and risk reduction for these various private entities. The funding is directed through the National Skill Development Fund. The NSDC funds both direct providers of skills training and support systems, such as initiatives focused on quality assurance, and provide training to trainer academies, or information systems.

Assessment

The NSDC has actively entered into a large number of skill development partnerships with the private sector since 2010. Through their partnerships, they have trained four million students and are funding 207 private-sector partnerships, each of which is estimated to train at least 50,000 people in 10 years.[15] Overall, the NSDC has been an agile and result-oriented organisation. It is probably the most robust government initiative in the VET space. The NSDC initiatives look promising and attempt to address most of the tasks they have been assigned. However, the NSDC's focus has been on quick capacity creation and this has sometimes led to a lapse in quality assurance, which in turn has led to serious mistakes in some cases.

One such case in point is the STAR scheme. The Standard Training Assessment and Reward Scheme was a national skill certification and reward scheme implemented by the NSDC and launched in August 2013. The objective of the scheme was to incentivise skill training by providing youth who had successfully completed an approved training programme with a monetary award. It was an ambitious initiative aimed to skill 10 lakh youth at an approximate total cost of Rs 1,000 crore to the government. With the intention of standardising certification and increasing productivity among the existing workforce, STAR certified 861,077[16] students before it was brought to an abrupt close in September 2014. This closure was attributed to 'unscrupulous people/institutes'[17] which had been scamming prospective students into enrolment to the scheme; presumably training programmes that had no right to do so and with no connection to the NSDC. There is limited publicly available information analysing the STAR scheme, representing an opacity which is stark since NSDC had positioned itself as a largely transparent institution otherwise. There is also limited accountability with no subsequent disclosure on where monitoring authorities had failed to meet their responsibilities.

The STAR scheme is a very good example of how a single-minded focus on capacity creation while compromising quality assurance and monitoring can be a serious setback to creating a skilling ecosystem in India. It is unfortunate that the correct regulatory framework and monitoring mechanisms were not in place before the implementation of STAR. The MSDE launched the Pradhan Mantri Kaushal Vikas Yojana (PMKVY) to address the same goals as STAR in July 2015. As of July 2016, official statements say that 17.94 lakh individuals were enrolled and 11.84 lakh were certified under this scheme.[18] A further 1.79 lakh individuals were trained under Recognition of Prior Learning (RPL). After rolling this programme out for one year, it was recently renewed for the period 2016–20. An ambitious programme, it has a total allocation of Rs 12,000 crore and is mandated to train 10 million youths in the five-year period. Six million of these are fresh youths, to be trained and brought into the workforce, while four million existing workers will be upskilled and certified under Recognition of Prior Learning. Interestingly, 25 per cent of both the financial and physical targets are being allocated directly to the states. This is an interesting way to ensure that the entire skills machinery works together, following the same targets, monitoring mechanisms and quality standards. This revised scheme is yet to be rolled out, and its impact on the skill development landscape and whether it successfully incorporates lessons from the failure of STAR and the pilot year of PMKVY is unknown.

In another such example, there have been cases of corruption and NSDC training partners mis-reporting their placement outcomes to access funds. This is driven by the fact that NSDC has linked funding for training partners to placement outcomes. It is important to pre-empt such instances; these can be avoided by putting in place and strictly adhering to strong quality assurance frameworks and monitoring mechanisms.

Setbacks such as these are dangerous and can potentially derail India's skill development plans, especially since India is at a critical point in consolidating an ecosystem that has traditionally been very fragmented. The equilibrium is fragile at best and quality assurance has to be the basis on which the entire ecosystem is built. Capacity generation cannot be pursued without a strong focus on quality.

National Skills Qualification Framework Description

The National Skills Qualification Framework has been structured as the overarching framework for skill development in India. It defines the learning outcomes that an individual should possess at different levels for various sectors, independent of whether the learner has gone through formal or informal learning. It will create a flexible system which will permit individuals to accumulate their knowledge and skills, and convert them through testing and certification into advanced diplomas and/or degrees. Class VIII graduates would, for example, have the option to enrol in certain courses, and there would be several levels of qualifications available, depending on the number of hours students spend on the subject.

The NSQF intends to address the issue of vertical (that is, within VET) and horizontal (that is, between VET and general higher education) mobility by creating a system of credits that would allow easy movement between vocational training, formal education and employment.[19] In the NSQF's official notification, it was stated that the framework would also provide greater transparency on progression pathways, so that students, employers and institutes would understand what a student's qualifications will be upon completion of a specific course.

A key aspect of NSQF will be facilitating a broader Recognition of Prior of Learning (RPL), allowing the assessment of skills acquired through informal means and consequently enabling pathways between the informal and formal economies.[20]

The NSQF is envisioned to act as a regulatory quality assurance framework. According to the NSQF's implementation schedule, by December 2016 no government funding will be provided to training or education programmes not aligned with the NSQF, and by December 2018 it will be mandatory for all training and education programmes to adhere to NSQF guidelines and define their criteria for admission according to NSQF qualification levels.

Assessment

The consolidation of the various existing government frameworks into the NSQF is a positive achievement. It also seems encouraging that with the creation of the MSDE, the NSQF will be administered by one body that intends to act as a nerve centre for all the key stakeholders in skill development. Pilots implementing the NSQF, such as the Vocationalisation of Secondary Education, have been launched, but are too early in their cycle for review. However, it should be noted that due to an immense push in capacity creation by the government, the skill development space is crowded with small, and in many cases low-quality, private organisations.

The MSDE will need to invest heavily in high-quality and transparent monitoring to ensure adherence to the NSQF by 2018. This will likely be the litmus test, given the historical challenges associated with corruption-free monitoring by government agencies on a large scale.

Sector Skill Councils Description

Sector Skill Councils (SSCs) are autonomous industry bodies and are central to the skill development ecosystem that MSDE and NSDC are trying to create. Working in close collaboration with NSDC to set the National Occupational Standards (NOS) is probably one of the most critical mandates given to the SSCs. Through this, employers rigorously define the key functions of a specific job role, combining all necessary NOS for a job into a single concise Qualification Pack. So far, 1,319 Qualification Packs with 6,625 NOS have been created, and these have been approved by over 1,000 companies. These NOS in turn feed into the NSQF in order to best align skills training with industry requirements. This places SSCs, and consequently industry participation, firmly at the centre of creating quality standards for skills training in India.

In addition to creating occupational standards, SSCs are additionally responsible for providing certification according to the National Occupational Standards, creating quality assurance and competency frameworks, researching existing skill gaps, and conducting training programmes for trainers. Till date, the NSDC has approved 37 SSCs. Currently, the sectors represented by SSCs consist of 19 of the 20 sectors that have been identified as high priority by NSDC, and cover the manufacturing, service, agriculture, allied service and informal sectors.

Assessment

The creation of Sector Skill Councils and the functions they are expected to carry out are well-conceptualised and, if successfully implemented, will ensure well-defined linkages between industry and skills training. The SSCs are envisioned as an interface between industry and training providers, and eventually as the leading quality assurance organisations in their respective sectors for skill development. The creation of one unified body for each identified sector will allow employers to work in a coordinated manner to ensure that the skill needs of their respective sectors are met. The SSCs are well-positioned to work closely with existing skill development organisations and initiatives at the national and state levels, in order to consolidate India's fragmented regulatory landscape and develop a unified strategy for skill development. Additionally, if implemented successfully, potential employers will be able to seamlessly evaluate potential employees against their skill requirements, thereby creating an efficient market solution to the skills landscape in India.

As of now, SSCs are at different stages of effectiveness, with some undertaking their mandates more proactively than others. SSCs for sectors such as Retail, IT/ITES and Security have been very active, while others are finding it difficult to mobilise industry participation. Traditionally, most Indian employers, especially those in the private sector, have not been directly involved in the skill development process. Together with MSDE and large industry associations, the

NSDC must play a central role in mobilising the private sector to work with the SSCs.

Conclusion

The supply side of skill development has seen landmark changes in recent years. The centralisation of decision-making in a single ministry is a welcome move and a necessary condition to improvements in this space. While a few years is too early to judge the efficiency and effectiveness of the programmes, one clear strength of the current framework is that it has clear and accountable mandates for the different agencies set up to solve different pieces of the problem. One could say that structurally, the appropriate foundations have been set in place. This has been supported by a material increase in urgency and a genuine focus on outcome-based solutions. This is, in itself, a marked change from the long-term doldrums that the skill development ecosystem was languishing in for several decades.

Going forward, two broad categories should be kept in mind for consideration. These are: (*a*) areas that require greater focus at a strategic level—vis-à-vis the provision of trainers and integration with the informal economy, and (*b*) from an execution aspect, the implications of a focus on outcomes as opposed to quality. These are set out below.

Creation of a Corpus of High-quality Trainers

Finding an adequate number of trainers who have the right levels of training themselves and are up to date with the latest developments in their fields has emerged as one of the most common challenges faced by training providers in India.

Traditionally, qualification requirements for trainers in skill development have been well-defined, and consequently limiting. For instance, trainers in the vocational education stream in schools need the same qualifications as teachers for general education, as opposed to relevant professional experience and/or qualifications. There are only a few part-time teachers who have the necessary professional qualifications. Instructors are rarely required to enrol in up-skilling courses to stay in touch with the most recent developments in their fields. They are thus often out of touch with current market needs and are unable to effectively teach students the skills required in the workspace.

In the ITIs and ITCs, instructors need to have a National Trade Certificate/National Apprentice Certificate/Diploma. This is further exacerbated by limited 'training the trainer' facilities in India. Pricing in the marketplace also reflects the challenges of attracting skilled trainers. Vocational trainers have traditionally been paid salaries that are well below par with what other professionals with similar skill sets would be paid in the industry, and this reduces personal incentives to seek out further training.

Private-sector skill development institutes are continuously facing the challenge of finding quality instructors. Consequently, they have been more innovative in this aspect. Large companies look for people with relevant professional experience, as opposed to formal qualifications. Some institutes also hire professionals who are employed in the relevant sector or have the necessary work experience on a part-time basis. They have an added advantage of being able to pay competitive salaries, thereby attracting and retaining faculty. This, however, is not true for smaller or newer companies, who are limited by their paying capacities. Skill development institutes with a focus on the unorganised sector or rural locations also have trouble locating and retaining good faculty.

All these signs point to the need for urgent innovation in the space of training the trainers in India. The NSDC has in the past explicitly stated its mandate to create 'training the trainer' institutes, where instructors would be up-skilled. It has commissioned detailed studies to analyse this space, which have returned with an extensive list of recommendations. It has also announced its intention to partner with training companies to create a hub and spoke model for training instructors. However, so far the NSDC has made very limited measurable progress.

Creating a corpus of high-quality trainers was also an important part of the MSDE's 2015 National Policy on Skill Development. Initiatives such as setting up training-the-trainer institutes as well as a portal which would act as a registration database for interested trainers, and working closely with industry to encourage working industry professionals to train part-time are all part of the MSDE's plans.

The paucity of adequately skilled trainers is one of the largest bottlenecks in creating incremental capacity for skills training. It poses serious challenges to the quality and effectiveness of the training that skills institutes (both government and private) impart to learners. The absence of any active intervention at scale to address this challenge over the past few years has been a considerable cause for concern. The successful and urgent implementation of these initiatives is going to be critical to the success of this government's ability to address India's skills challenge.

Integration with the Informal Economy

Addressing the training needs of the informal economy and creating pathways that link this vast population to the formal economy are paramount to creating a successful skill development ecosystem.

A majority of both government and private initiatives focus on the formal economy, with only a limited capacity being generated for the large informal economy relative to the magnitude of the gap. Also, a majority of the courses cater to the higher secondary and post-higher secondary levels, with the minimum qualificational requirement of Class X. Together, these two facts indicate the existing imbalances in the system, since 93 per cent of the Indian workforce operates in the informal sector,[21] and around 50 per cent of students drop out before completing Class X.

Additionally, the informal economy is difficult to account for, compounding the challenge of understanding the skill gap associated with this labour pool. Some government programmes have been in place for several years; yet, there has been little publicly available information to indicate their effectiveness. Concrete results are difficult to gauge due to the lack of transparency.

The most recent initiative to address the informal economy is the Recognition of Prior Learning (RPL), announced in July 2015. This newly devised programme aims to transform the existing skills in the unorganised sector into certified qualifications that can be used in the formal/organised sector. RPL is a function of the National Skill Qualification Framework, which integrates skill competencies and education in the hope of providing career mobility to populations that have acquired skills both formally and informally. The MSDE proposes to allocate adequate resources to RPL via various government initiatives. The PMKVY is one such channel through which the MSDE and NSDC hoped to provide RPL certificates to 10 lakh people in 2015. Data as of June 2016 suggests that 1.79 lakh people were trained under RPL.[22] Very little is known about the details of this initiative and the reasons behind the under-performance. Reasons such as trainees dropping out of the programmes mid-way due to opportunity cost or other personal reasons were cited for these numbers. The PMKVY has recently been renewed as an initiative for 2016–20 to skill and certify 10 million youths over the four-year period. This includes four million youth under RPL. Given the challenges associated with the erstwhile STAR scheme and the first round of the PMKVY, it is unclear how this target (which on an annual basis is five-and-a-half times what was achieved in 2015–16 under PMKVY) will be achieved. Given the magnitude of this initiative, it will most certainly be under close scrutiny by the different stakeholders in skill development.

Execution-related Considerations

The government's focus on capacity creation has on some occasions been at the cost of quality. The successful creation of a 'buzz' around skill development in the absence of an overarching quality framework has led to a large number of small and at times low-quality players being pulled into the market. In conjunction with the absence of high-quality trainers, the ecosystem may face a real hidden challenge around quality that will be obvious only a few years down the line. The mitigating factors—well-defined, comprehensive monitoring standards that are transparent and corruption free—need to be put in place and implemented urgently. The stronger focus on using short-term performance indicators around output when it comes to measuring the success of implementation typically imposes longer-term costs. The MSDE may benefit from enhancing focus on the harder question of ensuring quality, which will be key to the long-term success of skill development initiatives in India.

CONCLUSION

Material steps have been taken by the government to create a comprehensive skill development framework in India. They are working with a much needed sense of urgency to reduce the decentralised inefficiencies that have plagued the supply side of skill development. An equally thoughtful and energetic focus on how to generate, incentivise and develop a large pool of high-quality trainers will be hugely synergetic to this effort. Similarly, while there is a strong focus on the formal economy and on output-based indicators, the needs of the informal economy need to be more actively addressed. Additionally, a regulatory environment that incentivises the private sector to enter skill development is crucial. However, if unaccompanied by strong quality control and monitoring, it can be a recipe for disaster. Setbacks like the STAR scheme at this stage can potentially derail India's skill development plans, especially since India is at a critical point in consolidating an ecosystem that has traditionally been very fragmented. The equilibrium is fragile at best, and quality assurance has to be the basis on which the entire ecosystem is built.

NOTES

1. I would like to thank Arjun Raychaudhuri for his ongoing support. I would also like to thank Laura Harris, Leora Mincer and Eileen Shentu for their excellent research work.

2. US Census Bureau, International Database.

3. http://www.skilldevelopment.gov.in/National-Policy-2015.html.

4. Ibid.

5. Ibid.

6. In this chapter, the terms skill development and VET are used interchangeably.

7. http://mhrd.gov.in/sites/upload_files/mhrd/files/upload_document/REVISED-SCHEME-VHSE1.pdf.

8. https://c27web2.saas.talismaonline.com/NSDA/7.2%20-%20Haryana.pdf.

9. http://www.skilldevelopment.gov.in/National-Policy-2015.html, p. 16.

10. http://www.skilldevelopment.gov.in/school-education.html.

11. Ibid.

12. https://casi.sas.upenn.edu/casiworkingpaper/aggarwalkapurtognatta.

13. http://www.dget.nic.in/content/institute/key-statistics.php.

14. http://www.skilldevelopment.gov.in/National-Policy-2015.html.

15. http://www.skilldevelopment.gov.in/nationalskilldevelopment corporation.html#.

16. http://www.skilldevelopment.gov.in/star.html.

17. http://nscsindia.org/App_Documents/Documents/StarNoticeon-website16jan)(1).pdf.

18. http://economictimes.indiatimes.com/news/politics-and-nation/17-93-lakh-candidates-trained-under-pradhan-mantri-kaushal-vikas-yojna-as-on-july-18/articleshow/53318901.cms.

19. http://www.skilldevelopment.gov.in/nsqf.html.

20. http://mhrd.gov.in/sites/upload_files/mhrd/files/upload_document/NSQF-NOTIFICATION.pdf.

21. National Policy for Skill Development 2015, p. 9.

22. http://indianexpress.com/article/business/business-others/pradhan-mantri-kaushal-vikas-yojana-data-till-april-25-of-17-58-lakh-candidates-skilled-81978-get-placed-2877951/.

REFERENCES

Varma, Subodh, 'Survey: Even among skilled workers joblessness is high', *The Times of India*, 20 July 2015.

World Bank, 'Skill Development in India: The Vocational Education and Training System' (Washington, D.C.: Human Development Unit, South Asia Region, The World Bank, January 2006).

— six —

Employment and Education

An Exploration of the Demand Side Story[1]

Jeemol Unni and *Sudipa Sarkar*

India has seen a rapid growth in knowledge-intensive industries. At the same time, there appears to be a major surge in the demand for higher education, both technical and non-technical. The youth have now begun to understand that unless they acquire the relevant skills, they will not be able to gain from the current growth of knowledge- and technology-intensive industries. The challenge before India today is to match the education/skills of its youth with relevant jobs for them.

In the standard human capital theory, the causal relationship between education and earnings is viewed through productivity augmenting effects—education or human capital increases productivity, and so the earnings increase. Faced with imperfect market information, employers take the educational qualifications of prospective employees into consideration. This model's characterisation of the demand side is crude. While it acknowledges the role of physical capital, no other variable is used to characterise jobs (apart from wages and prices). Jobs or occupations play no role in production theory. The human capital model ignores the demand side, except for including dummy variables for occupation/industry or employing fixed effect models to capture the effect. It assumes that a mismatch between education and occupation arises from inadequate information and is temporary in a worker's career development, and omits human capital components. The literature on over-education attempts to analyse the mismatch between educations and jobs (Hertog 2000). This chapter is an attempt to fill the gap in the literature on the demand side of the relationship between education and occupation or jobs. We address three questions: Is the demand for higher education increasing rapidly in certain occupations? To what extent do technology and knowledge-intensive industries absorb (demand) workers in occupations requiring higher education? Does having a graduate degree affect the probability of being in a high-tech/knowledge-intensive industry (manufacturing plus services), and does this differ between occupations?

The chapter begins with a brief review of policy concerns and research on higher education in India. In the second section, we discuss changes in the percentage of graduates across occupations and construct occupational categories based on the share of graduate workers in each of the occupations. In the third section, we develop a classification of knowledge-intensive industries and discuss the growth of employment in these industries. In the fourth section, we explore the thickening and deepening of graduate occupations in knowledge-intensive industries. In section five, we discuss the determinants of participation in high-tech knowledge industries and compare the entry of graduates in occupation categories across manufacturing and service industries. We present our conclusions in the final section.

A Brief Review

Given India's age pyramid, with more than one-third of its population below the age of 14, and given its low literacy levels, the major debates in education have concentrated on elementary education. The arena of higher education is relatively under-researched. The literature suggests that once countries are in an advanced stage of economic development, the share of the manufacturing sector declines, while the share of the knowledge-based services sector increases (Fisher 1935; Kuznets 1971; Rowthorn and Wells 1987). As India grows rapidly into a knowledge economy, concerns have arisen about whether its higher education system can match up to the challenge of producing the kind of skilled workforce necessary for this growth.

The University Grants Commission (UGC) report on higher education (UGC 2003) discussed the issues and concerns facing higher education in India today. Two prominent reports have been brought out in recent years, by the National Knowledge Commission headed by Sam Pitroda (Government of India 2009a) and the Committee on Renovation and Rejuvenation of Higher Education headed by Yashpal (Government of India 2009b). A number of Bills were prepared by the earlier government in 2010: Foreign Educational Institutions (Regulation of Entry Operation) Bill, 2010; Prohibition of Unfair Practices in Technical, Medical Educational Institutions and Universities Bill, 2010; the Educational Tribunals Bill, 2010; and the National Accreditation Authority Bill, 2010. The Foreign Educational Bill is the most controversial, the basic premise of which is that every foreign educational service in India, existing or planned in the future, should register with a designated authority. The other bills propose to make accreditation mandatory, prevent malpractices in higher education and help the speedy disposal of disputes through a special tribunal (Anandakrishnan 2010). All of this points to the more recent concerns in policy circles around issues in higher education.

The literature on developed economies has dealt with the utilisation of skills acquired in college and analysed the social returns to higher education (Acemoglu and Angrist 2000; Moretti 2004). Another strand of literature has focused on the education/skill mismatch, mainly over-skilling (McGuiness 2006; Sala 2011), which investigates whether college graduates are employed in 'non-college' occupations (Gottschalk and Hansen 2003; McGuiness and Bennett 2007). However, such literature is not available for India.

An increasing skill premium in the Indian labour market has been attributed to a skill-biased technical change, which allows for a rapid increase in the supply of workers with graduate and postgraduate degrees/diplomas (Unni and Rani 2008). A section of the literature suggests that from the 1980s, there has been an increasing skill premium in India (Dutta 2005; Kijima 2006). The findings also suggest that this increase in the wage premium has come mostly from demand shifts in favour of workers with tertiary (college) or higher education. The supply of higher educated workers had remained almost unchanged during the period 1999–2004, while its demand was increasing (Azam 2010). However, others argue that this rapid increase in skill premium exposes a paradox in India's labour market, in the sense that this enormous pool of skilled workers is relatively shallow (Kapur and Mehta 2007). They argue that the higher education system produces poor-quality graduates, and serves neither as a screening or signalling device, nor prepares students to be productive and responsible citizens. A study of the links between higher education and high-technology industries shows that there is indeed a robust link between the two, although the quality of students from this system leaves much to be desired (Basant and Mukhopadhyay 2008).

It has been argued that the IT labour market has been deepening and thickening (Basant and Rani 2004). Labour market deepening occurs through extension and penetration into new areas, when diversity in the demand and supply of skills is enhanced. With increasing specialisation and expanding scale, the demand for skills in specific segments grows, which is referred to as thickening. This chapter discusses the extent to which these processes can be found in the knowledge-intensive industries.

GRADUATE EDUCATION AND OCCUPATIONS

To get an idea of the current interest in education among adults in each age group, we look at the percentage of the population currently studying at the graduate level and above. Nearly 17 per cent of adults aged 18 years and above were enrolled in graduate studies in 2009–10, and this had risen from little less than 14 per cent in 1999–2000 (Figures 6.1a and b). There was about a 10-percentage point increase

FIGURE 6.1a–b: Percentage of Adult Students Enrolled in Graduate Studies by Each Age Group

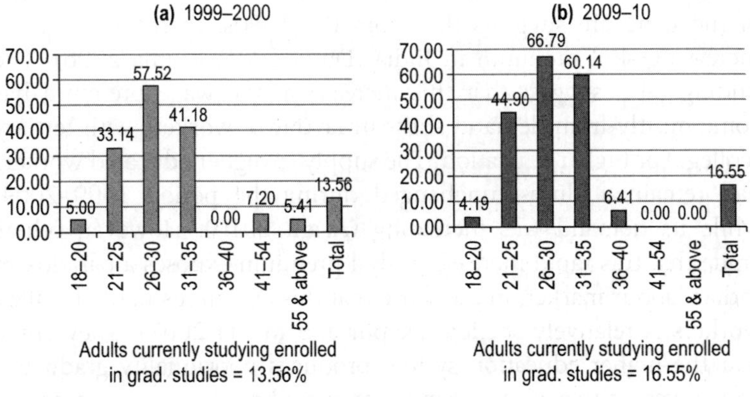

Source: Authors' own calculations based on National Sample Survey data of the years 1999–2000 (55th) and 2009–10 (66th round).

in graduate enrolments in the age groups 21–25 years and 26–30 years during this decade. Enrolments in graduate education increased by 20 percentage points among the 31–35 age group. This is indeed very encouraging for the growth of higher education.

Among the employed, there had been a rapid increase in the number of better-qualified occupations, such as professional, technical, administrative and clerical jobs, since 1999–2000 (Figure 6.2), whereas production, sales, service and agricultural occupations grew steadily up to 2004–05 and started falling thereafter.

FIGURE 6.2: Employment Trends by Broad Occupational Groups, 1993–94 to 2009–10 (in millions)

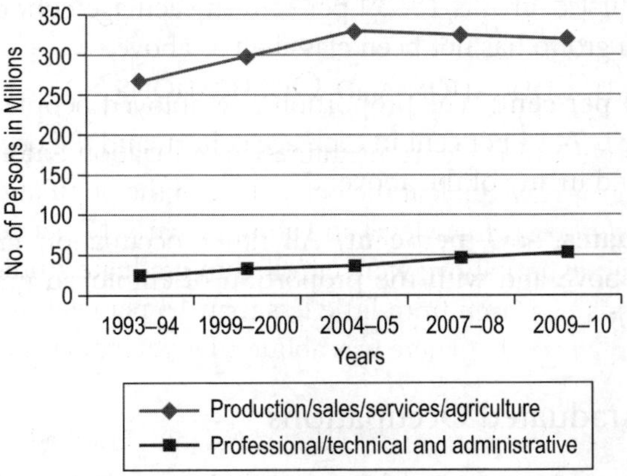

Higher Education and Occupational Structure

The question we ask ourselves here is: To what extent do various occupations require highly qualified labour, and how has this been changing over the past decade? Using graduate education as a measure of higher education, we divide occupations into graduate and non-graduate occupations. Occupations where less than 7 per cent of the workforce were graduates were noted as non-graduate occupations. Next, we observe the changes in these occupations over time in two ways: by comparing among the age cohorts 21–35 years and 40–54 years for 2009–10, and for the same age cohorts between 1999–2000 and 2009–10 using NSSO Employment and Unemployment Survey data.

Occupational groups are classified by graduate intensity, based on a study in the UK (Elais and Purcell 2004), as follows:

Very High, >= 60 per cent: The proportion of employed people holding a first degree is greater than 60 per cent in each age cohort in each occupation.

High, 40–59 per cent: The occupation group has not been classified as above, and the proportion of employed people holding a first degree is 40–59 per cent in each age cohort.

Medium, 15–39 per cent: The proportion of employed people holding a first degree is 15–39 per cent in each age cohort, and the occupation group has not been classified as above.

Low, 7–14 per cent: The proportion of employed people holding a first degree is 7–14 per cent in each age cohort, and the occupation is not classified in any of the above.

Non-graduates, < 7 per cent: All other occupation groups not classified above and with the proportion of employed graduates at < 7 per cent.

India's Graduated Occupations

Overall, nearly 71 per cent of the occupied population aged 21 years and above were in non-graduate occupations in 2009–10, having declined from 78 per cent a decade earlier (Table 6.1, column 5). The corollary is that nearly 30 per cent of the occupied persons were in graduate occupations. Among the graduate occupation categories, very high and high graduate intensity had 3 per cent each; the medium intensity category had 13 per cent; and low intensity constituted above 10 per cent of the occupied population in 2009–10. It was the medium graduate intensity occupations that registered the largest (around 10 percentage points) increase in the occupied population over the decade (Table 6.1, column 5).

The very high graduate intensity occupations had by definition the highest percentage of graduate occupations, about 63–73 per cent in both years and both age cohorts. The high intensity category was the only group that saw a classic 10 percentage points higher graduated occupations among the younger cohort compared to the older one, which was more or less sustained over the decades 1999–2000 to 2009–10. The medium occupations, which had registered a 10 percentage point increase in the occupied population, had a 10 percentage point decline in graduate intensity in the younger cohort in 1999–2000 to 20 per cent, but retained the same in both cohorts in 2009–10. The low intensity occupations, which had between 7–10 per cent of graduates, saw a nearly 3 percentage point higher graduate density among the younger age cohort in 1999–2000.

To sum up, the **very high graduate intensity occupations** retained their need for workers with higher education. These consisted of occupations that have always had a requirement for highly qualified people, for example solicitors, medical practitioners, higher education and secondary education teachers, biological scientists, architects/engineers, accountants, auditors, mathematicians/statisticians, senior administrators, directors, managerial executives, IT professionals and, surprisingly, poets, authors and journalists.

It was the **high graduate intensity occupations** that appeared to increase their demand for higher education in both the cohorts in India during this decade. High graduate density occupations were mainly those employing associate professionals, technicians, health professionals, clerks, technical salesmen, and primary and middle school teachers. There was definitely a change in the demand for better and highly qualified people among these occupations. We can say that with the advent of the knowledge economy in India, these jobs were being upgraded in terms of their need for better-qualified personnel.

Low graduate intensity occupations comprised merchants, shopkeepers, salesmen, chemical processors, rubber, plastic products, and paper and paper board workers. They also included farm plantation and metal processors, occupations that actually saw an increase in the graduate density among the younger cohort. It is possible that while the first set were occupations that required new skill sets in the new economy, the latter were occupations from which the young and better-educated were moving out.

Only a few occupations—two among the two-digit classification of nearly 27 occupation groups—actually showed a decline in graduate density over the decade.

TABLE 6.1: Summary Graduate Intensity Occupational Classification, 1999–2000 and 2009–10 (average percentage of graduates in each group)

Occupations by graduate intensity (1)	*Cohort 1 (21–35 years) (2)*	*Cohort 2 (40–54 years) (3)*	*21 years and above (4)*	*Percentage distribution (5)*	*Cumulative percentage (6)*
1999–2000					
Very High >=60%	73.2	71.7	71.9	1.4	1.4
High 40–59%	48.7	41.2	44.0	5.4	6.7
Medium 15–39%	20.6	27.6	23.0	3.8	10.6
Low 7–14%	10.3	7.7	8.9	11.3	21.8
Sub-Total Classes	*24.0*	*25.6*	*24.1*	21.9	
Non-graduate	1.9	1.0	1.5	78.1	100.0
Total	6.7	6.9	6.4	100.0	
2009–10					
Very High >=60%	71.7	63.9	72.1	2.7	2.7
High 40–59%	53.2	44.1	47.4	3.0	5.7
Medium 15–39%	20.8	20.1	19.6	13.1	18.7
Low 7–14%	7.6	7.0	7.0	10.6	29.3
Sub-Total Classes	27.2	*24.6*	22.7	29.3	
Non-graduate	2.4	1.5	1.8	70.7	100.0
Total	10.4	8.6	8.0	100.0	

Source: Computed from unit records of NSSO Employment and Unemployment Survey, 1999–2000 and 2009–10, by NCO 2004 classification in both years.

Employment in Knowledge-intensive Industries

Knowledge-intensive Industry Classification: Manufacturing industries and, more so, service industries in India are seen as increasingly technology and knowledge-intensive. Here, we address the issue of whether the growth of knowledge-intensive industries has led to a demand for higher educated graduates.

We use the Eurostat/OECD classifications to categorise the industries into various levels of knowledge intensity. For classifying manufacturing industries, the OECD classification is based on the ratio of R&D expenditure to GDP or R&D intensity (Felix 2006). Both direct and indirect expenditure on R&D are considered, including purchase of machinery, equipment and intermediary inputs. This is a proxy to capture the technological intensity of the manufacturing industry.

The service industries are classified based on the OECD proposal for knowledge-intensive services (Eurostat Metadata 2007a, 2007b). Knowledge intensity reflects the integration of a generic or service-specific science and technology base, and can be seen as a combination of the knowledge embedded in new equipment, personnel and R&D intensity (Felix 2006). The service industries have been classified broadly as knowledge-intensive, based on this OECD classification, and have been further split based on the types of services following Torres-Freire and Abdel (2010).

Using these classifications, we have grouped the non-agricultural industries using the National Industrial Classification (NIC 1998 for 1999–2000 and NIC 2004 for 2009–10) into eight knowledge- and technology-intensive groups, four each in manufacturing and services. Further, two other non-agricultural industries, construction and mining and quarrying, were retained separately (see Appendix 6.1, Table A6.1 for a detailed listing of the industries in each group). The primary activities—agriculture, dairy, fishing, forestry, etc.—were excluded from this classification.

Growth of Employment in Knowledge-intensive Industries

Of the total non-agricultural employment, about 48 per cent was in the less knowledge-intensive services (trade, transport, public administration) and 16.5 per cent was in the low technology manufacturing industries (mainly primary products) in 1999–2000 (Table 6.1). Both these low knowledge-intensive industry groups registered a small decline in the employment share of 6 and 2 percentage points, respectively, over the decade 1999–2000 to 2009–10, and accordingly registered lower annual growth in employment. Only about one-fifth of the total employment was in the high/medium technology-intensive manufacturing and knowledge-intensive service industry.

Manufacturing: The overall average annual growth of total non-agricultural employment was 2.7 per cent during 1999–2000 and 2009–10 (Table 6.2). In manufacturing, all the industry groups had shown less than 2.5 percentage annual growth of employment.

TABLE 6.2: Share and Growth of Employment in the Knowledge Industries, 1999–2000 and 2009–10

Knowledge Industry Groups (KII)	*Share of employment (%)*		*CAGR (%)*	*% of Graduates 2009–10*
OECD classification	*1999–2000*	*2009–10*	*CAGR*	
High-tech manufacturing	0.8	0.7	1.4	29.7
Medium-high-tech manufacturing	3.0	2.8	2.3	22.2
Medium-low-tech manufacturing	7.3	6.1	1.1	7.0
Low-tech manufacturing	16.5	13.9	1.1	4.9
Knowledge-intensive Services (KIS)	3.5	4.2	4.5	49.2
Social Knowledge-intensive Services	7.2	7.2	2.8	57.3
High-tech Knowledge-intensive Services	1.1	1.7	7.2	52.1
Less KIS	47.6	41.8	1.5	11.8
Construction	11.6	20.1	8.0	2.8
Mining & Quarrying	1.5	1.4	2.2	14.2
Total	100.0	100.0	2.7	14.7

Note: CAGR-compound annual growth rate.
Source: Computed from unit records of the Employment and Unemployment Surveys, National Sample Survey Organisation, 1999–2000 and 2009–10.

Services: Among all the industry groups, the highest annual growth, about 7.2 per cent, in employment was registered in high technology knowledge-intensive service industries. These included telecommunication, computer services and R&D, whose share was quite small, but increasing over the decade. The next highest growth was registered in the knowledge-intensive services (KIS), 4.5 per cent, with the share increasing from 3.5 to 4.2 per cent over the decade. These included financial services, real estate and other business, recreational and sporting services. This was followed by the social knowledge service industries, with a 2.8 per cent growth and share remaining at 7.2 per cent. This was mainly the education and medical services industries.

Overall, there was a rapid growth of employment in the knowledge-intensive service industries, whereas the technology-intensive manufacturing industries recorded a very slow growth in employment. This is understandable in that technology-intensive manufacturing industries were likely to be more capital intensive, and therefore likely to absorb less employment. It also reflects the nature of the high growth in the service sector, which is very knowledge intensive. This is important to our study as it probably implies the absorption of more educated workers, which is what we shall investigate in the rest of the chapter.

THICKENING AND DEEPENING OF GRADUATE OCCUPATIONS IN KNOWLEDGE-INTENSIVE INDUSTRIES

The simplest way of studying graduate intensity in industries is by the percentage of graduates in each industry group. This is presented in the last column of Table 6.2. About 60 per cent of occupied persons in the Social KI services are graduates, followed by about 50 per cent in the KIS and 52 per cent in the high-tech KIS. The next most graduate-intensive industries are the high-tech and medium high-tech manufacturing industries with about 30 per cent, with one-fifth of the workers in them being graduates. However, this does not tell us what types of graduate occupations are concentrated in each of these knowledge-intensive industries (KII).

The distribution of graduate intensity in occupations tells us which industry groups have a greater demand for higher educated/graduate workers. This also tells us about the demand for higher education in knowledge-intensive industries through the distribution of occupied graduates in each of the KII. This distribution is presented for the occupied population by age cohorts, 21–35 and 40–54 years (Tables 6.3a and b), and helps us to understand the deepening of knowledge intensity in each KII group.

TABLE 6.3a: Distribution of Workers in Knowledge Industries by Graduate Intensity in Occupation (21–35 years), 2009–10 (percentage)

Knowledge industry groups	*Graduate intensity in occupations*					
	Very high >=60 %	*High 40–59 %*	*Medium 15–39 %*	*Low 7–14 %*	*Non-graduate < 7 %*	*Total*
High-tech manufacturing	19.0	13.6	14.7	27.6	25.1	100
Medium high-tech manufacturing	12.5	9.6	10.0	50.0	17.8	100
Medium low-tech manufacturing	2.3	2.0	14.3	26.6	54.8	100
Low-tech manufacturing	1.0	2.1	12.5	10.4	74.1	100
Knowledge-intensive Services (KIS)	15.4	37.5	30.8	9.6	6.7	100
Social Knowledge-intensive Services	76.9	3.9	10.8	5.5	3.0	100
High-tech Knowledge-intensive Services	51.6	15.7	19.4	9.3	4.0	100
Less KIS	1.9	4.8	45.4	28.8	19.1	100
Construction	0.8	0.5	2.4	2.4	93.9	100
Mining & Quarrying	1.9	4.0	12.0	14.4	67.8	100
Total	9.7	5.2	24.2	18.0	42.9	100

TABLE 6.3b: Distribution of Workers in Knowledge Industries by Graduate Intensity in Occupation (40–54 years), 2009–10 (percentage)

Knowledge industry groups	*Graduate intensity in occupations*					
	Very high >=60 %	*High 40–59 %*	*Medium 15–39 %*	*Low 7–14 %*	*Non-graduate <7 %*	*Total*
High-tech manufacturing	12.3	15.9	9.0	40.4	22.4	100.0
Medium high-tech manufacturing	10.7	7.4	21.5	41.3	19.1	100.0
Medium low-tech manufacturing	2.9	2.8	15.9	25.1	53.3	100.0
Low-tech manufacturing	1.0	2.6	17.4	10.2	68.8	100.0
Knowledge-intensive Services (KIS)	10.9	32.7	41.9	7.0	7.4	100.0
Social Knowledge-intensive Services (SKIS)	68.4	6.4	8.7	11.7	4.8	100.0
High-tech Knowledge-intensive Services	24.3	34.3	16.1	20.2	5.1	100.0
Less KIS	3.3	9.0	42.7	22.9	22.1	100.0
Construction	0.8	0.4	4.3	1.4	93.1	100.0
Mining & Quarrying	3.4	4.7	7.9	23.3	60.8	100.0
Total	8.8	7.4	26.6	16.5	40.7	100.0

We had observed that more than half the occupied persons in the social KIS and 49 per cent in KIS were graduates (Table 6.1). Has there been a deepening of graduate intensity in the younger age cohort? In the services with a high concentration of graduates (KIS, social KIS and high-tech KIS), there was clearly a move towards more graduate-intensive occupations among the younger cohort (21–35 years, Tables 6.3a and b). However, subtle differences were noted.

KIS and business services showed an increase in very high and high graduate intensity occupations among the younger cohort. This implied a deepening of graduate-intensive occupations in these service industries, that is, the nature of jobs in the industry had changed to allow the entry of persons with lower graduate intensity. Financial services, banks and accounting services now perhaps produce products/services that are more technical, such as insurance products that require a variety of persons with varying graduate intensity to produce and market. Soft skills, such as knowledge of English, etiquette and style, are also important in the various occupations in this sector.

In social KIS and high-tech KIS, there was a concentration in very high (>60 per cent) graduate intensity occupations among the younger cohort compared to the older one. These occupations generally comprised educational and medical professionals, administrative/managerial, senior officers and technical engineers, computer programmers and scientists. This could be termed as labour market thickening or specialisation, when graduate intensity increases sharply in certain occupations and there is a greater absorption of such workers in these jobs. In industries such as education, medicine, software, hardware, and R&D, jobs are becoming more specialised and are requiring a larger proportion of highly qualified people.

We had observed that growth in employment was the highest in the high technology KIS, followed by social KIS and KIS industry groups. These industry groups also witnessed an increasing demand for higher educated graduates. This is clearly an impact of the demand for workers with higher education in the knowledge economy.

The deepening of knowledge intensity was witnessed in KIS, while social and high-tech KIS groups could be said to have more specialisation or a thickening of knowledge intensity. In the manufacturing sector, there was no real deepening or thickening of knowledge intensity. In medium-low and low-tech manufacturing, a status quo was maintained with more than 50 per cent non-graduates among both the younger and older cohorts.

One caveat, however, needs to be mentioned with regard to the changes observed in the services sector. There has been a decline in the quality of education delivered by institutions of higher education. The deepening of knowledge intensity may also occur if employers perceive this deteriorating quality of workers and, in certain occupations, use graduate education as a screening device. This might actually imply an over-education of workers in these occupation groups, that is, the occupation does not require a graduate degree, but employers prefer to employ graduates as there is an increasing supply of them and it becomes a convenient method to get better workers.

Participation in High-tech Knowledge-intensive Industry

The question we address here is: Does the effect of having a graduate degree on the probability of being in high-tech (HT) and knowledge-intensive (KI) industry (manufacturing plus services) differ between occupation groups? Our model is:

$E(\text{HT\_dummy}) = \text{Probability}(\text{HT\_dummy}=1) = \Phi(\alpha + \beta_1\text{edu\_dummy} + \beta_2\text{occupation\_category} + \beta_3\text{edu\_dummy\#occupation\_category} + \beta_4\text{sex} + \beta_5\text{social\_grp\_dummy} + \beta_6\text{region} + \beta_7\text{age})$

Where HT_dummy takes the value 1 for high-tech or knowledge-intensive manufacturing + service industries; the rest is 0. We also run the same model for HT manufacturing and HT/knowledge-intensive service industry separately. Here, age is the only continuous variable.

Our main variable of interest is *edu_dummy*, which takes the value 1 if the person has a graduate degree, and the value 0 otherwise. The nine occupational categories are coded as follows:

0—Elementary; 1—Legislators, Senior Officials and Managers; 2—Professionals; 3—Technicians and Associate Professionals; 4—Clerical; 5—Service Workers and Shop and Market Sales; 6—Skilled Agricultural; 7—Craft and Related Trades Workers; 8—Plant and Machine Operators and Assemblers. We have excluded category 6, farmers and other agricultural occupations, from the analysis.

To study the effect of a graduate degree on participation in the HT/KI industry in different occupations, an interaction variable is constructed by interacting the graduate dummy variable with each of the eight occupation category dummies (as there are nine occupation categories), and this is summarised by the term *edu_dummy#occupation_category*. The coefficient β_3 thus comprises eight coefficients for eight interaction terms in the model. We are interested in calculating the marginal effect of each explanatory variable.

In a non-linear model like probit, this marginal effect is an approximation of how much the dependent variable (in this case, the probability of being in the HT/KI industry) is expected to change for a unit change in the independent/explanatory variable. For a continuous independent variable, marginal effect is nothing but the first derivative of the dependent variable (y) with respect to the independent variable (say x_1). But the problem occurs when we want to compute the change of the effect of x_1 (an explanatory variable) on $E(y)$ (y being HT_dummy) for a unit change in x_2 (another explanatory variable), that is, the interaction effect of x_1 and x_2. This effect is actually the cross partial derivative of $E(y)$ with respect to x_1 and x_2, not the first derivative of $E(y)$ with respect to the multiplicative term (x_1 x_2) (for details on the model see Appendix 6.1).

Overall, there is a 17.4 per cent increase in probability of participation in the HT/KI industry (manufacturing + service) if the worker is a graduate (Table 6.4). The effect of higher education is more than double on the knowledge-intensive service industry than that on the high-technology manufacturing industry.

Within occupations alone, the probability of participation in high-tech industry was nearly 27 and 60 per cent higher among professional and technical occupations, respectively, compared to elementary. This was followed by clerical occupations (32 per cent higher probability). All these results were particularly true for the high-tech service industry, compared to manufacturing.

Among the control variables, age and the social group (caste/tribe) to which the worker belonged made no difference to overall participation in the HT/KI industry (Table 6.4). But workers in the knowledge-intensive service industry had a higher probability of being younger, male and from the upper social groups compared to their peers in the manufacturing industry. Gender has an impact on industry participation. Women have a greater probability (.021 or 5.5 per cent) of participation in the KI service industry, as well as in the HT/KI industry (3.3 per cent) than men. Women are also more likely to participate in the service industry, whereas men are likely to participate in the HT manufacturing industry (2.3 per cent higher probability than females). Further, the probability of participation in the knowledge-intensive service industry is more likely in south Indian states, while participation in high-tech manufacturing is more likely in west Indian states. This is intuitively correct, as the main knowledge-intensive IT service sector centres are the cities of Bangalore, Hyderabad and Chennai in the south, while the western states of Maharashtra and Gujarat are known to be manufacturing hubs.

TABLE 6.4: Determinants of Participation in HT Manufacturing and HT/KI Service Industries: Marginal Effects (*dy/dx*) of all Explanatory Variables except Interaction Term, 2009–10

Variables	*Probability of being in HT (Manu + Service) Industry*	*Probability of being in HT/KI Service Industry*	*Probability of being in HT Manu Industry*
Education dummy (Graduate or above=1)	0.174***	0.119***	0.0530***
	[0.000]	[0.000]	[0.000]
Occupation category (Reference group: 0-Elementary occupation)			
1—Legislators, Senior Officials and Ma	0.019	0.048***	–0.028***
	[0.122]	[0.000]	[0.000]
2—Professionals	0.273***	0.303***	–0.029***
	[0.000]	[0.000]	[0.000]
3—Technicians and Associate Profession	0.609***	0.629***	–0.026***
	[0.000]	[0.000]	[0.000]
4—Clerks	0.320***	0.311***	0.001
	[0.000]	[0.000]	[0.348]

(Contd)

Table 6.4 (Contd)

Variables	*Probability of being in HT (Manu + Service) Industry*	*Probability of being in HT/KI Service Industry*	*Probability of being in HT Manu Industry*
5—Service Workers and Shop and Market Sal	–0.035***	0.0138	–0.049***
	[0.000]	[0.118]	[0.000]
7—Craft and Related Trades Workers	0.008	–0.029***	0.036***
	[0.539]	[0.000]	[0.000]
8—Plant and Machine Operators and Assem	0.0002	–0.032***	0.025**
	[0.988]	[0.000]	[0.010]
Age	–0.0006***	–0.0003**	–0.0003**
	[0.000]	[0.038]	[0.020]
Female dummy	0.034***	0.055***	–0.023***
	[0.000]	[0.000]	[0.000]
SC/ST dummy	0.006	0.016***	–0.008**
	[0.240]	[0.001]	[0.014]
Region (Reference group: 0-Central)			
North	0.0251***	0.009	0.013**
	[0.000]	[0.212]	[0.030]
South	0.038***	0.033***	0.007
	[0.000]	[0.000]	[0.240]
West	0.049***	0.023***	0.025***
	[0.000]	[0.000]	[0.000]
East	–0.0154*	–0.002	–0.014***
	[0.081]	[0.745]	[0.008]
Observations	82,319	82,319	82,319

Note: Figures in parentheses denote the level of significance (p>|z|) *** p<0.01, ** p<0.05, * p<0.1.

The effect of a graduate degree (*edu_dummy=1*) for different occupational categories on participation in high tech and knowledge-intensive manufacturing and service industries are presented in Table 6.5. The marginal effects for the interaction terms are computed from the probabilities of being in the HT/KI industry for every combination of education and occupation category (*edu_dummy & occupation_category*) (for details, see Appendix 6.1, Table A6.2).

TABLE 6.5: Effect of Graduate Degree on Industry Participation (HT Manufacturing, HT and KI Service) for Each Occupation Category, 2009–10

Marginal effect of education (i.e., non-graduate to graduate) for different occupational categories	*HT/KI industry (Manufacturing + Service) participation*	*HT/KI service industry participation*	*HT Manufacturing industry participation*
graduate#0-Elementary–non-grad#0-Elementary	0.149 [0.005]***	0.090 [0.033]**	0.057 [0.067]*
graduate#1—Legislators, Senior Officials and Ma; non-grad#1—Legislators, Senior Officials and Ma	0.253 [0.000]***	0.212 [0.000]***	0.045 [0.000]***
graduate#2—Professionals; non-graduate#2—Professionals	0.503 [0.000]***	0.483 [0.000]***	0.018 [0.056]*
graduate#3—Technicians and Associate Profession; non-grad#3—Technicians and Associate Profession	0.102 [0.000]***	0.089 [0.000]***	0.016 [0.066]*
graduate#4—Clerical; non-grad#4—Clerical	0.060 [0.022]**	0.071 [0.006]***	–0.012 [0.340]
graduate#5—Service and Sales; non-graduate#5—Service and Sales	0.019 [0.252]	0.007 [0.584]	0.015 [0.263]
graduate#7—Craft and Related; non-graduate#7—Craft and Related	0.197 [0.000]***	0.063 [0.001]***	0.122 [0.000]***

(Contd)

Table 6.5 (Contd)

Marginal effect of education (i.e., non-graduate to graduate) for different occupational categories	*HT/KI industry (Manufacturing + Service) participation*	*HT/KI service industry participation*	*HT Manufacturing industry participation*
graduate#8—Plant and Machine Operators and Assem; non-graduate#8—Plant and Machine Operators and Assem	0.156 [0.000]***	0.054 [0.007]***	0.094 [0.003]***

Note: Figures in parentheses denote the level of significance.

The probability of being in the high-tech manufacturing/service industry is higher by 50 per cent for graduates compared to non-graduates among professional workers (occupation category 2); this is 25 per cent for legislators, senior officials and managers. This is perhaps because such workers are those who necessarily have a graduate degree. Having a graduate degree has no impact on participation in high-tech manufacturing as well as the service industry for service and sales workers. Overall, being a graduate does not make much difference in the high-tech manufacturing industry as compared to the knowledge-intensive service industry. The differences are particularly low in high-tech manufacturing: in occupations like legislator, senior officials and managers, 4.5 per cent as compared to 21 per cent in the knowledge-intensive service industry, and similarly 1.8 per cent compared to 48 per cent among professionals in the two industries, respectively. This implies that graduates in professional, administrative, executive and managerial occupations are more likely to participate in the high-tech/knowledge-intensive service industry. In the case of sales workers, we had noted earlier that the products of various business and financial services had become more sophisticated and required greater technical knowledge. Among administrators and managers, the service industry was the new growth sector, with perhaps more challenging jobs and also more remuneration.

Being a graduate created no advantage in industry participation for occupations such as merchants and service workers.

CONCLUSION

India has seen a rapid increase in higher education in recent decades. The question we ask is: Is there a demand for higher educated persons, graduates and above, or are we facing a situation of over-education in employment? This issue is addressed innovatively in terms of changes in the nature of jobs and in occupations within knowledge-intensive industries.

All but two of 30 occupations have had an increase in graduate intensity. Occupations with a high intensity of graduates, mainly engineering, medical and scientific technicians, social scientists and economists, technical salesmen, and primary and middle school teachers showed an increased demand for better and highly qualified people with the advent of the knowledge economy. The medium graduate intensity occupations comprised nurses, working proprietors (self-employed enterprises), village officials, artists and composers, and transport conductors, who showed a smaller increase in graduates among the younger cohort. The low graduate intensity occupations saw a large increase in the percentage of graduates among the younger cohort in 2009–10, for example, ticket collectors and checkers, merchants, shopkeepers, salesmen, and service workers. The nature of the activities in these occupations may have changed so as to require a more qualified workforce. This definitely indicates an increase in the demand for a better educated workforce in many occupations in recent years.

The industry groups, manufacturing and services were reclassified based on high-tech and knowledge intensity. We found that the service industries showed a greater demand for graduates. Within it, knowledge-intensive services (KIS), financial and business services, showed a deepening of graduate intensity, meaning that the nature of jobs changed to allow for occupations with lower graduate intensity as well. The social KIS, education and medical services, and high-tech KIS, R&D and computer services, showed a thickening or specialisation of occupations, reflected in the sharp increase in very high graduate intensity occupations.

Finally, having a graduate degree had a greater impact overall on participation in the service industry compared to manufacturing. Senior managerial officials and professionals with graduate and above degrees had a higher chance of being employed in the knowledge-intensive industry, mainly services. All this points to an increase in the demand for higher educated workers in particular occupations and within the knowledge-intensive industries, more so in the service sector.

APPENDIX 6.1

TABLE A6.1: OECD Classification of Knowledge-intensive Manufacturing and Service Industry

Knowledge-intensive Industry Classification	*Industry Groups (NIC, 1998 and 1987)*
High-tech manufacturing	Manufacture of office machinery and computers; radio, television and communication equipment and apparatus; medical, precision and optical instruments; watches and clocks
Medium high-tech manufacturing	Manufacture of chemicals and chemical products; machinery and equipment n.e.c.; electrical machinery and apparatus; transport equipment
Medium low-tech manufacturing	Manufacture of coke, refined petroleum products and nuclear fuel; rubber and plastic products; basic metals and fabricated metal products; other non-metallic mineral products; manufacturing n.e.c.
Low-tech manufacturing	Manufacture of food products, beverages and tobacco; textiles and textile products; leather and leather products; wood and wood products; pulp, paper and paper products; publishing and printing
Knowledge-intensive Services (KIS)	Financial intermediation; real estate, renting and business activities; recreational, cultural and sporting activities; water transport; air transport
Social Knowledge-intensive Services	Education; health and social work
High-tech Knowledge-intensive Services	Post and telecommunications; computer and related activities; research and development
Less Knowledge-intensive Services	Wholesale and retail trade; hotels and restaurants; land transport; transport via pipelines; supporting and auxiliary transport activities; activities of travel agencies Public administration and defence; compulsory social security; sewage and refuse disposal, sanitation and similar activities; activities of membership organisation n.e.c.; other service activities; activities of households as employers of domestic staff; extra-territorial organisations and bodies
Construction Industry	
Mining and Quarrying	

MODEL AND INTERPRETATION OF RESULTS

The purpose of the model is to learn whether the effect of having a graduate degree (x_1) on the probability of being in a high-tech industry (y) (both manufacturing and services) differs between occupation groups (x_2). And to do so, we use an interaction term of graduate dummy and occupation category ($x_1 . x_2$) dummy. We are interested in calculating the marginal effect of each explanatory variable which, in a non-linear model like Probit, is an approximation of how much the dependent variable is expected to change for a unit change in that explanatory variable. For a continuous independent variable, marginal effect is nothing but the first derivative of the dependent variable with respect to the independent variable (say x_1). But the problem occurs when we want to compute the change of the effect of x_1 on $E(y)$ for a unit change in x_2 (another explanatory variable). This effect is actually the cross-partial derivative of $E(y)$ with respect to x_1 and x_2.

Linear Model: In linear models, the coefficient of the interaction term between x_1 and x_2 gives exactly this cross-partial derivative. So if we consider the interaction term ($x_1 . x_2$) to be another variable q and compute the marginal effect of q, then it is the same as the cross-partial derivative (coefficient of interaction term) of $E(y)$ with respect to ($x_1 . x_2$),

i.e., $\partial E(y)/\partial q = \partial^2 E(y)/\partial x_1 \partial x_2$

Non-linear Model: In non-linear models (Probit or Logit), since the functional form is not linear, the coefficient is not equal to the marginal effect,

i.e., $\partial^2 E(y)/\partial x_1 \partial x_2 \neq \partial E(y)/\partial (x_1 . x_2)$.

So far, this illustration has been given for continuous independent variables, but the same holds true (that is, the coefficient ≠ marginal effect) with differences instead of differentials (partial derivatives) of the independent variables in case they are discrete or dummy in nature. Hence, the computation of marginal effects in Probit or Logit models, which include interaction terms (with discrete values), requires a different methodology as compared to those followed in general.

Generally, STATA commands '*mfx*' and '*dprobit*' are useful in estimating the marginal effects. But these commands do not give the correct marginal effects when interaction terms are included in the model. The command '*margins, dy/dx(*)*' (which is a post command, run after Probit) can give us the marginal effects of all other independent variables, except the interaction terms. The marginal effects of the interaction terms can be obtained from the command '*margins*'.

Instead of taking the derivative of the expected probabilities of any occupational category with respect to *edu_dummy*, we will calculate the marginal effect as the difference between the expected probabilities (which are called margins) of any occupation group with and without graduate degree, since the *edu_dummy* is a categorical variable which takes values 0 or 1. The command '*margins*' gives us the estimated probabilities in STATA. The results copied from the STATA output on running the command '*margins edu_dummy#occupation_category*' are presented in Table A6.2.

TABLE A6.2: Margins of Interaction Terms

	Margin	*Std. Err.*	*Z*	*P>z*
Education*occupation (0—Non-grad, 1—Grad)				
00	0.089	0.005	18.26	0
01	0.090	0.007	12.68	0
02	0.300	0.015	20.66	0
03	0.708	0.014	50.92	0
04	0.426	0.018	24.08	0
05	0.078	0.004	19.07	0
07	0.089	0.005	18.27	0
08	0.088	0.006	13.88	0
10	0.238	0.052	4.55	0
11	0.342	0.018	19.56	0
12	0.803	0.011	71.73	0
13	0.809	0.012	68.32	0
14	0.486	0.019	25.37	0
15	0.097	0.017	5.89	0
17	0.285	0.038	7.57	0
18	0.244	0.037	6.69	0

The margins command shows the probabilities of every combination of occupational category and education (*occupation_category & edu_dummy*) being in a high-tech industry. The probability of elementary workers (occupation code 0) being in the HT industry without a graduate degree is 0.089, while that probability for workers with graduate degrees is 0.238. The marginal effect of having a graduate degree (*edu_dummy*) for production workers is thus 0.149 (see Table 6.5).

NOTE

1. This chapter was presented at the conference on 'Higher Education: New Trends and Challenges', Centre for Policy Research, New Delhi, 28–29 July 2011. This chapter is the product of a larger research project titled 'Pathfinder Brazil India—Assessing the Impact of Higher Education Expansion on Economic Restructuring, Occupational Change and Access to Opportunities in Brazil and India', funded by the Economic and Social Research Council (ESRC), UK.

REFERENCES

Acemoglu, D. and J. Angrist, 'How Large are Human Capital Externalities? Evidence from Compulsory Schooling Laws', *NBER Macroeconomics Annual* 15, 2000, pp. 9–59.

Anandakrishnan, M., 'Grappling with Core Concerns of Higher Education', *The Hindu*, 15 June 2010.

Azam, M., 'India's Increasing Skill Premium: Role of Demand and Supply', *The B.E. Journal of Economic Analysis and Policy* 10 (1), 2010, pp. 1–28.

Basant, R. and P. Mukhopadhyay, 'An Arrested Virtuous Growth? Higher Education and High-tech Industries in India', Annual Bank Conference on Development Economics, Cape Town, 2008.

Basant, R. and U. Rani, 'Labour Market Deepening in India's IT: An Exploratory Analysis', *Economic and Political Weekly* 39 (50), 2004, pp. 5317–26.

Dutta, P. V., 'Accounting for Wage Inequality in India', *Indian Journal of Labour Economics* 48 (2), 2005, pp. 273–95.

Elais, P. and K. Purcell, 'SOC (HE): A Classification of Occupations for Studying the Graduate Labour Market', Research Paper No. 6, Warwick Institute for Employment Research, Warwick, 2004.

Eurostat Metadata, 'High-Technology' and 'Knowledge-Intensive Services', 2007a. Available at http://epp.eurostat.ec.europa.eu/cache/ITY_SDDS/EN/htec_esms.htm (last accessed 3 April 2011).

_____, '"High-Technology" and "Knowledge Based Services" aggregations based on NACE Rev.2', 2007b. Available at http://epp.eurostat.ec.europa.eu/cache/ITY_SDDS/Annexes/htec _esms_an3.pdf (last accessed 3 April 2011).

Felix, B., 'High Tech Industries and Knowledge Based Services: The Importance of R&D and Human Resources in Science and Technology', *Eurostat Statistics in Focus: Science and Technology*, 2006.

Fisher, A. G. B., *The Clash of Progress and Security* (London: Macmillan, 1935).

Gottschalk, P. and M. Hansen, 'Is the Proportion of College Workers in Non-college Jobs Increasing?' *Journal of Labor Economics* 21 (2), 2003, pp. 449–71.

Government of India (GoI), *National Knowledge Commission: Report to the Nation, 2006–09*, New Delhi: Government of India, 2009a.

_____, *Report of the Committee on Renovation and Rejuvenation of Higher Education*, New Delhi: Government of India, 2009b.

Hertog, J., 'Over Education and Earnings: Where Are We, Where Should We Go?', *Economics of Education Review* 19, 2000, pp. 131–47.

Kapur, D. and P. B. Mehta, 'Indian Higher Education Reform: From Half-Baked Socialism to Half-Baked Capitalism', Brookings-NCAER India Policy Forum, New Delhi, 2007.

Kijima, Y., 'Why did Wage Inequality Increase? Evidence from Urban India 1983–99', *Journal of Development Economics* 81 (1), 2006, pp. 97–117.

Kuznets, S., *Economic Growth of Nations* (Cambridge, MA: Harvard University Press, 1971).

McGuiness, S., 'Over-education in the Labour Market', *Journal of Economic Surveys* 20 (3), 2006, pp. 387–418.

McGuiness, S. and J. Bennett, 'Overeducation in the graduate labour market: A quantile regression approach', *Economics of Education Review* 26 (5), 2007, pp. 521–31.

Moretti, E., 'Estimating the Social Return to Higher Education: Evidence from Longitudinal and Repeated Cross-sectional Data', *Journal of Econometrics* 121 (1–2), 2004, pp. 175–212.

Rowthorn, R. and J. R. Wells, *Deindustrialisation and Foreign Trade* (Avon: Cambridge University Press, 1987).

Sala, G., 'Approaches to Skills Mismatch in the Labour Market: A Literature Review', *Sociologia de la Salud* 42 (2), 2011, pp. 1025–45.

Torres-Freire, C. and A. Abdel, 'High-tech industries and knowledge-intensive services: why are these activities the core businesses for

Sao Paulo's competitiveness?', VIII Triple Helix Conference in the Development of Cities of Knowledge, Expanding Communities and Connecting Regions, Madrid, 2010.

University Grants Commission (UGC), *Report on Higher Education in India: Issues, Concerns and New Directions* (New Delhi: UGC, 2003).

Unni, J. and U. Rani, *Flexibility of Labour in Globalizing India: The Challenge of Skills and Technology* (New Delhi: Tulika Books, 2008).

— *seven* —

Financing of Higher Education in India

The Way Forward

K. P. Krishnan

Introduction

Today, India is poised at a critical juncture of its development. On the one hand, it is ready to take its position as an important player in the global economy, while on the other, it is facing the challenge of harnessing its demographic advantage by educating and training its over 140 million people in the 18–24 age group. The crucial role of education and skill development in the emerging knowledge society makes it all the more important to pay attention to expanding education and promoting skill formation. Higher education has made a major contribution to the economic and social development of India. Looking ahead, its quality and reach will be a major determinant of India's capacity to become a better society, evolve into a knowledge economy and help in the sustained participation in the global economy.

The Current Scenario

The 1990s and the first decade of the twenty-first century saw numerous policy changes in higher education. A relative decline in public expenditure on higher education (per-student public expenditure on higher education increased in nominal terms, but declined in real terms; see Prakash 2007), greater private-sector participation, especially in technical education, upward revision of student fees, and the introduction of a new student loan programme have been some important milestones. Simultaneously, the demand for higher education has been growing rapidly with faster growth in enrolment in higher educational institutions; however, there is a growing mismatch between supply and demand in higher education institutes of repute.

The growth rates among students enrolled in postgraduate courses and research have doubled, while the number of institutions for postgraduate and research studies grew at a slower rate in the 1990s than it had in the 1980s. Although enrolment has been increasing in absolute terms, only 8–9 per cent of the population in the age group 17–24 attended higher educational institutions in India, as against 92 per cent of the eligible age-group population attending higher educational institutions in the USA, 52 per cent in the UK and 45 per cent in Japan. The Gross Enrolment Ratio (GER) has increased significantly in recent years and is now clocking over 20 per cent. This jump of over 8 per cent in GER over an eight-year period will call for a serious increase in the funding requirements of higher education.

PREVAILING FUNDING PATTERNS

Appropriate public policy support for higher education remains essential in a knowledge-based society. The funds for higher education in India come mainly from three different sources, viz., the government, fee income from students, and philanthropy, industry, etc. Reliance on government resources almost doubled, from 49.4 per cent in 1950–51 to 75.9 per cent in 1986–87. On the other hand, fee income as a source drastically declined, from 36.8 per cent to 12.6 per cent, during the same period (Rani 2014). Other sources contributed around 10 per cent throughout the period. Thus, until the 1980s higher education was largely a state-funded activity, with about three-quarters of the total expenditure being borne by the government.

The expenditure per student (in real terms) fell by 28 per cent between 1990–91 and 2002–03. Decline in per-student expenditure means a decline in the real resources available per student on an average, seriously affecting the quality of higher education (GoI 2005). The trend of decline in plan allocations that had started prior to economic liberalisation was arrested with the increased allocations to the higher education sector during the period 1997–2000. However, since 2006 there has been a steady increase in the allocation to higher education. While funding by state governments has been relatively constant (at about half per cent of GDP), central government funding doubled (as fraction of GDP) and has been the principal driver in the increase in the percentage share of public expenditure on higher education (Figure 7.1).

FIGURE 7.1: Expenditure on Higher Education (as % of GDP)

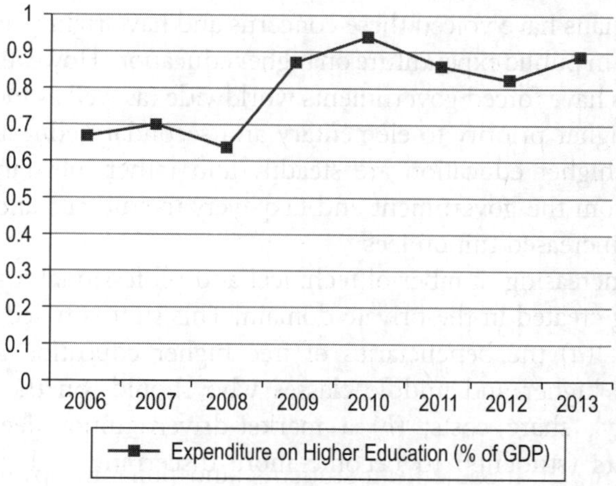

Source: Annual reports of the Ministry of Human Resources Development, Government of India, for the relevant years.

While India's expenditure on higher education as a percentage of GDP is comparable to other countries, it is extremely low when assessed on a per-student basis (Ernst and Young and FICCI 2009). Even for the very low enrolment ratios in higher education in India, it is increasingly realised that public budgets cannot adequately fund higher education, particularly when sectors of mass education require more resources. Hence the need for several public policy alternatives such as an increase in student fees, student loans, etc.

SHIFTING RESPONSIBILITY

Concerns have also been raised about the access, equity and quality dimensions in the field of education in the country. India has one of the largest networks of higher education in the developing world (China, which was behind India in the 1980s, is now significantly ahead), but barring a handful of Indian Institutes of Technology (IITs) and Indian Institutes of Management (IIMs), none of them feature in the list of top-level institutions in the world, giving rise to issues about standards. In addition, there are important questions of access, in terms of how an individual's participation is dependent on his/her religion affiliations, socio-economic status and demographic characteristics (Basant and Sen 2010). Successive committees and academicians have voiced these concerns and have rightly argued for increases in public expenditure on higher education. However, limited resources have forced governments worldwide (as well as in India) to accord higher priority to elementary and secondary education. The costs of higher education are steadily and rather inevitably being shifted from the government and taxpayers to students and parents through increased tuition fees.

An increasing number of technical and professional institutions are being created in the private domain. This shift is based on three premises: (*a*) the beneficiaries of free higher education are often from the higher and middle classes who should, on the grounds of 'equity', share costs; (*b*) a market-driven tuition fee enables consumers (students) to become more discerning and producers (colleges and universities) to become more cost-conscious and driven by individual needs; and finally (*c*) higher education, as distinct from basic education, brings more private benefits through increased incomes and status, and hence individuals and families must bear the burden of higher fees. However, it may also be argued that under imperfect market conditions, a rise in the net cost of higher education restricts the access of the underprivileged and exacerbates the existing inequalities. It is observed that the proportion of the population with higher education rises sharply with rising levels of household economic status, both in rural and urban areas (GoI 2005).

In a bid to reconcile these seemingly contradictory objectives of reducing public expenditure and improving access to the economically backward, governments internationally have been increasingly moving away from funding institutions to funding students via student loans. Student lending can take the form of conventional mortgage-type loans or income-contingent loans, which link repayments to the earning capacity of the borrower (a variation of the latter are the 'graduate taxes'). The current Education Loan Scheme operational in India is structured like a conventional mortgage loan. However, before we evaluate the current scheme, it might be useful to look at a few international examples of how student loans have been structured and how successful they have been in achieving the twin objectives outlined above.

INTERNATIONAL EXPERIENCE[1]

The world over, higher education financing has been moving towards greater cost sharing, which *inter alia* has led to a greater financial burden on students and/or parents. While some argue that this is a result of market-oriented policies, the causes are more basic. As noted in Chapter 1 of this book, the number of students enrolling has skyrocketed and the cost per student has been increasing as well, which means that unless governmental funding increases substantially, increased cost sharing is inevitable. But given the multiple pressures on the government purse, while public expenditure on higher education has been increasing, it is insufficient to meet the enormous increase in demand. This story is not specific to India alone. It is a global phenomenon, as some of the country experiences illustrate below (Johnstone and Marcucci 2010).

Australia

The Higher Education Contribution Scheme (HECS) in Australia is a combination of tuition plus income-contingent loans available to most Australian students. The loan covers the full amount of tuition, which is regulated by the Government of Australia. The loan carries a zero real rate of interest and repayments are collected like income tax dues. The system, therefore, is cost-efficient to administer and is characterised by a low default rate.

China

China's loan programmes have undergone many modifications since their experimental beginnings in six cities in 1999. The Government Subsidized Student Loan Scheme (GSSLS), in operation since 2004, provides student loans to 20 per cent of enrolled students. The interest payment is shared between the students and the government. The scheme is operated through participating banks, and the risk is shared by the university, the government and the bank.

Germany

Germany has an extensive system of means-tested, or 'need-based', study assistance, known colloquially as BAfoG. Close to half the amount provided is a grant, and the balance is a loan at a zero nominal rate of interest.

Japan

The newly created independent administrative institution, Japan Student Services Organisation (JASSO), administers the recently revised student loan system. It consists of two schemes. The first is an interest-free loan for needy, meritorious students, and the second is a deferred interest carrying loan, based solely on economic need. Loan repayments are collected automatically from the *student's bank or postal account.*

The Netherlands

Student loans are provided in the Netherlands to cover tuition and maintenance. One component of the loan is not 'means-tested'. There is a second means-tested component, which can be converted to a grant if satisfactory academic progress is maintained. Interest varies annually at the government's borrowing rate, plus about 1 per cent to cover administrative costs.

South Africa

Student loans are given by the government sponsored Tertiary Education Fund of South Africa (TEFSA). These are need-based and carry a high interest rate of inflation-plus-two-percentage-points. However, depending on academic performance, nearly half the loan is converted to a grant. Repayment is income contingent. The national tax system is not used for collection, but the government has authorised the tax agency to *report borrower incomes to TEFSA* for purposes for income verification.

Sweden

Sweden has no tuition fee and has relied on universally available student loan programmes since the 1960s to cover student living costs. The programme has undergone many changes, with the latest one being introduced in 2001; this carries a one-third interest rate subsidy and a minimum repayment of 5 per cent of the annual income.

United States of America (USA)

Loans and parental contributions are the bedrocks of the very extensive reliance in the United States on cost sharing. The United States provides federally guaranteed conventional, fixed-schedule loans, available to all students with some financial need (defined quite liberally) at minimally subsidised rates of interest. Even the unsubsidised loans available to students without financial need carry the implicit subsidy of governmental guarantee and the benefit of an interest rate that is near the government's borrowing rate. Most student loans in the United States are provided by the private banking sector, and are securitised and sold to other investors in the secondary markets. Sallie Mae, a Fortune 500 company originally created in 1972 as a government-sponsored entity (GSE), provides a good part of federal and private student loans, along with a host of other financial services ranging from servicing of loans, to default aversion, to philanthropy. It manages over US$ 180 billion in debt for nearly 10 million student customers and administers more than $11 billion in college savings accounts for customers.

The Project on Student Debt estimated that the average college senior in 2009 graduated with $24,000 in outstanding loans. In August 2010, student loans surpassed credit cards as the nation's single largest source of debt, edging ever closer to $1 trillion (Harris 2011). Since 1978, the price of tuition at US colleges has increased over 900 per cent, 650 points above inflation. To put that number in perspective, housing prices, the bubble that nearly burst the US economy, increased only 50 points above the Consumer Price Index during those years.

> The loans and costs are caught in the kind of dangerous loop that occurs when lending becomes both profitable and seemingly risk-free: high and increasing college costs mean students need to take out more loans, more loans mean more securities lenders can package and sell, more selling means lenders can offer more loans with the capital they raise, which means colleges can continue to raise costs. The result is over $800 billion in outstanding student debt, over 30 per cent of it securitized, and the federal government directly or indirectly on the hook for almost all of it (Harris 2011).

STUDENT LOANS AS A FINANCING OPTION FOR HIGHER EDUCATION IN INDIA

For access to higher education, equity and social justice demand that newly emerging beneficiaries of the secondary education sector, who increasingly represent vulnerable groups, are able to afford higher education. It is to be realised that 'Higher Education is no longer a luxury; it is essential to national, social and economic development' (UNESCO 2000). It is a fact that macro-economic reforms imply profound changes in the relationship between government and higher education, and also a considerable expansion of the private sector in higher education.

Nevertheless, there are three important economic justifications for government funding of higher education:

1. Higher education investments generate external benefits important for economic development, such as the long-term returns from basic research and from technical development,

which are essential for long-term economic competitiveness. However, it should be recognised that public subsidies for research is a pure public good, whereas public subsidies for teaching in higher education have a mix of private and public benefits. The case for greater public funding of the former is strong, but that of the latter is weak, especially if public policy facilitates a good, well-designed and accessible student loan programme.

2. Private investment alone in higher education would be socially *sub-optimal*.
3. An increased role of the market undermines the participation of meritorious students from economically disadvantaged groups.

It has been argued that a number of countries in the developing and developed world have established student loan programmes in order to safeguard poor students from the rising costs of higher education (both tuition fee and maintenance cost). However, the implementation of cost recovery in an equitable manner requires a scholarship programme that ensures (to begin with) necessary financial support to academically qualified poor students. Further, it is important to note that unlike in the United States, in India, conventional university courses are unable to cater to the immediate demands of the market. This academic inflexibility boosted the rapid development of private initiatives in higher education. However, apart from a few reputed private higher learning institutions, the majority of them are education shops catering to a mass of students, who are willing to pay in the hope of being trained to enter the job market.

Student loan schemes should meet the twin criteria of being '*need-based*' and '*generally available*.' This is especially important when declining public expenditures and extensive private participation exert an upward pressure on fees and living expenses, which, in the absence of a liberal student loan programme, can create major access barriers with reference to family incomes, caste and gender.

The current 'Education Loan Scheme' for pursuing higher studies in India and abroad, as amended in 2011 and implemented through the banking sector, meets the first criterion well, as it is available to any student with an established need, that is, a student who has secured admission to a higher education programme either through a competitive exam or a merit-based selection process. The policy document of the scheme is also very liberal in the scope and coverage of academic programmes, which may range from a simple graduate course to a highly ranked full-time professional course conducted by the IIMs and IITs. Furthermore, the scheme has a comprehensive coverage for the complete range of expenses, including living and other expenses, in addition to the basic tuition fee, and for studies in India, provides an amount up to Rs 4 lakh without any security or even margin money.

However, with regard to the second criterion of '*general availability*', these liberal provisions perhaps make the banks highly apprehensive about repayments. Consequently, loan appraisals, apart from looking at the future income streams of the student (justifiably), also include a provision for 'means testing' of the parent/guardian's repayment capability. The latter provision is clearly at divergence with the 'general availability' principle, and encourages adverse selection against students with perceived non-bankable backgrounds, who were perhaps the primary target beneficiaries of the scheme.

The number and amount of education loans disbursed have been indicated in Table 7.1.

TABLE 7.1: Education Loans Disbursed under the Student Loan Scheme of Banks

Year	*Number of A/Cs*	*Total amount (in Rs Crore)*	*Average loan amount (in Rs)*
2004	3,19,337	4,550.06	1,42,485
2005	4,68,207	6,713.16	1,43,380
2006	6,79,945	10,012.49	1,47,254
2007	9,44,397	14,282.56	1,51,235
2008	1,246,870	19,816.54	1,58,930
2009	1,603,385	27,645.58	1,72,420
2010	1,928,350	35,628.33	1,84,761
2011	2,237,031	43,074.00	1,92,550
2012	2,460,493	49,069.00	1,99,428
2013	2,509,465	53,520.00	2,13,273
2014	2,235,532	58,256.00	2,60,591

Source: Indian Banks' Association: Social Banking Department.

The 'security' on these loans is as follows:

- Up to Rs 4 lakh—co-obligation of parents
- Between Rs 4–Rs 7.50 lakh—co-obligation of parents; suitable third-party guarantee
- Above Rs 7.50 lakh—co-obligation of parents; tangible collateral security; and assignment of future income of student.

A cursory look at Table 7.1 shows the following trends:

1. Outstanding loans have grown from Rs 4,550 crore (as on 31 March 2004) to a little under Rs 60,000 crore (as on 31 March 2014). This is a 10-fold growth in about a decade.
2. A state-wise analysis reveals that the four southern states of Tamilnadu, Kerala, Karnataka and Andhra Pradesh account for more than 50 per cent share of the accounts. During 2009–10, these four states accounted for 64 per cent of the total educational loan accounts, which declined to 57 per cent during 2010–11 and rose again to 60.88 per cent as on 31 December 2014. Tamilnadu accounted for around 36–39 per cent of the total in 2010–11, and now stands at 31.86 per cent of the total. These states have emerged as a hub for higher technical education and attract students not only locally, but from all over the country. The two other states with a significant share hovering around 6–7 per cent are Maharashtra and Uttar Pradesh. Table 7.4 on the state-wise distribution of education loans brings this out very clearly. During the five-year period for which data is shown in the table, it is evident that there was very little change in the rank-ordering of the top six states. These continue to be Tamilnadu, Kerala, Andhra Pradesh, Maharashtra, Uttar Pradesh and Karnataka.
3. With regard to participating banks, as expected and brought out in Figure 7.2, nationalised banks, followed by the State Bank of India (SBI) and its associates, overwhelmingly dominate this activity. Foreign banks and private-sector banks continue to be very minor players, with their combined shares declining over time.

FIGURE 7.2: Education Loans—Bank Group-wise Distribution

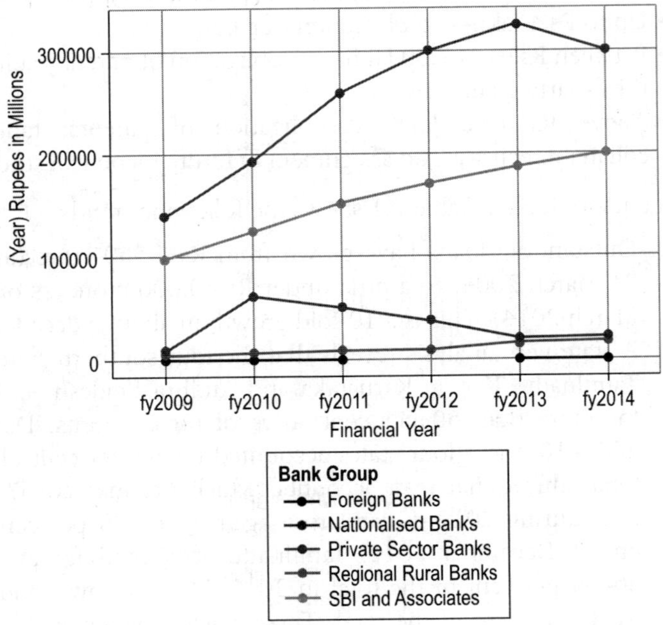

Source: This figure was constructed for some of the years on the basis of the data presented in Table 7.1, by grouping banks according to the RBI's classification of banks.

4. An analysis of the distribution of loans in terms of geographical areas shows that semi-urban areas have recorded the highest rates of growth, followed by urban areas. Figure 7.3 highlights this distribution. This is perhaps a reflection of both the location of higher education institutions and the location and origin of students in these institutions.

However, what is disconcerting is the trend wherein the total outstanding is more than or equal to the loans disbursed in a year. The problem, therefore, is of NPA in education loans rising at a faster rate. The higher education loan NPA percentage increased from 2.74 per cent in 2008–09 to 3.72 per cent in 2010–11, to clock 5.68 per cent in 2013–14. As per the Indian Banks' Association, the gross NPA position in higher education loans and the annual growth rate is shown in Table 7.2. A comparison of the NPA position in the overall banking sector and also in the higher education segment is given in Table 7.3.

FIGURE 7.3: Education Loans—Population Group-wise Distribution

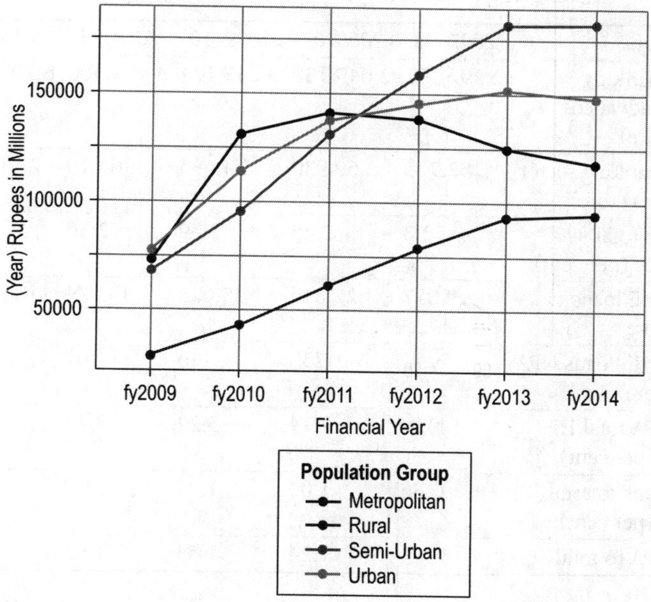

Source: This figure was constructed on the basis of the data presented in Table 7.1 by disaggregating the data by bank location. The disaggregation was done by the Indian Banks Association (Social Banking Department).

TABLE 7.2: Gross NPA Position and its Annual Growth

Category of loan	*Amount (in Rs Crore)*				*Annual growth rate*		
	2008–09	*2009–10*	*2010–11*	*As on 31/12/2014*	*2009–10*	*2010–11*	*2013–14*
Less than 4 lakh	612.43	918.47	–	3,320.39	49.97	–	
Between 4 to 7.5 lakh	83.65	127.55	–	299.52	52.48	–	
Above 7.5 lakh	61.81	100.25	–	202.29	62.19	–	
All	757.89	1,146.20	1,600.80	3,822.19	51.24	39.65	21.70 (approx)

TABLE 7.3: Overall NPA Position Compared to Higher Education (HE) Loan NPAs

Category	*2007–08*	*2008–09*	*2009–10*	*2010–11*	*2013–14*
Total banking sector advances (Rs crore)	2,292,391	2,649,130	3,247,174	4,287,400	8,101,775
Total banking sector NPA (Rs crore)	52,725	60,930	74,685	98,610	2,51,000
NPA to total advance (per cent)	2.3	2.25	2.39	2.30	4.11
Total HE loans (Rs crore)	19,817	27,646	35,628	43,074	59,834
Total HE Loans NPA (Rs crore)	N.A.	758	1,146	1,601	3,398
HE NPA total HE loans (per cent)	N.A.	2.74	3.22	3.72	5.68
HE loans to total loans (per cent)	0.86	1.04	1.09	1.0	0.74
HE NPA to total		1.24	1.53	1.62	1.35

While the average NPA-to-loan ratio was 2.39 per cent in 2009–10, that for education loans was 3.22 per cent. The same declined to 2.30 per cent in 2010–11; however, for the education loans, it increased to 3.72 per cent and further to 5.68 per cent in 2013–14, despite the fact that the size of education loans is comparatively smaller (see Table 7.1).

Currently education loans are one of the sectors with the highest growth rate, despite constraining factors like parents' repayment capability and restrictive repayment schedules, which are not meaningfully related to the income levels of the borrower. It also does not rope in educational institutions, which are important beneficiaries of the scheme, in any meaningful fashion. Their role has been restricted to certification and passive provision of information. Last but not least, student loan schemes worldwide have government participation in the form of guarantees on default (as discussed in the section on international experience), interest rate subsidies and servicing of loans during the 'in-school' period. Moreover, it is also a sector where NPAs are rising faster than banking sector NPAs,

Table 7.4: State-wise Distribution of Education Loans

State	*2014*	*2013*	*2012*	*2011*	*2010*	*2009*
Tamil Nadu	1,29,476.963	1,35,039.222	1,17,762.481	91,821.094	67,824.11	43,618.47
Andhra Pradesh	51,926.832	52,858.918	54,340.568	54,637.271	50,381.82	36,244.34
Kerala	75,915.325	77,844.151	68,154.754	57,567.001	46,891.57	32,153
Maharashtra	39,296.509	37,073.645	38,934.91	40,876.674	38,607.81	21,235.59
Karnataka	31,694.427	37,412.659	36,350.789	32,503.45	29,245.3	19,742.97
Uttar Pradesh	35,682.11	36,013.599	34,705.499	30,921.573	22,712.5	14,907.21
Gujarat	13,413.068	12,885.602	14,464.537	16,582.865	13,712.72	8,983.022
NCT of Delhi	10,250.652	13,930.772	16,032.387	22,157.906	20,482.25	8,418.283
West Bengal	15,869.011	15,722.421	15,569.646	15,594.27	12,812.25	8,342.639
Madhya Pradesh	18,302.7	17,676.742	16,023.255	12,520.85	9,685.96	7,843.546
Odisha	16,670.497	17,171.848	15,875.437	14,070.911	10,755.2	6,893.895
Rajasthan	14,181.957	13,319.29	14,900.461	12,204.255	10,102.25	6,576.044
Punjab	9,529.336	9,373.092	9,614.557	9,820.493	7,920.077	5,723.393
Bihar	27,235.007	24,275.097	19,727.526	15,675.802	9,569.224	5,370.473
Haryana	9,658.512	9,639.672	9,406.863	9,049.816	6,581.217	4,963.965
Jharkhand	13,602.069	12,598.783	11,385.173	9,691.977	7,251.087	4,365.784
Uttarakhand	6,434.692	6,233.459	5,908.926	5,111.33	3,967.818	2,808.195

(Contd)

Table 7.4 (Contd)

State	*2014*	*2013*	*2012*	*2011*	*2010*	*2009*
Himachal Pradesh	3,366.374	3,284.865	3,536.225	2,562.534	1,932.088	1,851.986
Assam	4,139.214	4,141.514	3,919.777	3,854.52	2,956.931	1,830.026
Chhattisgarh	3,841.266	3,519.235	3,233.703	3,088.702	2,285.807	1,608.825
Chandigarh	1,695.255	1,986.403	2,296.167	2,551.918	2,518.057	1,228.62
Jammu & Kashmir	2,504.163	2,321.6	2,168.668	2,007.2	1,709.647	1,214.913
Puducherry	2,967.402	2,922.464	2,689.073	2,037.701	1,647.51	1,004.882
Goa	871.956	890.835	993.543	1,082.963	944.453	604.604
Manipur	417.754	422.913	391.472	419.31	312.849	249.088
Meghalaya	564.465	466.481	388.682	332.923	250.259	178.229
Tripura	686.906	544.642	474.972	337.178	216.983	154.879
Mizoram	268.158	270.769	261.965	252.346	189.509	127.429
Sikkim	121.771	128.989	119.065	187.989	68.144	59.738
Nagaland	119.893	107.662	100.999	103.134	76.28	52.633
Andaman & Nicobar Islands	140.225	137.134	132.568	100.925	75.261	45.809
Arunachal Pradesh	151.497	125.748	102.377	90.598	59.632	35.19
Daman & Diu	38.882	36.735	30.611	31.588	24.537	22.955
Dadra & Nagar Haveli	57.722	60.207	52.295	47.551	31.32	20.778
Lakshadweep	2.476	4.684	3.681	1.247	1.246	0.831

and hence future modifications need to factor this in. In summary, the current scheme depends completely on the banking sector for funding, operationalising and servicing.

RETHINKING THE FUTURE FUNDING OF HIGHER EDUCATION

In the absence of government participation, it is difficult to envisage the scheme becoming accessible to *the large number of students* now completing their secondary education, who are not in a position to provide acceptable co-obligant/collateral security. While the business of student loans will continue to grow rapidly, it will further enhance the 'adverse selection' of students benefitting from greater access to secondary education.

In terms of the IBA data, for the nearly 30-plus lakh student borrowers at present, the average loan amount is about Rs 2.5 lakh. If the government measures are successful and the GER reaches 20–25 per cent in the coming decade, the number of students who are eligible and seeking access to loans would be a mere 150 lakh students. Assuming an average loan of Rs 2.5 lakh, it would mean loan requirements of over Rs 3,00,000 crore. This, in the absence of higher government outlays, would probably be a low estimate.

A simple correlation analysis between enrolment in higher education, the number of loan accounts, the amount and availability, and access, measured in terms of the average population per bank branch, reveals a significant relationship between enrolment, and the number of loan accounts and the amount. Surprisingly, the relationship between the availability of banks and enrolment in higher education is not significant. What this signifies is that, more than access, what the sector craves is a well-designed product that would help meet the twin criteria of being *need-based* and *generally available*. With appropriate risk reduction measures, such a product would be an ideal instrument for securitisation, with a very high rating. However, with the growing defaults in these loans (Table 7.3), it is unlikely that the earlier growth rates can be maintained in the *absence of effective risk reduction strategies*.

Balance Between Risk Reduction and Meeting Higher Education Loan Demands

The education loan industry is growing, and the current outstanding of education loans is a little over Rs 60,000 crore. The current product being offered by the banks is a plain vanilla version, with scope for innovation to facilitate easier access. The increase in the cost of education means that a number of talented students may find it difficult to afford the education on their own. As a result, educational institutions may also face the challenge of attracting talented students who can afford the higher fees and living expenses.

At the same time, for the lenders, understanding the quality of the course and the institution as well as the student's potential employability is vital for the quality of the portfolio. Coupled with the objectives of access and equitability, these issues make the perceived risks relatively complex for a lender.

Recent debates on the subject indicate that considering the mammoth task at hand, the current financing models may not be able to meet the demand without the participation of the private sector and international financial and strategic partners. As India's current expenditure on education is at 5 per cent of the average household income, it possibly makes it more attractive for these types of players to participate in the financing of higher education. However, simply making easy credit available may not address all the issues at hand, as the recent experience worldwide has indicated that easy credit can be used as a palliative without addressing systemic problems.

The various challenges associated with the present education loan model are: a high default rate; need for better due diligence by banks; non-participation of the universities/institutes to assume part of the financial risk; equity in access; standardising loans for securitisation; improper data collection; and poor administration.

Proposed Design Parameters to Address Equity, Access and Affordability

The proposed National Academic Depository (NAD) Bill, 2011 sought to put into place an institutional mechanism for the maintenance of a national database of academic awards in electronic format in a depository. This would also facilitate authenticated access, online verification and an efficient retrieval system for degrees. The Bill also envisages online interaction and exchange of information with the Central Identities Data Repository created by the National Identification Authority of India, under the National Identification Authority of India Act, 2011, for persons whose academic awards are maintained in the national database. The Central Identities Data Repository also captures bank account details, and linking this with NAD can help to link it with the student loan information. There has been no further progress on the enactment of this Bill.

However, there is also a need to redesign the strategy for meeting the higher education loan requirement. Of foremost importance is the collection of good-quality and nuanced data, which is required for this complex policy analysis. There is a need to formulate an empirically backed policy as the present system of depending on bank data may not capture the actual requirement across various socio-economic strata. The present system leads to mass commoditisation of the product being offered without addressing the issue of equity. For example, in reality there may be a need to offer loans with less financial commitment but with more flexibility in repayment. Superior underwriting capabilities based on strong research into educational institutions, courses, potential employability and compensation, along with cross-border tracking and collection abilities may ensure that the portfolio quality is at the highest level.

Discussions between the Indian Bank Association and educational institutions on the rating model for institutions of higher education are a step in this direction. Criteria like placements, academic standards, intellectual capital and connections with industry will be used to rate the institutes, as such rating, based on the placement records of students, would help the banks to structure their loan products better. A good placement record with higher salary would make the loan less risky for the bank and may offer better security terms, which can translate into lower interest rates.

The fixed repayment schedules (beginning course period plus one year or six months after getting a job, and to be repaid in five to seven years) with uniform EMIs spread over the entire repayment period are more restrictive than they are in developed economies. This has recently been addressed, with repayments being allowed to stretch up to 15 years. However, these recent changes are also rather mechanical and more in the nature of one size fits all. Worldwide *successful student loan programmes have government participation* with two objectives: first, to ensure greater access to deserving students purely on 'need', and second, the high risk of default due to the absence of collateral to encourage the participation of the commercial banking sector. Hence, the broad design parameters for the new scheme can look at the following points:

- Setting up an institutional mechanism to encourage access to economically backward students.
- The *educational institutions*, especially in the private sector, are major stakeholders in the success of the student loan programme. Their becoming *co-signatories* to the loan with certain responsibilities would decrease defaults and improve default tracking mechanisms. It would also dissuade them from increasing their fees in view of the easy availability of loans.
- A guarantee fund with the participation of the government and educational institutions, and the operation of the same by a separate agency like a private credit insurance company, so that student loans could be guaranteed, reducing the cost to borrower. The corpus can be built up by *charging a one-time guarantee fee* of the sanctioned amount and a *nominal annual service fee* of the outstanding credit from the borrower. This corpus fund can then be used to reimburse the banks for defaults. Such a model would encourage banks to lower the interest rate, which currently stands at Benchmark Prime Lending Rate (BPLR) for loans up to Rs 4 lakh and BPLR plus 1 per cent above Rs 4 lakh.

The announcement by the government in 2012 regarding the setting up of a Higher Education Credit Authority for providing limited credit guarantees through risk-pooling for educational loans seems to be a step in this direction. However, the other idea of a government-owned Higher Education Financing Corporation does not seem very good, in light of what is happening to the public-sector banks-led education loan scheme. Neither seems to have moved ahead, and hence their impact is difficult to assess. The budget speech of 2015 had a new announcement on this subject:

> [W]ith a view to enable all poor and middle class students to pursue higher education of their choice without any constraint of funds, it is proposed to set up a student Financial Aid Authority (SFAA) to administer and monitor scholarships as well as education loan schemes through the Pradhan Mantri Vidya Lakshmi Karyakram. Administration of the SFAA would be done through a single IT based portal for all scholarships and loan programmes which will minimize the need for personal interaction between the student and the disbursing agencies. All Government scholarship schemes and loan schemes shall be administered through the portal. Application forms will be designed to minimize the requirement to file any kind of supporting documents.

The role of widespread basic as well as higher education has been crucial in the development of the fast-growing economies. But the high cost associated with higher education can be a major deterrent to participation in higher education. This is particularly true for the economically disadvantaged, across religion, caste or gender lines. The high incidence of poverty and low participation in higher education feed on each other (GoI 2011). This vicious circle can be broken through the adoption of a multi-pronged approach, which may include greater public investment, either by setting up more institutions or by the government standing as guarantor in an ecosystem where information asymmetries are addressed by the creation of a credit information bureau and the rating of educational institutions for educational loans.

NOTE

1. This section on international experience summarises the comparative insights from Japan, Germany, and other nations. It draws heavily from the following online sources:

http://gse.buffalo.edu/FAS/Johnston/loans.html;

http://www.eastwestcenter.org/fileadmin/resources/education/ed2020_docs/Johnstone_Financing_Higher_Ed_01.pdf;

https://books.google.co.in/books?id=DtafVAl7S1kC&pg=PA185&lpg=PA185&dq=the+newly+created+independent+administrative+institution,+Japan+Student+Services+Organization+%28JASSO%29,+administers+the+recently+revised+student+loan+system.+The+system+is+made+up+of+two+types+of+student+loans:+the+first+class+scholarship

+loan&source=bl&ots=nubkFK97VD&sig=acDJEB-f2Pa5mK0pkRwbho VT4mc&hl=en&sa=X&ved=0CB0Q6AEwAGoVChMIgtnH5-yExg IVT5y8Ch2IkAAW#v=onepage&q=the%20newly%20created%20 independent%20administrative%20institution%2C%20Japan%20Student %20Services%20Organization%20(JASSO)%2C%20administers%20the %20recently%20revised%20student%20loan%20system.%20The %20system%20is%20made%20up%20of%20two%20types%20of%20 student%20loans%3A%20the%20first%20class%20scholarship %20loan&f=false.

References

Basant, R. and G. Sen, 'Who Participates In Higher Education In India? Rethinking the Role of Affirmative Action', *Economic and Political Weekly* 45 (39), 2010, pp. 62–70.

Ernst and Young and FICCI, 'Making the Indian Higher Education System Future Ready', New Delhi: FICCI Higher Education Summit, 2009.

Government of India (GoI), 'Report of the CABE Committee on Financing of Higher and Technical Education', New Delhi: Central Advisory Board of Education, 2005.

———, 'India Human Development Report, 2011: Towards Social Inclusion', New Delhi: Institute of Applied Manpower Research, Planning Commission, 2011.

Harris, M., 'Bad Education', *n+1*, 2011. Available at https://nplusonemag.com/online-only/online-only/bad-education/ (last accessed 3 April 2012).

Johnstone, B. and P. Marcucci, *Financing Higher Education Worldwide: Who Pays? Who Should Pay?* (Baltimore: Johns Hopkins University Press, 2010).

Prakash, V., 'Trends in Growth and Financing of Higher Education in India', *Economic and Political Weekly* 42 (31), 2007, pp. 3249–58.

Rani, P. G., *Economic Reforms and Financing Higher Education in India*, New Delhi: National Institute of Educational Planning and Administration, 2014.

UNESCO, 'Higher Education in Developing Countries—Peril and Promise', UNESCO and World Bank Report of the Task Force on Higher Education and Society, 2000.

— eight —

The Supreme Court and Private Higher Education

Litigation Patterns and Judicial Trends

Devesh Kapur and *Madhav Khosla*

Introduction

In recent years, the Indian Supreme Court has emerged as a critical institutional actor, intervening in a range of areas traditionally regarded as the domain of the executive and legislative branches of government. While the reasons for this greater activism and intervention are complex and have been discussed elsewhere, their consequences have been profound, with the Court's interventions shaping policy and not simply adjudicating (Mehta 2007; Sathe 2003). In this chapter, we examine a relatively neglected area of the Court's interventions, namely its role in the field of higher education.[1] The number of disputes relating to higher education has increased manifold in recent years, yet there has been little attention devoted to adjudicatory approaches in this realm. The role of the Supreme Court, and the judiciary more generally, is also missing from the now burgeoning literature on the changing character of Indian higher education. Much recent scholarship has examined the evolution of higher education in India, unpacking its shortcomings and challenges (see, for example, Agarwal 2009; Kapur 2010; Kapur and Mehta 2008). Yet, far less has been said about the regulatory role that courts play in this process.

This chapter addresses this lacuna in two distinct ways. We first analyse empirical patterns in both litigation and adjudication in higher education by analysing litigation trends in higher education cases over the past six decades (since the Indian Constitution came into being), and map changes in education-related litigation and changing trends in the specific nature of disputes being litigated and the party structure to the disputes. We find that a major development has been the rise of the regulatory arms of the state and private educational institutions as litigants, reflecting the changing roles of the state and the private sector in the provision of higher education. We then examine how courts have grappled with this change, identifying interventions that the Supreme Court has undertaken in the field of higher education. In particular, we reflect upon how judges bring to bear a certain vision of the state and education in their assessment of higher education disputes, and its implications for higher education.

LITIGATING HIGHER EDUCATION

Our analysis of the trends in higher education focuses on litigation over the past 60 years (1950–2009). We began by populating a list of cases of the Indian Supreme Court that dealt with higher education during this period. Two leading law reporters—Supreme Court Cases and Manupatra—were used for this purpose, and every judgement that included the word 'education', along with either of the words 'university' or 'college', was noted. This keyword search consequently accounted for cases dealing specifically with higher education. Of course, if the case sources are incomplete (in that certain judgements may not be reported), our data will be less robust, although we believe that by using two exhaustive case law reporters, our list is comprehensive. Moreover, it is important to map out the scope of our analysis. By focusing on the Indian Supreme Court, we hope to consider cases that have ramifications throughout India, and learn how the judiciary operates as an arm of the state. Needless to say, however, the High Courts and other lower courts which have been excluded may provide important insights of their own, which this chapter will be unable to articulate. Finally, we also do not consider ongoing petitions or cases currently pending; it would be premature to include these in our analysis.

Through this methodology, we arrived at a list of 507 judgements delivered over the past six decades. Being sensitive to the complexity that legal issues possess, we did not simply focus on the ultimate remedy that was delivered in the judgements. For instance, we may have been able to demonstrate that the Supreme Court decided a higher percentage of cases on a certain issue against the state in one decade as compared with another. However, without a substantive analysis of the issues involved, this heterogeneity of outcomes may simply reflect, *inter alia*, the rise of frivolous litigation on a certain issue. In other words, it would confirm little as there would be no homogeneity of inputs. Accordingly, we delved into each judgement that our search provided, analysing in detail the type of party before the court, the nature of the legal dispute at issue, and so forth. This reading also allowed us to eliminate judgements which, although having appeared in our search, did not in fact involve a higher education dispute.

Our analysis reveals, at the outset, a steady rise of higher education cases over this period, and a seven-fold increase in the past three decades, from 29 higher education cases in the period 1970–79 to 206 from 2000–09 (Figure 8.1). To put it differently, in the first three decades after independence (1950–79), the Supreme Court

FIGURE 8.1: Supreme Court Cases on Higher Education: Number of Cases and %age of Constitutional Cases

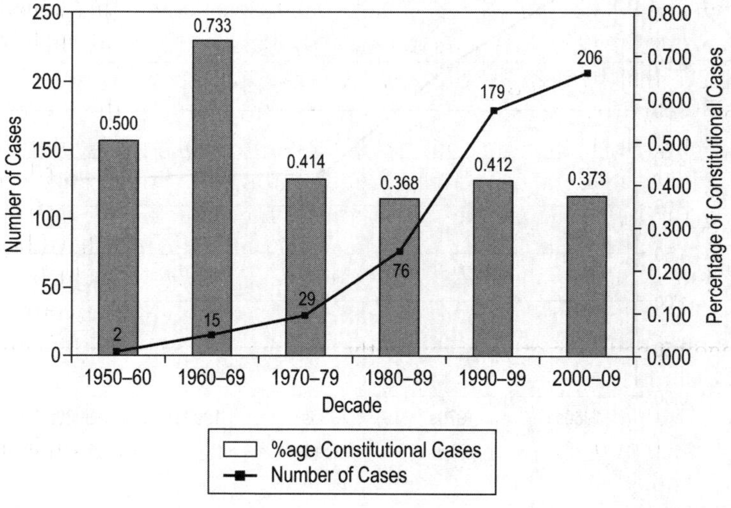

addressed itself to about 1.5 higher education cases annually. In the most recent decade (2000–09), the average was 20.6—a *14-fold* increase. The reasons, as we note later, stem from a combination of factors, ranging from the massive growth of higher education itself, the multiple governance challenges in the sector, and a broader trend of seeking judicial remedies to the numerous governance challenges in the country, reflecting the weaknesses of the legislative and executive organs of the state.

Nonetheless, on two indicators there seems to be a degree of stabilisation in higher education matters before the Supreme Court. The first relates to the bench strength of higher education cases. Unlike courts like the United States Supreme Court, which sits *en banc* (as a full bench), the Indian Supreme Court operates in separate courtrooms. Different benches are constituted by the Chief Justice and the size of a bench reflects the legal significance of the issue before the Court.[2] Over the past three decades, the average bench strength of higher education has consistently been just above two (Figure 8.2).

FIGURE 8.2: Supreme Court Higher Education Cases: Average Bench Strength Per Decade

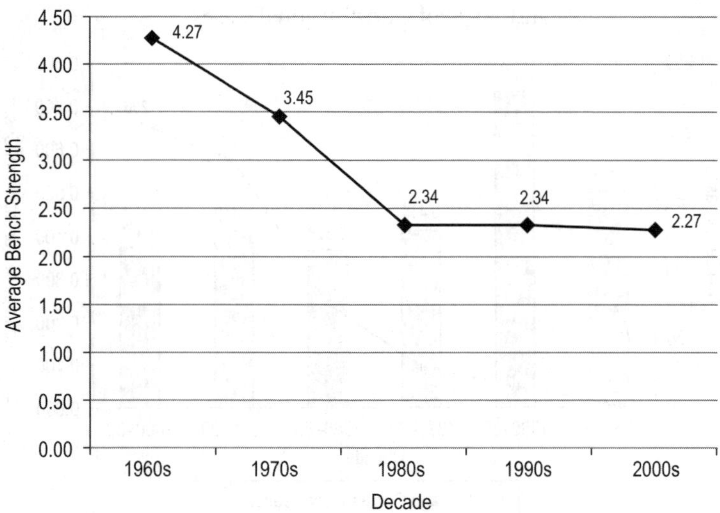

This stabilisation over the past three decades may be indicative of at least two factors. The first is the increasing caseload of the Indian Supreme Court and a tendency to resolve cases through small benches. The second reason may represent the repetition of claims over time, and therefore the limited number of new legal issues that have emerged. This need not, of course, represent the political importance of the claim being litigated. Further, the probable repetition of claims should not obscure the fact that several new issues have indeed arisen, which in turn have been decided by large benches. A series of decisions in the 1990s and onwards examining the rights of private educational institutions are cases in point, which we discuss later.

The second way in which higher education-related claims have stabilised has been with regard to the number of higher education cases involving a constitutional dispute. Naturally, such a dispute may take several forms. It may deal with an issue involving federalism, and how the Constitution undertakes power-sharing between the Indian union and the several states on the subject of education;[3] it may involve an affirmative scheme in higher education and therefore give rise to an equality-based challenge;[4] and so forth. As Figure 8.1 reveals, after the 1960s, the number of higher education cases before the Supreme Court that raised constitutional questions seems to have settled at around 40 per cent. This percentage appears to be relatively stable, even though the number of cases rose rapidly.

Although the percentage of higher education cases involving constitutional challenges has declined since the first two decades of India's independence, the reasonably constant figure of 40 per cent over the past three decades indicates that a sizeable amount of higher education cases involve claims that are central to either the Constitution's model of institutional design or to rights considered fundamental. What is the character of the litigants involved in such cases and how can we understand the nature of the claims being adjudicated? In our study, we categorised the parties involved in higher education cases before the Supreme Court into six groups: the central government; a central-run university; a state government; a state-run university; private educational institutions; a miscellaneous category involving a party that does not fall under the aforementioned heads (Table 8.1).

TABLE 8.1: Cases with Given Party (%)

	Central govt.	*State govt.*	*Central univ.*	*State univ.*	*Private univ.*	*Other*
1950–59	33.3	33.3	0.0	33.3	0.0	0.0
1960–69	0.0	6.7	13.3	73.3	0.0	6.7
1970–79	0.0	10.3	6.9	79.3	0.0	3.4
1980–89	1.3	6.5	9.1	75.3	1.3	6.5
1990–99	1.8	14.1	1.8	61.8	6.5	14.1
2000–09	12.7	41.2	3.0	17.0	18.8	7.3

Since there were just two cases in the first decade (1950s), we look at trends subsequently. Our categorisation carries us to three important conclusions. First, for most of this period, state-run universities constitute the majority. If we add state governments as well, nearly 70 per cent of all litigation before the Supreme Court involved either a state government or a state-run university. The large presence of the sub-national state rather than the centre as a litigant indicates that most disputes involve non-federal state educational institutions, and is indicative both of state universities (and state-run affiliated colleges) as the major provider of higher education and the increasing malfunctioning of such institutions.

Second, there has been a major rise of private educational institutions as litigants in higher education cases, concomitant with their explosive growth in the past two decades. The share of central universities as litigants barely increased from 1.8 per cent to 3 per cent from 1990–99 to 2000–09. On the other hand, while the central government was a party in only 1.8 per cent of higher education cases during 1990–99, its share grew manifold during 2000–09 to 12.7 per cent. The increasing regulatory role of the state, in contrast to its delivery role, is a phenomenon that is also reflected at the sub-national level. The percentage of cases in which a state university was a litigant decreased from 61.8 per cent in 1990–99 to 17 per cent in 2000–09, whereas the percentage of cases in which a state government was a litigant increased from 14.1 per cent to 41.2 per cent, reflecting a more invasive—and malfunctioning—regulatory role.

These figures reflect the rise of private educational institutions and the relative decline of the education-delivery arm of the state, and a concomitant increase of its regulatory arm as a litigant in higher education disputes. Thus, although constitutional disputes in higher education cases have stabilised at around 40 per cent, the character of these disputes has changed. Earlier, the state-run character of educational institutions made higher education disputes constitutional in nature, whereas now the state's regulatory role is increasingly doing so.

These figures help us to understand the party structure before the Supreme Court in higher education cases. They do not, however, explicate the nature of the dispute in question before the Court. In order to understand the specific claims before the Court in higher education disputes, we formulated 10 categories under which cases may be included: reservations, minority institutions, right to education, faculty and administrative staff and curricula, remuneration, fees, admissions, disciplinary action against students and examinations, grant-in-aid, and establishment/recognition/affiliation disputes. Cases that could not be included under any of these categories were inserted in a miscellaneous section (Figure 8.3).

It is striking to note that the largest number of issues involve internal governance, related to faculty and administrative staff issues and disputes involving curricula. If we add other issues that should also be internal to a university, such as fees, admission and disciplinary actions, then about 70 per cent of cases reflect the abject state of internal governance of India's higher education institutions.[5] On a subject like reservations and affirmative action, judicial intervention cannot be considered surprising. However, the major presence of faculty and staff-related issues—typically involving their appointment—indicates the extent to which such issues are not resolved within the college or university sphere. The high level of litigation illustrates both the internal governance failures of educational institutions and the willingness of the judiciary to translate such disputes into justiciable claims. A noteworthy variation in the kinds of issues in higher education disputes has been with regard to the recognition/establishment/affiliation of educational institutions. In 2000–09, disputes related to recognition/establishment/affiliation formed 16 per cent of the cases, whereas during 1990–99, they constituted only 3.3 per cent of the cases and virtually none before that (Table 8.2).

Figure 8.3: Supreme Court Higher Education Cases, Frequency of Issues (1950–2009) (471 cases)

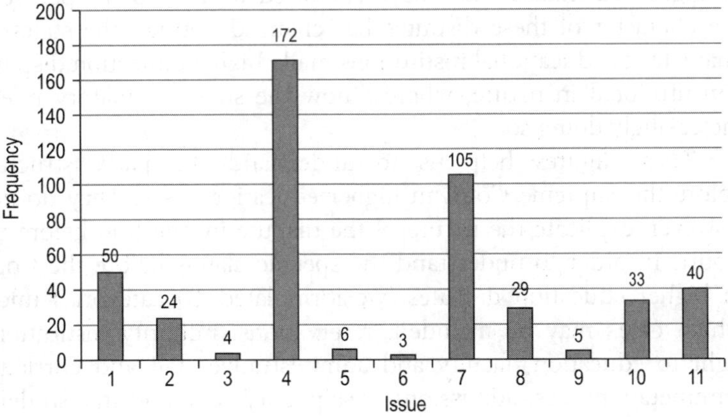

Issue	*Description*
1.	Reservations
2.	Minority Institutions
3.	Right to Education
4.	Faculty, Administration and Curricula
5.	Remuneration
6.	Fees
7.	Admission
8.	Disciplinary Action against Students and Examinations
9.	Grant-in-aid
10.	Recognition, Establishment, Affiliation
11.	Other

The rise in disputes involving the recognition/establishment/affiliation of educational institutions again points to the rise in litigation involving the regulatory arm of the state. Many of these disputes have, expectedly, involved private educational institutions. Our analysis of both the nature of litigants and the kinds of disputes in higher education cases over the past 60 years reveals how the growing presence of private educational institutions and the expanding regulatory role of the state have been the prime drivers of litigation in higher education. In the next section, we examine how the Supreme Court has addressed the growth of private educational institutions.

TABLE 8.2: Cases by Issue (%)

Issue % Time series	*Reservation*	*Minority Institutions*	*Right to Education*	*Faculty & Administrative Staff*	*Remuneration*	*Fees*	*Admission*	*Disciplinary action against students and examinations*	*Grant-in-aid*	*Recognition, Establishment, Affiliation*	*Other*
1950–59	0.0	33.3	0.0	33.3	0.0	0.0	0.0	0.0	0.0	33.3	0.0
1960–69	12.5	18.8	0.0	31.3	0.0	0.0	0.0	18.8	6.3	0.0	12.5
1970–79	6.9	13.8	0.0	62.1	0.0	0.0	3.4	13.8	0.0	0.0	0.0
1980–89	7.6	5.1	0.0	25.3	1.3	0.0	49.4	5.1	2.5	0.0	3.8
1990–99	12.7	3.9	1.1	39.8	1.7	0.6	19.9	7.7	0.6	3.3	8.8
2000–09	10.4	3.1	1.2	34.4	1.2	1.2	17.8	2.5	0.6	16.0	11.7

THE PROFITEERING PUZZLE

As Table 8.1 demonstrates, the growing presence of private educational institutions and the burgeoning regulatory role of the state have been the principal drivers of litigation in higher education during the past decade. How has the Supreme Court dealt with the increasing role that private educational institutions have begun to play in Indian higher education and the litigation in this sector? In this section, we focus on one way in which the judiciary has, since the 1990s, regulated higher education and private educational institutions: through articulating a purpose for higher education and holding that educational institutions cannot engage in 'profiteering'.

What precisely does the word 'profiteering' mean and how has it come to occupy such a central place in the Supreme Court's conceptualisation of higher education? Over the past six decades, 'profiteering' has appeared in a significant number of judgements. These judgements can, for the most part, be divided into two categories. The first set of judgements involves the sale of certain commodities.[6] These cases include food adulteration, the black marketing of medicines, agricultural produce, the Essential Commodities Act, 1955, and so forth. In these cases, 'profiteering' is typically used to indicate malpractice on behalf of a seller, which unjustly benefits him in a sale transaction (often in violation of applicable statutory provisions).

The second set of judgements in which 'profiteering' figures prominently relate to the regulation of land. The diverse issues involved in this set include the urban land ceiling, land acquisition, rent control and eviction, land transfer, land acquisition, and so forth.[7] In these cases, 'profiteering' is largely used to describe the 'exploitative' use of land, and to define an activity that must be prevented to ensure the equitable distribution of land and the recognition of property rights. In both sets of cases, we find that 'profiteering' is used pejoratively to define an activity that does not simply involve the making of profit. Indeed, the Supreme Court has often recognised this distinction, holding that while one may be entitled to make a reasonable profit, one cannot resort to profiteering.[8]

Interestingly, although our search has not been exhaustive, the term 'profiteering' appears to be *sui generis* to the Indian Supreme

Court (at least amongst the major common law jurisdictions). While the term appears to have a rough equivalence to 'monopoly rents', the latter term has a precise definition, especially in the large case law in antitrust. In contrast, the Supreme Court's view of 'profiteering' lacks any analytical precision—like the old definition of pornography, they know it when it offends their sensibilities.[9]

The higher education cases in which 'profiteering' has been used stand in sharp contrast to the aforementioned type of cases, and it is interesting to note how the word has found its way into higher education disputes. The first case to consider in this context is *St. Stephen's College v. University of Delhi* ([1992] 1 SCC 558). Although the Supreme Court, in *St. Stephen's College*, did not expressly use the word 'profiteering', this case was the first to seriously articulate the *necessarily charitable* nature of education. The case arose out of a dispute between St. Stephen's College and the University of Delhi, to which the college was affiliated. The legal dispute centred around whether the College was entitled to follow an autonomous admissions procedure distinct from that adopted by the University. The College argued that it was a religious minority educational institution, and therefore entitled to special protection under the Constitution. Moreover, it was pointed out that it was merely an affiliated college which was not maintained by the University. The University of Delhi, on the other hand, posited that every college that is part of the University must comply with its directions, and relevant legal instruments. It further argued that under Article 29(2), no minority educational institution could discriminate in its admissions procedure purely on the grounds of religion. Similar issues in the case also arose with regard to the Allahabad Agricultural Institute.

Briefly put, the three core issues before the Court involved the minority character of St. Stephen's College, the College's power to admit students through a process contrary to instructions issued by the University of Delhi, and St. Stephen's College and Allahabad Agricultural Institute's power to reserve seats for students from their own minority community. On the first two issues, the Court found St. Stephen's College to be a minority educational institution and held that it was not bound by the circulars of the University of Delhi as regards the procedure for admission. For present purposes, the doctrinal tools that the Court developed to arrive at these conclusions are of limited concern; it is more interesting to unpack the Court's examination of the third issue: the preferential treatment towards students belonging to the institution's minority community.

The question before the Court was whether Article 30(1) of the Constitution—which gives minorities the right to administer and establish educational institutions—necessarily gave such institutions the right to adopt preferential treatment in admissions processes towards candidates from their minority. The difficulty arose because both institutions were receiving government aid, and Article 29(2) of the Constitution appeared to prohibit such preferential treatment. As a textual matter, Article 29(2) appears unequivocal: 'No citizen shall be denied admission into any educational institution maintained by the State or receiving aid out of State funds on grounds only of religion, race, caste, language or any of them.'

Despite Article 29(2), however, the Court held that the right to prefer minority candidates was 'a necessary concomitant right' flowing from Article 30(1) (*Stephen's College* v. *University of Delhi*: 611). What is noteworthy is the Court's reasoning. Rather than providing an elaborate justification for why Article 30(1) overrides Article 29(2), or why we should read against the text of Article 29(2), or why reading different provisions as a whole may prove more instructive than a clause-bound reading of Article 29(2), the Court's interpretive decision was based on an assessment of the political economy of higher education. Article 29(2) could not rob minority educational institutions of their rights under Article 30(1) because, the Court held, no minority educational institution could exist without state funding. The Court observed: 'The educational institutions are not business houses. They do not generate wealth.... It is not possible to have educational institutions without State aid.... The minorities cannot therefore, be asked to maintain educational institutions on their own' (*Stephen's College* v. *University of Delhi*: 609–10). The belief that no educational institution can generate profit was the foundation for the Court's decision.

The argument that it was not possible to have educational institutions 'without State aid' demonstrated a puzzling ignorance of the history of higher education institutions, whether worldwide or in India. Prior to independence, private philanthropy played a major role in the establishment of new higher education institutions, be it the landed gentry funding Aligarh Muslim University, the princely states and businesses whose financial support underlay the creation of Banaras Hindu University, the Jesuits establishing a string of colleges, Tagore's personal contributions and fundraising for Vishva-Bharati, or the philanthropic efforts of Indian business, such as Jamsetji Tata (IISc-Bangalore), Rajah Annamalai Chettiar (Annamalai) and the Birlas (BITS-Pilani), to take a few examples. While it is certainly the case that a higher education institution with a *research* focus will almost always require public funding in the long run, this is not necessarily the case with teaching institutions. And in any case, it is unclear why state aid, even if essential to supporting higher education, should necessarily support institutions rather than students (in the form of scholarships).

By adopting this proposition, the Court made its interpretive approach seem necessary: if state funding is a *sine qua non* for the existence of a minority educational institution, then surely state funding cannot limit the institution's autonomy, for there is no other option available; and if an institution's autonomy is limited, then Article 30(1) seems entirely meaningless. This strategy to square the circle ignores the significance of Article 29(2). Further, its flawed reasoning is easily exposed by the fact that Article 29(2) specifically refers to educational institutions maintained by the state or receiving state funds—if this was the only way for institutions to survive, then such a reference would have been unnecessary. In other words, by referring to institutions maintained or aided by the state, the Constitution envisages the existence of institutions *not maintained* or *aided* by the state, and necessarily imposes different constitutional obligations on those institutions. The proposition that one cannot have educational institutions without state aid therefore runs against the very essence of Article 29(2). Further, Article 30(1) does not begin with a non-obstinate clause. Without it, it is difficult to see why it provides any sort of exception to Article 29(2). The only explicit exception to Article 29(2) is provided in Article 15(4), which deals with reservations for backward classes. Article 30(1) is meant to protect a minority educational institution's autonomy in circumstances like a distinct admissions procedure; an autonomy question distinct from those that are at issue in Article 29(2). Through its technique, we also notice, therefore, that the Court ignores the two very different kinds of institutional autonomy questions that *St. Stephen's College* invites.

St. Stephens College's central principle—that educational institutions cannot generate profit—took an even more baffling turn in a decision that soon followed. In *Unnikrishnan*,[10] the Court came to accept that educational institutions could exist without state support, but introduced the word 'profiteering' in higher education cases. The Court in *Unnikrishnan* considered whether citizens had a right to establish an educational institution. The petitioners appealed to Article 19(1)(g) of the Indian Constitution, which guarantees all citizens a right 'to practise any profession or to carry on any occupation, trade or business'. They argued that Article 19(1)(g) provided the right to establish an educational institution, and that this institution could have a profit motive. Such an educational institution should be treated, it was suggested, like any other business venture. The respondents, the Indian Medical Council and the All India Council for Technical Education, alternatively argued that the 'very concept of collecting the cost of education—that is what the concept of cost-based or self-financing educational institutions means—is morally abhorrent and is opposed to public policy' (*Unnikrishnan* v. *State of A. P.*: 741). Interestingly, key staff in both organisations were later found to be engaging in widespread corruption, demanding bribes for regulatory approvals, providing some insight into why they had insisted that the very concept of collecting the cost of education was 'morally abhorrent'.

In determining whether there exists a right to establish an educational institution, the Supreme Court ruminated over the problems in education delivery that were plaguing India. Placing emphasis upon the limited capacity of the state and its inability to increase the budgetary allocation towards education, the Court observed that '[b]ecause, the State is in no position to devote more resources and also because the need is constantly growing, it is not possible to do without private educational institutions (*Unnikrishnan* v. *State of A. P.*: 747)'. But what, if any, fee structure must private educational institutions conform to? In answering this question, the Court distinguished between two kinds of private educational institutions—aided and unaided. As regards aided institutions, the Court held that they must conform strictly to the fee structure adopted in state-run institutions. It went so far as to say that aided private educational institutions 'shall not be entitled to charge any fees higher than what is charged in governmental institutions for similar courses' (ibid.: 749). This, the Court held, would be a *condition* upon which grants would be provided, since 'public funds cannot be donated for private purposes' (ibid.).

With regard to unaided private educational institutions, the Court conceded that such institutions were not required to charge the same fee as state-run institutions. The facilities that such institutions could provide would vary considerably from one another and from state-run institutions, and so one could not stipulate a blanket fee structure to which such institutions must be required to conform. The Court held, however, that the fee structure of unaided private educational institutions would be regulated through one important factor: the *commercialisation* of education would be unconstitutional. Thus, it was observed that 'in light of our tradition and from the standpoint of interest of the general public, commercialization is positively harmful; it is opposed to public policy ... this is one of the reasons for holding that imparting education cannot be a trade, business or profession' (*Unnikrishnan* v. *State of A. P.*: 750).

In other words, the Court held that no private unaided educational institution could operate for profit, and that running an educational institution could not be considered a trade, business, or profession for the purposes of Article 19(1)(g). It chose not to answer the question of whether it could be considered a 'profession' under Article 19(1)(g) (*Unnikrishnan* v. *State of A. P.*: 751). In support of this conclusion, the Court offered no justifying reason to demonstrate why the Constitution treated education differently. Justice Reddy merely stated, 'Education has never been commerce in this country. Making it one is opposed to the ethos, tradition and sensibilities of this nation' (ibid.), and further proceeded to make the bizarre claim that India has always treated education 'as a religious duty' (ibid.). Justice Mohan, who delivered the concurring opinion, introduced the word 'profiteering' into the judgement, holding that: 'It cannot be gainsaid that profiteering is an evil. If a public utility like electricity could be controlled, certainly, the professional colleges also require to be regulated' (ibid.: 702). He cited precedent on the desired nature of public utilities, without any explanation for why they should be instructive with regard to the regulatory structure governing private educational institutions. Even the most basic distinction—that unlike higher education, electricity is regulated because of the natural monopoly intrinsic to the sector—appears to have missed the learned judges. Equally, if not more troubling, for a country whose social structures, long sanctified by purported religious beliefs, ensured that the vast majority were denied access to education and whose citizens pay large sums to purchase private education (now running into tens of thousands of crores), whether in the form of private tuitions or elites purchasing expensive higher education abroad, the reference to 'tradition' and 'religious duty' is at best inexplicable and a caricature of Indian realities.

These cases laid the foundation for *T. M. A. Pai* v. *State of Karnataka*,[11] in which an 11-judge bench of the Indian Supreme Court reflected upon the regulatory structure of higher education. In *T. M. A. Pai*, the Court reversed itself, declaring the scheme formulated in *Unnikrishnan*—which had prescribed conditions under which the state could grant recognition or affiliation to an educational institution—to be unconstitutional. The Court found that the scheme failed to appropriately distinguish between public and private educational institutions. It emphasised the importance of autonomy for private educational institutions, on matters ranging from faculty appointments to fee structure. However, it continued to maintain that the act of establishing an educational institution was a charitable act, and thus no profiteering could take place. Consequently, it evolved an innovative strategy for giving private unaided institutions more autonomy in formulating their fee structure: institutions were allowed to have a 'reasonable surplus to meet costs of expansion and augmentation of facilities' (*T. M. A. Pai* v. *State of Karnataka*: 590). The generation of a revenue surplus would not amount to profiteering—the requirement became that funds generated must be put back into the institution.

T. M. A. Pai's many conclusions, which we shall not delve into here, led to numerous interpretive disagreements. Ultimately, a five-judge bench in *Islamic Academy* v. *State of Karnataka*[12] was constituted to clarify *T. M. A. Pai*. Chief Justice Khare, who delivered the majority opinion, held that, as per *T. M. A. Pai*, the 'imparting of education is essentially charitable in nature' and no profiteering or capitation fee can take place: 'Thus the surplus/profit that can be generated must only be for the benefit/use of that educational institution. Profits/surplus cannot be diverted for any other use or purpose and cannot be for personal gain or for any other business or enterprise' (*Islamic Academy v. State of Karnataka*: 721).

Islamic Academy reveals how the Supreme Court evolved from its stance in *St. Stephen's College*, but nonetheless did not depart from the view that private higher education cannot operate as a business. We observed the mode of constitutional reasoning in *St. Stephen's College* and how the Court's understanding of the political economy of higher education led to a flawed sense of the relationship between Article 29(2) and Article 30(1) of the Constitution. The 'revenue surplus' strategy that the Court confirmed in *Islamic Academy* is not justified through any institutional or interpretive reason. The Court relied on a particular conception of education, without concern for whether the Constitution treats the imparting of education differently from other activities. Although 'profiteering' was traditionally a term adopted in cases dealing with either essential commodities or land usage, over time the term has cemented its place in the Court's higher education jurisprudence. It is also worth noting that while the term 'profiteering' is almost invariably used alongside the term 'capitation fee', the latter is a practice involving a differential fee structure for different candidates, while generating profit does not involve an issue of discrimination. In other words, if 'capitation fee' is problematic, it is because it raises an equality concern and involves an Article 14 challenge, while the generation of profit from an educational institution invites no such concerns. Indeed, the first major capitation fee decision, *Mohini Jain*,[13] involved both an equality challenge and the right to education challenge. The Supreme Court's repeated analogising of profit generation with capitation fee ignores the issues at stake in both instances.[14] Equally, it is presumptive that the precise criteria for 'profiteering' can be laid out, given the ease with which revenues can be lowered by inflating costs, especially through higher transfer prices to firms supplying goods and services and where the promoter has direct or indirect financial interests, or simply higher salaries to the promoter and his kin.

Judicial Craftsmanship and Private Educational Institutions

The prohibition on 'profiteering' presents but one example of how the judiciary has regulated private educational institutions and embraced a certain vision of education while performing the task of constitutional interpretation. In this part, we illustrate the nature of this phenomenon through a discussion of two cases over the past decade.

The first of these is *Govt. of A. P.* v. *J. B. Educational Society*.[15] The writ petitioners in this case were private educational institutions which sought to establish colleges in the State of Andhra Pradesh. They applied for permission under the All India Council for Technical Education Act, 1987 (AICTE Act), and received approval from the AICTE Council. They then applied for permission under Section 20 of the Andhra Pradesh Education Act, 1982 (A. P. Act), in order to establish the sought institutions. Permission under the A. P. was, however, denied on the ground that there were already several colleges in the locations in which the petitioners had sought to establish them, and thus the state government was not convinced that there was any pressing educational need in the concerned localities. Subsequently, the private educational institutions challenged the constitutional validity of the A. P. Act on the ground that the State of Andhra Pradesh lacked the legislative competence to enact the law, as it dealt with a subject already covered by a central enactment—the AICTE Act. This contention was accepted by the High Court of Andhra Pradesh, and the matter came up before the Supreme Court.

The ostensible purpose of the A. P. Act was to develop the educational system in Andhra Pradesh. The Act provides that no educational institutions can be established except in accordance with its provisions, the most notable of which is Section 20. Under this section, a competent authority appointed by the state government shall conduct regular surveys for ascertaining the local educational needs, and thereafter seek applications from entities that wish to establish education institutions. As per the section, 'any educational agency' intending to 'establish an institution imparting education' must apply for permission, and 'before the permission is granted, satisfy the authority concerned' of the fact 'that there is a need for providing educational facilities to the people in the locality'.

The legal source of power for this law was Entry 25 of the Concurrent List in the Seventh Schedule to the Constitution, a list of items on which both Parliament and state legislatures are competent to pass laws. This Entry, which deals with 'Education', is explicitly 'subject to the provisions of Entries 63, 64, 65 and 66 of List I', the list on which Parliament has the exclusive power to enact legislation. It was under Entry 66 of List I that Parliament enacted the AICTE Act, the aim of which was to coordinate the standards and norms for technical education throughout India. Under Section 10 of the Act, the All India Council for Technical Education, appointed under Section 3 of the Act, has a wide range of powers and functions. These include undertaking surveys on the state of technical education, laying down of norms for courses, curricula, etc., formulating schemes for the training of teachers, and so forth. Regulations regarding the granting of approval for new technical institutions are framed by the Council through Section 23 of the Act.

In *J. B. Educational Society*, the petitioners argued that no permission could be sought by the state government under Section 20 of the A. P. Act since the AICTE Act controlled this legislative field. The state government, on the other hand, argued that there was no repugnancy between both statutes as no conflict appeared in their application. Assessing these competing claims, the Supreme Court examined the AICTE Act, and how it aimed to coordinate and determine the standards of technical education. In light of this legislative intent, it held that Section 20 of the impugned A. P. Act 'does not in any way encroach upon the powers of the authorities under the Central Act' (*Govt. of A. P. v. J. B. Educational Society*: 220). It proceeded to observe that the state government alone could 'decide about the educational facilities and needs of the locality' (ibid.), and therefore the A. P. Act was essential. Even though Entry 25 of the Concurrent List was subject to Entries 63, 64, 65 and 66 of List I, Justice Balakrishnan found that the State of Andhra Pradesh had 'the legislative competence to pass the legislation in respect of education including technical education and Section 20 of the Act is intended for general welfare of the citizens of the State and also in discharge of the constitutional duty enumerated under Article 41 of the Constitution' (ibid.: 221).

Article 41 is part of the Directive Principles of State Policy chapter and calls upon the state to work towards education. But it refers to the 'state' in general, and has nothing to say on whether its guidelines are to be fulfilled by the Union or state governments. That assessment deals with the Constitution's federal scheme, involves the distribution of legislative and executive power between the Indian Union and her constituent parts, and is dealt with by other provisions of the Constitution.

However, there are more serious concerns. First, by legitimising the Andhra Pradesh government's regulatory strategy, it confers permanent rents on first movers. And since most of these institutions are owned or run by politicians, the Court effectively rewards the very sources of the problems of Indian higher education. The idea that competition may improve the welfare of students or that a spatial concentration of educational institutions might beget network externalities is not at all a part of the Court's thinking.

A second problem with the Court's interpretive approach is its impoverished understanding of legislative repugnancy. The Court cited an earlier 1973 decision, in which it was held that in order for repugnancy to arise, there must be clear inconsistency between the central and state enactment, that this inconsistency must be irreconcilable, and that obeying one statute would lead to the disobeying of the other.[16] But it refused to investigate or apply this test in any considered fashion, and held that the two statutes were not repugnant to one another because Section 10 of the AICTE Act did not relate to the particular educational needs of a particular geographical area in a state; the AICTE Council's approval was merely 'general' (*Govt. of A. P. v. J. B. Educational Society*: 221).

Repugnancy under the Indian Constitution is dealt with by Article 254. In the case of a Union and State law conflict, the former gains precedence and the latter is, to the extent of the repugnancy, void. A historical excursion into the interpretation of this provision is unnecessary for now, but we may observe that early decisions did not require a direct conflict for repugnancy to arise; even if two laws spoke differently on the same question but didn't lead to different outcomes, they could be repugnant. Over time, this standard was tightened, and a direct conflict was considered a requirement for repugnancy to exist.[17] The precedent that the Court relied upon reflects this development, and therefore for the question of repugnancy to be answered, we must ask whether or not the AICTE Act and the A. P. Act conflict.

Regrettably the Court, after citing the requisite test, failed to ask this question: it simply asserted that the two statutes did not conflict as the AICTE Act did not deal with local educational needs. But this is precisely the point. *Because the AICTE Act does not address the question of local educational needs, it does not make this a requirement for setting up an institution.* The reality is that the two statutes conflict and lead to diametrically opposite outcomes because a private educational institution is subject to entirely different criteria under the two laws; in other words, the institution gains permission under the Union law but not the State one, and therefore cannot be set up. The outcomes are different because, *ceteris paribus*, one has the right to establish an institution under one law, but does not have the right to do so under the other. This is precisely why the private educational institutions came to court in *J. B. Educational Society*. But rather than engaging with this factual scenario, the Court seemed taken in by the importance of educational institutions to meet local needs. The Court cited sections from *T. M. A. Pai Foundation* and *Islamic Academy of Education*, which spoke about the importance of catering to local needs in the sphere of education.

What is striking are the limitations of the Court's imagination with regard to the goal of catering to local needs in education; the judgement fails even on its own terms. It is based on a belief that proscription rather than incentives (for the private sector to establish institutions in underserved areas), and monopolies rather than competition (to improve the provision by existing institutions), would result in better social outcomes. Just what evidence the Court in its majesty based its reasoning on, is unclear.

Whatever the merits of this claim, the key point is that it had nothing to do with whether or not the AICTE Act and the A. P. Act were repugnant to one another. The fact that the question of repugnancy was perfunctorily dealt with, and that the legal dispute was answered by turning to the importance of education to meet local needs, reveals how the Court's vision of education fashioned its interpretive approach. The second case we shall consider, *Prof. Yashpal* v. *State of Chattisgarh*,[18] confirms this with even greater force.

Yashpal involved a challenge to the constitutionality of the Chhattisgarh Niji Kshetra Vishwavidhyalaya (Sthapana Aur Viniyaman) Adhiniyam, 2002 (hereinafter 'the Act'). The petitioners asserted that the Act enabled the state government to incorporate and establish private universities through a gazette notification, as a result of which universities had been indiscriminately established throughout the State of Chhattisgarh. These universities lacked basic infrastructure and teaching staff, and were awarding a bizarre set of degrees (for instance, 'Fellow of the International Institute of Medical Sciences'). It was further asserted that these universities had entirely ignored guidelines under the University Grants Commission Act, 1956, and several were running professional courses without receiving permission from regulatory authorities like the Medical Council of India (MCI), Dental Council of India (DCI), and so on. The state government, on the other hand, argued that the impugned legislation sought to facilitate the creation of private universities in Chhattisgarh, and was within its legislative competence as per Entry 32 of List II of the Seventh Schedule to the Constitution (dealing with, *inter alia*, the incorporation of universities). It was further argued that the state had granted universities permission based on certain expectations, that it was unfortunate that in several cases these expectations had not been met, and that the state had taken requisite action by amending the statute and even de-notifying several institutions.

The Court upheld the contention of the petitioners and declared the Act unconstitutional. The primary reason for unconstitutionality was the fact that 112 universities had been established without any application of mind, and that educational fraud was being committed with ease. Although the Court failed to clearly articulate the legal problem here, the facts make it clear—the impugned Act was unconstitutional because it suffered from excessive delegation, too much discretion was vested in the executive, and consequently that discretion could be arbitrarily exercised, and thus universities were being established which existed only on paper.[19]

Ideally, the Court should have made this narrow and appropriate ruling, and invalidated the impugned law. It should have asked the state to craft legislation more carefully. However, what is troubling is that it did far more (a tendency not limited to this case). To begin with, the Court considered the relationship between Entry 32 of List II and Entry 66 of List I (dealing with the coordination of standards). These two entries suggest that Parliament may lay down standards of education while a state may establish a university; precedent supports this and, citing earlier cases, the Court observed that,

> in spite of incorporation of universities as a legislative head being in the State List, the whole gamut of the university which will include teaching, quality of education being imparted, curriculum ... will not come within the purview of the State Legislature on account of a specific entry on coordination and determination of standards in institutions for higher education or research and scientific and technical education being in the Union List for which Parliament alone is competent (*Prof. Yashpal* v. *State of Chattisgarh*: 444).

It is unclear what this discussion on the power-sharing scheme between the centre and the states hoped to achieve, but perhaps it had something to do with the Court's conclusion that the impugned law was unconstitutional since it stifled the operation of the UGC Act. The Act had resulted in the creation of universities without campuses, teachers, and so forth; hence, it made it impossible for the UGC to monitor, and consequently enforce, the standards of education in these institutions. No state law could, the Court argued, prevent the proper functioning of a central law, and this was one of the reasons why the Chhattisgarh legislation was unconstitutional. But the problem here is that the Court left unsaid the extent and the fashion in which the UGC binds private institutions. Importantly, the Court ignored the fact that the impugned law dealt with private educational institutions.

Rather than simply positing that the Act should have been more detailed, the Court launched into a discussion on the meaning of a 'university'. It did this with the ostensible purpose of ascertaining legislative competence, and considered how the word 'universities' in Entry 32 of List II should be interpreted. In undertaking this task, it referred to a broad range of materials, including the *Encyclopaedia Brittannica*, the report of the University Education Commission which was set up in 1948 and headed by Dr S. Radhakrishnan, and the report of the Kothari committee, constituted in 1961. Through these materials, it constructed a vision of what universities must look like: they must have, for instance, playgrounds; there must be a 'plurality of teachers teaching more than one higher faculties'; there must be sports facilities 'for overall development of the personality of the students', and so forth (*Prof. Yashpal* v. *State of Chattisgarh*: 451).

What we notice from this discussion is that although the Court's overall conclusion was correct—the Act was unconstitutional—it entirely misunderstood the legal issue in question. It did not use the words 'excessive delegation' anywhere in the decision, and launched into a lengthy discussion on the meaning of 'universities' and a 'degree' because, according to it, the impugned law didn't establish universities at all. That is to say, the law lacked legislative competence under Entry 32 of List II because that entry deals with universities and the universities that had been established under the law did not conform to the Court's conception of what a university should look like. The entire legal conversation here becomes about what universities are, rather than whether or not the law says too little and enables the executive to get away with too much.

Conclusion

Of the many players who have driven the regulation of higher education in modern India, the judiciary has emerged as a central figure. Litigation patterns illustrate the changing character of legal disputes involving higher education and the growing involvement of private educational institutions in such disputes. The data is particularly stark on the number of disputes involving matters that one would regard as internal to the administration of an educational institution, revealing both the failure of such institutions to resolve matters within their competence and the judicial willingness to convert such matters into justiciable claims.

While litigation patterns tell one part of the story, adjudicatory trends reveal another. One chief way in which the Supreme Court has sought to regulate higher education has been through the articulation of a normative vision—educational institutions cannot indulge in 'profiteering'. We have unpacked the curious manner in which this term has made its way into the Court's higher education jurisprudence, how the Court's view on this matter has oscillated with the changing political economy of higher education, and the implications that this has had for the task of constitutional interpretation.

Although our data covers the first six decades of India's constitutional experience, recent decisions are equally revealing. Consider *Teerthanker Mahaveer Institute of Management* v. *Union of India*, a 2011 Delhi High Court case in which the petitioners sought to increase their intake of students for the MBBS course.[20] They argued that the regulator (Medical Council of India [MCI]) had wrongly rejected their application as they had satisfied the infrastructural requirements for the additional intake. The Council argued, however, that the petitioner colleges had only been granted approval for running an MBBS course, rather than recognition for the same. Under MCI regulations, the argument went, recognition could only be granted after the completion of five years of the course, and without it they were ineligible to be granted permission for additional intake. The case thus involved the technical legal question of what precisely the MCI regulations mandated. However, rather than directly addressing this interpretive question, the Court instead chose to ruminate over the state's incapacity to meet health education demands, and the need for additional intake. For the Court, the question became how best to respond to the crisis in Indian medical education—and the answer was that, if institutions can accommodate extra students, they should be permitted to do so.

The point here is not whether this argument succeeds on its own terms—although the argument is certainly suspect. If the concern is to improve healthcare for the vast majority of Indians, the focus should be on public health; there is ample evidence that India's problem is not too few doctors, but far too few nurses and public health personnel. Furthermore, the Court's argument assumes that if there are more doctors, they will serve the large rural majority where they are desperately needed. However, this ignores the political economy of the medical profession—nearly three-fourths of India's doctors legally permitted to practice operate in and around urban areas, serving less than 30 per cent of the population. And of those who do serve in rural areas, it is arguable just how many of them show up in the first place. With absenteeism rates ranging from a quarter to a third, the few become even fewer. And of those who do show up, the quality of care provided by India's doctors leaves much to be desired.[21]

Rather, our effort has been directed towards revealing how the Court's regulatory vision has shaped this sector. The challenges facing Indian higher education are serious, and the sector is struggling with a crippling regulatory regime (Kapur 2011; for more detailed analyses, see Agarwal 2009; Kapur 2010; Kapur and Mehta 2008). This chapter suggests that it might be worth asking to what extent courts have, through the act of resolving disputes, contributed to the problem. For the Indian Supreme Court, sometimes less might be more.

Notes

An earlier version of this chapter was presented at the 'Higher Education: New Trends and Challenges' Conference, Centre for Policy Research, New Delhi, 28–29 July 2011. We are grateful to the participants for comments and suggestions, and to Rohit Chandra, Shruti Aji Murali, Brunda Rao, and Raeesa Vakil for excellent research assistance.

1. The select few contributions include Chandrasekhar 2005, Dam 2006 and Wright 1985.

2. The enabling provision dealing with the rules that govern Supreme Court practice is Article 145 of the Constitution. For a recent discussion on the Chief Justice's role in constituting benches, see Robinson, et al. 2011.

3. See, for example, Osmania University Teachers' Association v. State of Andhra Pradesh, (1987) 4 SCC 671.

4. See, for example, A. K. Thakur v. Union of India, (2008) 6 SCC 1.

5. For an excellent analysis of internal governance issues, see Chapter 9 in this volume.

6. See, for example, A. N. Lakshman Shenoy v. ITO, 1959 SCR 751; Diwan Sugar & General Mills v. Union of India, AIR 1959 SC 626; Mishrilal Jain v. Distt. Magistrate, (1971) 3 SCC 693; CIT v. Himangshu Sekhar Chakravarty, (1972) 4 SCC 576; Shree Meenakshi Mills v. Union of India, (1974) 1 SCC 468; Prabhu Dayal Deorah v. Distt. Magistrate, Kamrup, (1974) 1 SCC 103; Ramappa Gundappa Sahakari Samyakta Besava Sangha v. State of Mysore, (1974) 2 SCC 221, Mohd. Rajab Gujari v. State of J&K, (1974) 2 SCC 190; Kamla Prasad v. Distt. Magistrate, (1975) 1 SCC 314; Mohd. Rajab Gujari v. State of J&K, (1975) 2 SCC 323; Nathmal v. State of Rajasthan, (1975) 2 SCC 591; Satya Deo Prasad Gupta v. State of Bihar, (1975) 3 SCC 736; Dwarika Prasad Sahu v. State of Bihar, (1975) 3 SCC

722; Bankatlal v. State of Rajasthan, (1975) 4 SCC 598; State of M. P. v. Galla Tilhan Vyapari Sangh, (1977) 1 SCC 657; Union of India v. Cynamide India, (1987) 2 SCC 720.

7. See, for example, State of Punjab v. Ramji Lal, (1970) 3 SCC 602; Distt. Council of United Khasi and Jaintia Hills v. Sitimon Sawian, (1971) 3 SCC 708; Venkatamma v. City Improvement Trust Board, (1973) 1 SCC 188; Dwarka Prasad v. Dwarka Das Saraf, (1976) 1 SCC 128; Velji Lakhamsi v. Benett Coleman, (1977) 3 SCC 160; Union of India v. Valluri Basavaiah Chowdhary, (1979) 3 SCC 324; Thumati Venkaiah v. State of A.P., (1980) 4 SCC 295; Bhim Singhji v. Union of India, (1981) 1 SCC 166; Precision Steel Engg. Works v. Prem Deva Niranjan Deva Tayal, (1982) 3 SCC 270; State of U.P. v. L. J. Johnson, (1983) 4 SCC 110; Narain Khamman v. Parduman Kumar Jain, (1985) 1 SCC 1; State of Gujarat v. Parshottamdas Ramdas Patel, (1988) 1 SCC 132; Accountant and Secretarial Services v. Union of India, (1988) 4 SCC 324; A.V. R. v. Fairfild Coop. Housing Society, (1988) 4 SCC 408; Bharat Singh v. State of Haryana, (1988) 4 SCC 534; Dattatrya Shankarbhat Ambalgi v. State of Maharashtra, (1989) 4 SCC 532; Shantistar Builders v. Narayan Khimalal Totame, (1990) 1 SCC 520; Raju Kakara Shetty v. Ramesh Prataprao Shirole, (1991) 1 SCC 570; Meera Gupta v. State of W.B., (1992) 2 SCC 494; S. Vasudeva v. State of Karnataka, (1993) 3 SCC 467; Govt. of A. P. v. H. E. H., The Nizam, (1996) 3 SCC 282; T. R. Thakur v. Union of India, (1996) 3 SCC 690; Maharani Shantidevi P. Gaikwad v. Savjibhai Haribhai Patel, (2001) 5 SCC 101; State of A. P. v. N. Audikesava Reddy, (2002) 1 SCC 227; Jamshed Hormusji Wadia v. Board of Trustees, Port of Mumbai, (2004) 3 SCC 214; Parvinder Singh v. Renu Gautam, (2004) 4 SCC 794.

8. For a recent articulation, see Ashoka Smokeless Coal India v. Union of India, (2007) 2 SCC 640.

9. To the extent that 'profiteering' is indicative of market power, the issue should come under the ambit of the Competition Commission of India.

10. Unnikrishnan v. State of A. P., (1993) 1 SCC 645.

11. (2002) 8 SCC 481.

12. (2003) 6 SCC 697.

13. Mohini Jain v. State of Karnataka, (1992) 3 SCC 666.

14. For a recent example, see Cochin University of Science & Technology v. Thomas P. John, (2008) 8 SCC 82, at 91.

15. (2005) 3 SCC 212.

16. M. Karunanidhi v. Union of India, (1979) 3 SCC 431, at 444.

17. See State of Maharashtra v. Bharat Shanti Lal Shah, (2008) 13 SCC 5.

18. (2005) 5 SCC 420.

19. Shubhankar Dam's scathing critique of the decision also fails to acknowledge the problem of excessive delegation, and his discussion on the

use of discretionary power is mistaken. But on other points he does—as our discussion reveals—accurately identify concerns with the decision. See Dam 2006.

20. For a more detailed analysis, see Kapur and Khosla 2011.

21. For an excellent study on this issue, see Jishnu, et al. 2012.

REFERENCES

Agarwal, P., *Indian Higher Education—Envisioning the Future* (New Delhi: Sage Publications, 2009).

Chandrasekhar, C. P., 'Chipping at the Margin: Judicial Institutionalisation of the Privatisation of Higher Education in India', *Social Scientist* 33 (9–10), 2005, pp. 90–99.

Dam, S., 'Unburdening the Constitution: What has the Indian Constitution got to do with Private Universities, Modernity and Nation-States?', *Singapore Journal of Legal Studies* 48, 2006, pp. 108–47.

Das, J., A. Holla, et al., 'In Urban and Rural India, A Standardized Patient Study Showed Low Levels of Provider Training and Huge Quality Gaps', *Health Affairs* 31 (12), 2012, pp. 2774–84.

Kapur, D., 'Indian Higher Education', in Charles T. Clotfelter (ed.), *American Universities in a Global Market* (Chicago: University of Chicago Press, 2010), 305–34.

———, 'Addressing the Trilemma of Higher Education', *Seminar* 617, 2011, pp. 87–92.

Kapur, D. and M. Khosla, 'Courts and Colleges: A Problematic Relationship', *Seminar* 627, 2011, pp. 2–5.

Kapur, D. and P. B. Mehta, 'Mortgaging the Future? Indian Higher Education', Brookings-NCAER India Policy Forum, 2008.

Mehta, P. B., 'The Rise of Judicial Sovereignty', *Journal of Democracy* 18 (2), 2007, pp. 70–83.

Robinson, N., et al., 'Interpreting the Constitution: Supreme Court Constitution Benches since Independence', *Economic and Political Weekly* 46 (9), 2011, pp. 27–31.

Sathe, S. P., *Judicial Activism in India: Transgressing Borders and Enforcing Limits* (New Delhi: Oxford University Press, 2003).

Wright, E. C., 'Courts and Universities: The Impact on Litigation on University Autonomy', *Journal of the Indian Law Institute* 27, 1985, p. 35.

— nine —

Governance in Higher Education

A Contested Space (Making the University Work)

Pankaj Chandra

Introduction

Contemporary universities in India are relatively young (that is, dating back to the early nineteenth century) by the standards of some of the well-known universities of the world (although the tradition of a formal university education dates back to the fifth century CE at Nalanda). Yet, while the older global counterparts grow in strength, Indian institutions are struggling to maintain the relevance of their vision and its purposeful execution once the founding generation has left the institution. What shapes these mechanisms to manage the development of academic institutions and where are Indian institutions falling short? I explore this question here. I present a conceptual exploration of how to place issues of governance amongst several factors that impact higher education, its role in defining the relatively low level of effectiveness and quality that have come to define the Indian higher education system, and the role that a university as an organisation plays in building a superior learning ambience.[1]

All of the three significant committees set up by the Government of India since independence to advise on reforms in higher education—the Radhakrishnan Commission of 1948, the Kothari Commission of 1964, and the Yashpal Committee of 2009—expressed concern about the quality of higher education, its governance and the purpose of education (Kothari 1970; Radhakrishnan 1962; Yashpal 2009), the ranking of Indian universities, the extent of research and knowledge generation, and the inward-looking science and arts education. In recent times, many have lamented the loss of recognition of Indian academia on the global stage.[2] Did India become so self-absorbed with its own cultural history and its search for an indigenous paradigm that defined its own environment that it started to pay scant attention to developments around the world? Or did it fall so far behind that it could not pay attention to what was happening elsewhere? Perhaps it was both. Post-independence, India started lagging behind global developments in knowledge generation, despite some interesting experiments involving the setting up of standalone institutions and research centres. The most unfortunate outcome has been the deterioration of intellectual energy and vibrancy of thought in Indian academic institutions. (One cannot deny, however, that there are pockets of excellence in what would otherwise be an intellectually colourless coat of higher education.) Visible signs of this deterioration range from decrepit buildings with posters stuck on walls, or poorly stocked libraries, or closed faculty offices and barricaded administration areas, or students hanging outside the colleges during college hours, to more dangerous signs of decay—conversations bordering on gossip and bereft of intellectual analysis, politicking on issues of admission, grades or faculty recruitment, lack of a shared vision on the future of the institution, and vanishing space to craft interesting experiments in managing institutions. There appears to be a decline in the belief that merit is the basis of the academy's development. This has been accompanied by a lack of recognition of the fact that academic institutions are stimulated by the advancement of knowledge generation, and that such knowledge generation plays an important role in ensuring that institutions remain relevant, both in preparing the youth for the country and in addressing society's challenges.

Much has been written about the role that governmental agencies like the University Grants Commission (UGC), All India Council for Technical Education (AICTE), or the various state government departments of education have played in determining the state of affairs of universities. They range from regulatory overreach and high control of a university's decisions (for example, in admissions, choice of leadership, recruitment of staff) to defining its financial health and opportunities that have resulted in under-achievement by the universities (Hatekar 2009; Singh 2004; Deshpande 2000). The functioning of both the MHRD and the UGC has been severely criticised for creating inefficiencies in universities (Kapur and Mehta 2004). However, an analysis of the management of universities, that is, governance within the university, has been noticeable by its absence.[3]

In this chapter, I address the issues of governance within institutions and their relationship with the larger governance structures of the state. Universities are unique organisational forms that are peer-managed, and hence require a governance structure and ethos that are different from a bureaucracy or a commercial organisation (Bess and Dee 2007). The construction of such learning organisations should include the articulation of clear goals and enabling mechanisms to ensure that individual and organisational goals are aligned (Garvin 1993). In both a bureaucracy and a commercial organisation, this is done with the top management defining strategic directions, and middle management intrapreneurship driving the execution. Academic organisations are peer-group governed and work more through influence and persuasion. Consequently, this organisational form takes more time to change as it functions through its cultural DNA. Rules attempt to circumscribe the functioning of public institutions, while the founder or sponsor defines directions in the case of private institutions. Both have had a debilitating impact on Indian higher education.

In the following section, I first outline the notion of governance in the higher education ecosystem and its impact on the quality of education. In section III, I define the state of governance in Indian institutions and inquire into the interrelated factors that have led to this state. I argue that the model of governance adopted for higher educational institutions was incomplete and incapable of delivering quality education. By analysing the governance system, one may be able to better understand the state of our academia. Section IV provides a framework for understanding the governance system of a university organisation, and the issues therein. In section V, I suggest ways to re-design the governance mechanism in order to enable the university to deliver higher value, both to the individual and society. Conclusions are presented in section VI.

THREE QUESTIONS

I posit that the characteristics embedded in the structure of the governance system of higher education have played a crucial role in defining the state of higher education in India. I also argue that, over the years, the governance system and its practice have become ineffective, and that it no longer supports the charter of providing quality education. Moreover, its current form creates tensions and pressures that academic institutions are unable to withstand.

This leads me to three questions on governance that have to be addressed before their implication on the quality of higher education in India can be understood:

1. What is 'governance' about in the context of higher education? Is it any different from 'institution building'?
2. What are the elements of the governance system of higher education in India?
3. What is it about governance in academia that makes it vulnerable to both control and anarchy?

I address these questions in a relatively general sense. Governance in an academy is about:

- Ensuring that the university is being true to its charter;
- Creating an environment of excellence in learning and innovation;
- Developing and steering the institution on the basis of a shared vision;
- Defining the roles of various stakeholders: students, employees, university leadership, boards/executive councils, alumni, government, funding organisations, recruiters, etc.
- Securing and safeguarding its autonomy: academic, administrative, financial;
- Enforcing the accountability of various stakeholders;
- Navigating through organisational management and influence; and
- Managing long and short-term finances.

Governance is also about having and exercising the authority to achieve the above objectives in the service of the academy. Academic organisations are in some ways different from other organisations—

the low volatility in the demand for their services, long tenure of employees, and high intellectual ability require governing processes that will ensure that both renewal and growth remain a concern for key stakeholders. Moreover, the role that they play defines how the institution is governed and whether its objectives will be met. Governance processes come into conflict with institution-building processes when the institutional agenda is made subservient to an individual agenda (or to a sect within) without reference to the broad vision of the institution. The question of roles and the responsibility for governance is more muddled than anything else in the Indian academy.

The governance system of an academic institution comprises the structure of governance (that is, the sponsoring agency and their intermediaries, the governing bodies, the executive, current employees, and the students), the policies/rules/processes that govern the institutions, the interrelationships between various groups comprising the governance structure, processes for reconciling short-term and long-term objectives, and the renewal system. It is the interplay of these elements that defines how well the institutions will be able to meet their objectives. Amongst Indian institutions, four types of governance situations seem to be prominent. The first is dominated by the bureaucracy of the state government (for example, University of Mumbai), which largely defines the agenda of the institution in very narrow terms of admissions, teaching, examinations, and the hiring of the vice-chancellor, the registrar, and the faculty and staff, and controls most of the related processes; this organisational form also struggles through the management of a large number of affiliated colleges. The second governance form can be seen in central universities (for example, University of Delhi), where the university leadership establishes norms of engagement and faculty are largely passive or act in opposition to higher-level mandates from the vice-chancellors. The vice-chancellors of these institutions govern through rigid rules and are in turn dependent on the philosophy of education and its governance as practised in agencies like the University Grants Commission (UGC) (as are the state institutions) or the Ministry of Human Resource Development (MHRD). The state institutions are in the same situation, except that they have to deal with the thinking of their state's educational bureaucracy as well.

A third group is represented by standalone institutions (for example, an Indian Institute of Technology, an Indian Institute of Management, or a Tata Institute of Fundamental Research) in all areas, but particularly in engineering, management and medicine—these institutions are small in size and are seen to be 'faculty governed', where the institute leadership is expected to largely implement what the faculty decides. Deviations almost always lead to conflicts. In recent times, these have been some of the more celebrated and sought after institutions in the country. These standalone institutions do not enjoy a smooth relationship with agencies like MHRD or AICTE. These sponsoring agencies have played the role of enlightened owners who control through the choice of board of governors, the choice of institute leadership and funds. The fourth and final group is private institutions, which are largely controlled by their promoters, are mostly run like family businesses with low faculty participation in governance, are generally low on transparency, and have yet to establish quality in both academics and governance (of course, a few exceptions do exist here as well; obviously, the question is whether the Indian higher education system runs on exceptions). The colleges amongst them that are affiliated to a university face the added control from the university. The preponderance of government agencies rather than educational bodies (for example, accreditation bodies or association of universities or association of vice-chancellors or education think-tanks) in defining how universities are managed sets the tenor of engagement in this domain.

The quality of governance defines the quality of education that will be imparted by the university. It should be designed to deliver the charter of the institution. Academic institutions are organisational forms that require a governance environment which balances academic freedom with accountability through a process of participative decision-making. This balance can be easily disturbed by extreme positions. An aggressive and control-driven leadership or board or sponsor would turn the other stakeholders hostile and destabilise this fine balance. Similarly, an institutional agenda driven by the self-preservation of employees creates permanent fissures in the relationship between leadership and staff, thereby weakening the governance system. What makes this governance system so vulnerable to an imbalance in this relationship? Academic governance works on the principles of mutual persuasion, demarcation of academic and administrative roles, and the primacy of merit in ideas and actions. An overreach by any stakeholder violates these principles, destroys the ability to dialogue, weakens the appreciation of the various skills required to run an institution, and develops institutions that are sectarian, based on personal exchange and low morale. Along with permanency in employment, the above can create a potent mixture of entitlement, whimsical decision-making and low accountability. Such an environment creates a barrier to learning and to the advancement of knowledge and change in general. This balance appears to have been severely shaken in the Indian higher educational scenario.

STATE OF GOVERNANCE

The state of governance has to vary with changing times in order to address the changing aspirations of stakeholders (including the society) as well as the challenges and opportunities that arise from the social, economic and political environment. While much of the observations in this chapter are anecdotal, we use them to create a conceptual frame for studying such issues. The current state of governance in the Indian academy can be evaluated along the following dimensions.

Purpose of the University

At the turn of the previous century, the purpose of higher education was to create Indians who would serve the British bureaucracy, and perhaps run the government once the British left. However, from the late nineteenth century to the early twentieth century, the Indian scientific leadership wanted to prove that excellence in teaching and research could be achieved in India.[4] With the establishment of new technology centres in the mid-1950s, the foundation of engineering was expanded. With it came the expansion of the university system to prepare manpower for newly independent India. But the scientific leadership also convinced the political leadership of the value of separating research from the university education system via the establishment of a series of research centres, in the natural sciences, applied technology, and social sciences and humanities. The standalone institution or research centre became the new norm (Bok 1982).[5] One of the driving arguments was that these could be governed better to meet the new objectives. The growing population as well as the changing economic environment, particularly from 1980 onwards, led to purpose being focused around the preparation of manpower for India, particularly the technical kind. By the dawn of the twenty-first century, this philosophy was down to a fine art in the country.

The Government of India's focus moved towards training the largest number of people and providing the greatest access to higher education. This may have been the reason for the standardising role that UGC has played, which is indeed the model for the large-volume production of manpower. It was probably assumed that quality would be taken care of by people in these universities (which normally happens); unfortunately, however, the standardising processes of the government reduced their influence and flexibility to experiment. The standardisation of knowledge delivery had several unintended impacts. The university became very narrowly purposed. From strengthening the 'learning ambience' of an institution to an examination-driven environment, from engagement with stakeholders to politics and lawlessness, from developing world-renowned researchers in Indian institutions to the large-scale emigration of high-quality potential researchers, from acceptable physical infrastructure to decrepit infrastructure due to paucity or poor utilisation of capital investment, the changes in higher education had become very visible. They had a dramatic impact on the way these institutions would be managed—who would lead them, how they would be run, and how the stakeholders, particularly the state and the academics themselves, would change the governance regime of universities. At some point, the causality became bi-directional.

Roles of Various Stakeholders

Traditionally, the stakeholders have been the state, the faculty and staff, the students, and members of the civil society. Alumni have rarely been engaged with Indian institutions. The government was the founding trustee of state and central universities. Bureaucrats with a partial understanding of the higher education governance system through the various agencies, that is, the MHRD, UGC, AICTE, the state education departments and even registrars (whom the state appointed, directly or indirectly), controlled the curriculum, the rules governing the academy and academics, and finances and capital expenditures (including who would be the agency to execute capital projects). It was (and often is) not uncommon for bureaucrats and politicians to influence the recruitment of faculty and staff, the admission of students and appointment of university leadership. The role of the government changed from guardian to chief decision-maker. Another feature of this violence on the governance system came in the form of the roles played by the chancellor (in the case of state universities) and the visitor (in the case of central universities)—the former being the Governor of the State and the latter, the President of India. These roles opened up opportunities to politicise the processes of the university and intrude in its governance, especially in appointments by ignoring the recommendations of search committees; or it simply introduced delays in decisions relating to the university. One wonders how an organisation can survive such ravages when the entry process for its key stakeholders has been adversely affected.

In the early years, private institutions were established by very tall local and national leaders from all walks of life. The purpose was to contribute to the building of a new nation. People like Lala Sriram in Delhi, Madan Mohan Malaviya in Banaras, Sir Syed Ahmed Khan in Aligarh, Munshi Kali Prasad Kulbhaskar in Allahabad, and Kasturbhai Lalbhai in Ahmedabad were of this kind. Their institutions became leading national centres of learning, attracted the best of faculty and students, and were managed effectively. Over the years, most of these institutions of the past became pale shadows of the promise presented by their founders and their performance in early years, in terms of scholarship, national character, learning opportunities and ideas. There are very few private institutions from the post-independence era that could become models of higher education in India. Private institutions have been accused of becoming teaching factories, of many kinds of malpractices, and of becoming money-making ventures for their 'promoters'.

Civil society has also played a role in disabling the university. Its engagement moved away from viewing the university as a potential place for generating ideas for society. It began to view the academy only from the vantage point of its own beneficiaries—children who needed admission to earn degrees for a job, businesses that could supply the needs of the university, politics that could secure influence from voters or supporters within the university. Once these needs had been met or rendered unnecessary, civil society walked away from the university. It saw the university less and less clearly as an agent of social change, spurred on by its scholarly thought and ideas.

There has been a significant deterioration in the quality, aspiration and values of one of the most key stakeholders, the faculty. Academics plays two important roles—the advancement of knowledge and impacting the world through scholarship; and training young minds to learn to think, and thereby contribute to the development of society. On both counts, academics has failed to excel, although the failure of the first point has been far more visible. To fill this gap, academics took over the task of managing all aspects of their institution, ranging from security to placement to finances to building construction to campus maintenance to overseeing examinations, while devaluing the use of professionals or mistrusting them in the management of services and facilities in universities. Interestingly, this is a key area of tension in university governance. Two situations have arisen in the country today—first, where the vice-chancellor is held hostage to the administration led by the registrar, and second, where s/he is held hostage by the faculty (of course, a third option also exists: in a small number of cases, the vice-chancellor, in conjunction with one of the other two, has marginalised the third), thereby leading to a very difficult governance environment.

Executive councils (or boards) as trustees and protectors of the university charter have failed to perform their role of providing strategic direction and oversight of the academia (Freedman 2014).[6] The faculty plays another role: performing a gate-keeping function by keeping non-meritorious and undeserving candidates from becoming academics. And here, the failure has been colossal. Another truth has emerged in India—whether it was opportunities in other professions or other countries, whether it was the absence of role models in the university, whether it was disillusionment with the state or any other sponsor, whether it was a lack of resources available to the academy or their lack of impact, the academia in India no longer remains the profession of choice for bright young people.

So from strong and involved trustees, the university is now managed by indifferent or self-serving stakeholders; from being governed by the university, it is now being governed by the state/central government; from being centres of scholarship, the university has become another centre of employment for a certain kind of people. The most important question, however, is: Why did this happen? There are indeed several hypotheses that need to be tested to answer this question. They range from a loss of national purpose, to control of institutions by the government through grants, to the destruction of academic and institutional autonomy (although private institutions have as bad a record), rent-seeking by individuals, criminalisation of the university, the rapid growth and lack of expansion of faculty resources, and low accountability of various stakeholders. One other factor requires mention: there are lots of gaps in the relationship between various actors in the university organisation and in the common understanding of their roles. Consequently, no one feels responsible or even empowered enough to improve the governance environment, and thereby steer the institution away from its deterioration.

Nature of Leadership

One of the major casualties of Indian society has been the decline in the number of strong leaders in all walks of life. The university is no exception. Each of the older institutions can boast of people like S. Radhakrishnan (Banaras Hindu University), Satish Dhawan (the Indian Institute of Sciences), Vikram Sarabhai (Indian Institute of Management, Ahmedabad), P. C. Mahalanobis (Indian Statistical Institute), Asutosh Mookerjee (University of Calcutta), etc., as their vice-chancellors or founders/directors in the early years. Similarly, on the faculty of institutions were C. V. Raman, Meghnad Saha, S. N. Bose, J. C. Bose, Amartya Sen, and C. K. Prahalad. The nature of academic leadership has changed quite dramatically in Indian institutions, and academics of a global stature have practically vanished from the Indian academic stage. Why did this happen?

While many consider state control of academic institutions and the consequent deterioration in autonomy, control of resources by bureaucrats and administrators, and the growth of academic vibrancy in North America and Europe as some key reasons for the change in the academic scenario in Indian universities and the flight of academics from India, a few other possible reasons need study. One relates to the loss of power and decision-making on the part of the university leadership to nurture, reward and protect scholars in universities. The second is the shift in defining what would be the proving grounds for academics in India. Within a few decades of independence, Indian academics moved away from generating knowledge that would be judged by the standards of the world to those within India. Third, institutional leaders were beginning to be selected on the basis of their proximity to the government or other stakeholders, and not on merit or academic stature. And lastly, the university governance system had been damaged to such an extent that even so-called 'reasonable' leaders found it impossible to lead their institution towards improvement.

It would be instructive to look at who becomes the head of an institution. Since the decision-making happens at the level of the government, influence often plays a role, particularly at the state level. Such leaders are found to be compliant, distracted and not focused on creating a vibrant learning ecosystem. Leading an academic institution is quite a complex task, and it is highly unlikely that one will be able to understand its complexities until one steps into that role. To manage this transition successfully, institutions globally help the leader in the transition by providing faculty advisors (Kadane 2004),[7] board-level initiation, strong senior administrative support, and a long transition into the job to understand the culture, traditions and processes of the university. All these processes are missing from the Indian academic environment. A vice-chancellor learns on the job and often through mistakes, which prove costly at times. The short tenures of vice-chancellors (often three years) do not allow a worthy person to make a lasting impact.

The leadership hierarchy in Indian institutions is poorly structured. It is not designed to address the needs of a modern university. The vice-chancellor is rarely allowed to operate like the chief executive officer that s/he is. S/he is poorly supported by her/his office (which largely comprises clerks and low-skilled administrators) and other academic leaders at the institution. The vice-chancellor struggles to manage the day-to-day affairs of the institution (which should be taken care of by a provost or a pro-vice chancellor), while strategic issues, external relationships, growth and new initiatives suffer. One can ask why institutions fail to change this state of affairs. Two answers become apparent—first, structural change is so cumbersome, tedious and time-consuming (given that University Acts require the approval of the state or central legislature) that no vice-chancellor attempts it. One wonders what the boards and executive councils are doing. Second, the faculty body protests any such change[8]—a clear case of a poor demarcation of roles. Consequently, maintaining the status quo becomes the best option, leading to the stagnation of the university. A word on the executive councils—these are some of the most ineffective bodies, and have not been proactive in building consensus for change at their institutions. Their engagement is limited to a few meetings each year. These meetings are hardly attended, and the agenda is often very tactical and focused on approvals. An engaged organisational hierarchy permits different levels of decision-making to be undertaken by different groups of people, and prevents the usurping of institutional power by any one group. This aspect is missing in Indian institutions. This vacuum is filled by the government bureaucracy at times and employee groups at others—the two groups who have longer sojourns with respect to the university. The outcome is self-interest. Long-term vision and strategic change-making together become the biggest casualty as no one desires a major course correction. It would be interesting to study the percentage of leaders who served more than one term, or served as leaders in multiple institutions, in order to understand whether governance can improve through experience imparted to the leadership. Anecdotally, most leaders finish their careers with a single term at a single institution.[9] Has the governance of academia been affected by this state and nature of the leadership? The answer would be—most certainly.

Rules, Processes and Scale

Governance at an institution is as good as the processes it has developed—processes for admissions, recruitment and promotion, programme approvals, financial accountability, academic renewal, evaluating growth, and for managing stakeholders and convocations. Somehow, Indian institutions have been very reluctant to become process-oriented. Instead, they are either dependent on people to define ways of doing tasks, or are comfortable with rule-based systems. While rules of any significance can be implemented by a clerk, process implementation seeks to use judgement to moderate guidelines—and this requires insights, wisdom and honesty.

As the government took control of institutions, the first casualty was institutional autonomy. One of the features of this autonomy is process orientation. Many people are required to carry out processes and make judgements. As a consequence, a higher degree of consultation is involved in this approach to governance. Rules, on the other hand, require individuals for administration, and are designed by a hierarchical formulation. External control from a distance can only be exercised through explicit rules. The underlying assumption is that the rules will ensure that fair decisions are made. Moreover, one can monitor whether rules have been followed. Unfortunately, rules create bureaucracies in academia. As the number of universities grew and student enrolment increased, this need to control through rules grew even stronger. Standardisation was desired across institutions in various activities, such as the selection of vice-chancellors or faculty, or admissions of students, or financial expenditures or investment processes. This was achieved by subjecting all institutions to Government of India service rules, purchase policies, salary structures, finance rules, and audits by the Comptroller and Auditor General (CAG). Academic institutions that were supposed to innovate, experiment and change suddenly started to look, operate and smell alike. This critique is not of the need for oversight or fairness or transparency in decisions—all of these are necessary for healthy governance. These rules reduced the university leadership and administrators to bureaucrats and took intelligent judgement (supposed to be the hallmark of academia) and innovation out of university governance. Unfortunately, the rules did not prevent the appointment of rotten leadership, corruption in admissions, rent-seeking in universities, the hiring of mediocre people as academics; and they did not prevent mediocre academics and poor scholarship from defining the norms of promotion and reward. It did not keep nepotism and influence away from universities. Some institutions, however, have done better than others.

Institutions consequently moved away from student-centric processes of learning and discretion in decision-making to intense bureaucracy, from seeking excellence to meeting minimum norms, from complete ownership of activities to complete amnesia on accountability, and from a strong financial planning model to a CAG mindset of control and mistrust.

There is another aspect of these processes that needs mention. Universities survive for centuries when they develop a vibrant and questioning culture. Building such a cultural organisation requires the establishment of soft processes and traditions. Soft processes like annual faculty reviews, programme reviews, teaching evaluations, pedagogy workshops and teaching support, external academic reviews, and tutorials were all meant to enhance the quality of the learning environment in the academy. You can hear many a dean or vice-chancellor complain of low attendance in faculty seminars, university-wide lectures, and similar academic activities on their campuses. Similarly, institutions collectively celebrate certain values, events, achievements, and people—orientations, convocations, award dinners, etc., were traditions that built a sense of pride in the community. Unfortunately, these traditions have been lost in many institutions and soft processes never took root in most. Perhaps the most important tool at the disposal of the university to move towards excellence was lost.

Competition for Excellence and Resources

Universities are unique organisations that link the past to the future. The richer the past, the brighter 'appears' to be the promise of the future. Academics live in the future as they deal with young people, who are there to build a future. That is what is exciting about academic research and innovation. This curiosity drives excellence in universities. Competition around ideas between research groups has always challenged universities to out-perform each other and drive discoveries. Centres, faculty positions and research funds are created to bring leading scholars from other places to the universities. Unfortunately, there are not many stories emerging from Indian academia and the agencies of government that create and fund grand challenges for the university. From an aspirational point of view, it appears that at some point in time in modern Indian history, these two critical stakeholders decided that their proving ground was not going to be the world. For the most part, we stopped comparing our academic practices, our research methods, our systems, our reward/incentive/evaluation processes, and even our knowledge-based systems with those of others around the world. Very soon, work on many of the issues arising in the East was being done by people outside India, and not within. Our best started to be hired away from India. The divorce between research and teaching became commonplace. Indian journals lost their global appeal, and soon their good Indian contributors. The cost of attending an international conference grew considerably (most institutions would provide support for one international conference every three years; some did not even do that). Domestic conferences and journals struggled to elicit quality papers. The research grant system has been in tatters for a long time. Soon, the country fell off the academic map (of course, there were few exceptions, as in any case). India was largely in the news for sending bright students abroad! There were very few centres in the country and a handful of individuals in most disciplines who were respected both within and outside the country for their scholarship.

Renewal Systems

One interesting aspect of organisations is their ability to renew themselves. Academic institutions do so by constantly questioning the relevance of their output and focus, by changing their curriculum and programmes based on the needs of the society, by subjecting their academic output, programmes, departments and faculty to external reviews, by participating openly in debates on the changes in institutional priorities, by bringing in fresh talent as academics and administrators into the university, and by utilising the facility of sabbaticals on a regular basis to rejuvenate and retool themselves (many places do not even offer sabbaticals). Very few institutions in the country have a comprehensive renewal system embedded in their institutional strategy. What is equally important is the seriousness and care with which these processes are executed. Similarly, universities rarely review their administrative processes to enhance their effectiveness.

Why did academics and academic institutions not find it valuable to invest their time and resources for renewal, and who should demand it? Could it be that the complete control of universities by the government over a long period of time has created an environment where academics have either forgotten, or not been initiated into, the practices and traditions of academic excellence, or consider it the responsibility of the government to rejuvenate them? Is renewal purely a good practice, or should it be mandatory? Or was a paucity of financial resources responsible for many of these practices being set aside?

In conclusion, years of neglect and bad practices, poor leadership and mediocrity in academia, lack of innovation in academic administration, unprincipled expansion, real or perceived control of the administration by the government, and increasing disparity in compensation between opportunities within universities and outside have led to this putrid state of governance in universities.

VARIOUS VIEWS OF GOVERNANCE

Governance in higher education can be viewed through multiple lenses of decision-making and influence. They help us understand the complex interaction of issues that define the governance system in the Indian university. They also support the argument that governance is about the ways of doing things. There is a strategic view of governance at the university that allows universities to establish a long-term view of their own activities and make choices that support it. The university as an organisation imposes its own constraints and challenges on the way it is governed and on the processes needed to keep it healthy. This is reflected in the organisational view of the university. Finally, governance is as much about vision and processes as it is about their execution. Issues of capacity, tactics and performance for managing the university effectively are captured in the operational view of the university. In this section, we raise issues that fall within each of these three perspectives on governance.

The Strategic View of Governance at the University

The choice of a certain governance form and its deployment to achieve long-term objectives in a changing environment is a strategic task. Institutions that are strategic in nature create impact. They make choices about programmes, directions of research and size of the school, and then deploy resources to develop this environment of excellence while using various mechanisms to safeguard their values and vision. The choice of a Jawaharlal Nehru University to not offer undergraduate or professional education is a strategic one, with long-term implications. Rigidities imposed by the regulators have led to Indian institutions becoming more opportunistic and less strategic. Several questions arise around the strategic view of Indian institutions. These relate to the purpose of the university and the roles of each stakeholder; the structure of the university and the related aspects of autonomy, relationship between stakeholders (within the university and outside) and its accountability; and the task of curating university values and processes of governance.[10]

The Organisational View of Governance at the University

As an organisational form, the university is far more complex than other organisations because of its matrix structure, its knowledge ethos, its cultural openness, its lack of perceived hierarchy, its consensual decision-making processes, its tolerance for variance, its continuous youthful character and accompanying impatience, and its single-minded pursuit of new knowledge. Where did this thinking become muddy in India? Students ransacking university property, or faculty sitting by the roadside on a strike, or university leadership operating behind secure offices and guarded by the police are a complete anathema to learning and the advancement of knowledge. It is not uncommon for these stakeholders to express disagreement by bringing academic activities to a halt. Politicians in the country have frequently used this absence of agreement on how the institution should be run to foment dissatisfaction and interfered in its functioning, much to the institution's detriment. It lends credence to the view that Indian academic organisations appear rigid and unwilling to change, are unwilling or unable to manage the complex issues that arise in such environments, and are unable to navigate the ship towards excellence and goal seeking. Several issues that relate to the structure and management of the organisation, which in turn affect the well-being of the academia, are: organisation design and accountability, including incentives for merit; power, politics and the transformation of academic organisations in India; and preparing the leadership to build institutions.

The Operational View of Governance at the University

A significant weakness in India in general, 'execution' is an area of major concern in the academy. Getting things done or the logistics of running the institution is as crucial, if not more, than the policies designed to run them. Whether it is the process of admissions or scheduling classrooms and courses or introducing a new programme, organising a faculty recruitment process or a sports event or conference, the submission of grades or information on staff privileges, campus security or food service or building maintenance, the bursar's office or counselling or staff advising, development or fundraising and alumni engagement or budgeting, Indian institutions do a terrible job of managing institutional resources and services. The real use of information systems and technology to improve productivity and enable the better utilisation of university resources is limited.

Most leaders do not understand the need for managerial systems that will enhance operational capabilities, and consequently help to achieve the objectives of the university. Low wages deter high-quality managerial talent from seeking employment at the university. Those who choose university administration as a career find themselves at a dead end as far as career growth and excitement are concerned. Faculty have to step in to undertake many administrative roles (ranging from managing computer centres, project offices, development offices, career development, admissions, to conference centres, etc.) in order to make the university work with a certain degree of effectiveness. This role has been most debilitating for academia in India. It distracts the faculty from their role as academics, affects the quality of their teaching and research, and changes their aspirations—from winning Nobel Prizes and creating an impact through their thinking to becoming administrators (some are surely needed, but it cannot be an aspiration for most). Worse still, the faculty as voluntary administrator tends to reject accountability. Operational excellence in governance is a key area of reform as far as Indian academia is concerned. Several issues and questions that need to be addressed in this regard are planning for capacity and growth; constructing decision-making processes; and instituting operational excellence and performance systems.

Many tensions exist in the Indian university—between competing visions of higher education, between the stakeholders, in striking a balance between research and teaching, between competing resources, and between competing opportunities within and outside the university. They impact the governance of the university, and consequently its health and excellence. Hence, it needs to be re-designed.

REDESIGNING THE GOVERNANCE SYSTEM

The governance system of a university represents the ecosystem that helps to make the university work. It forms a supply chain of connected entities, people, processes and perspectives that ensure that the strategic vision is translated into decisions at the university. The Indian higher education system needs to address the following issues in order to overhaul its governance system into one that will foster excellence.

Defining the Purpose of the University

A competitive and modern economy is as much about good governance, quality infrastructure and a judicious utilisation of resources as it is about the exploration of nature, an appreciation of diverse cultures, respect for public commons, modernisation, and enlightened citizenship. The role of education is to help the individual reflect on such issues. Universities become the platform for such enquiry and reflection. The university's role as premier thought centre for the country or the region has to be re-established. This would require changing the charter of each institution and re-crafting their vision. Manpower development, research and constant experimentation to address the issues facing the country and the world will have to be strongly articulated. The repatriation of research centres to the university, conversion of standalone educational institutes into multidisciplinary colleges with the status of a university, the linking of grants to research output, external achievements and contribution to national issues, and the preparation of graduates for the society would ensure that the focus on quality is not lost. An absence of quality in education has proven to be as pernicious as lack of access.

Defining the Proving Grounds and Benchmarks

Indian higher education must lead the efforts to rid society of poverty and make the economy competitive and modern. This will require articulating the roles of various institutional types, providing for mobility between types, and excelling in what one purports to do. Institutions may be classified as research universities, teaching central universities, professional institutions or vocational colleges based on what they propose to do and how well they do it. A research university must be multidisciplinary and must benchmark itself globally, and measure itself by world standards. Given the available resources, such universities will be limited in number and will require a higher deployment of resources for research. Research must be part of the educational experience, even at the undergraduate level. A teaching central university will also be a multidisciplinary institution that aims to become a cutting-edge teaching institution. Such an institution will enrol a larger number of students and provide them with a high-quality learning experience. Faculty will innovate around teaching, but will also be encouraged to undertake research. Professional institutions would be existing single-discipline ones that are applied in nature, provide the best of class industry practices and bring global knowledge into the classrooms. Both the teaching central and professional institutions will become the main suppliers of manpower for industry. Vocational institutions would impart skills in traditional and modern crafts, geared towards self-employment and direct use by industry and society.

If such an ecosystem is to be of high quality, institutions of each type will have to benchmark with their equivalent counterparts globally. The ecosystem architecture must allow mobility for both individuals and institutions to move from one type to another, based on performance; this will make institutions aspire to become better. This perspective will permit all types of institutions—small and big, research and teaching, professional and vocational—to experiment (for example, a professional institution may develop a programme where students spend six months in the industry every year, or which gives college credits to students admitted with a vocational diploma and/or some work experience).

Delivering Autonomy

Autonomy of the institution is the *sine qua non* for excellence. Autonomy is the ability to make one's own decisions in a transparent manner with appropriate oversights. Both governments and private promoters have to recognise that once they set up mechanisms of governance through internal structures and processes, a governing board, a process for strategic planning, and financial oversight through statutory auditors, their role in directly governing the university diminishes. This will help to strengthen internal governance and develop professionals to run the institution. Government and promoters must seek stringent external academic and financial reviews from institutions, subject them to a serious accreditation process, allow boards to undertake the hiring of university employees, including the university leadership (and not see universities as places of patronage), and allow them to develop their own curriculum and programmes (it should be the task of the accreditation agency to look at quality). Funding should be in the form of block grants based on the approval of multi-year plans, and a financial delivery system should be created wherein the grant is automatically deposited in an account for five years with the university being able to draw only the requisite amount each year, with a five-yearly review for determining funding requirements for the next five years. The salary structures set up by the Pay Commissions should serve only as the floor, with institutions having the ability to pay more based on the availability of their own funds (the same principle may be applied to the number of employees). Each institution should be encouraged to establish an endowment, and their boards should be empowered to review the elements of the governance system and establish broad policies on structuring the financial model of the university, including fees. Universities are dynamic organisations—attempts to control them should be curbed, as this slowly destroys their vibrancy, their meritocracy and their creativity.

Defining Roles and Accountability

Academic institutions need to clearly articulate the roles of various stakeholders and have an understanding of the extent to which each can have an influence on the governance of the institution. This will minimise areas of conflict and help to move the institution forward; this is an area where Indian institutions have fared rather poorly. It is also important to re-design the structure of the university so that a coordinated yet decentralised decision-making can emerge (for example, reinstating the positions of pro-vice chancellor/provost as the academic head, establishing a council of deans as the key leadership council, pushing hiring decisions to the level of the deans, circumscribing the role of the Senate—the highest academic body in several Indian institutions—etc.).

Restoring accountability within the university system is even more crucial. Processes relating to annual reviews, hiring and promotion need to be strengthened and made meaningful. The practice of open advertisement for promotion breeds insecurity and leads to influence-seeking. On the other hand, competing against oneself for promotion[11] has led to dropping of standards due to familiarity. The latter is a superior strategy, but needs to be made more serious and stringent. Academics are provided with tenure to enable them to research issues that are important to society but are not marketable, or publish their research without fear of retribution. It was felt that this was required to advance knowledge. But the key question remains: What must be done if a faculty member stops generating knowledge post-tenure, or stops producing quality research? Most institutions, globally, use a stringent tenure system as a proxy to ensure that those who get tenure have worked very hard and smartly, and that this would become a habit as they progress through their careers. Indian institutions follow a probation system post-appointment, which is of a short duration and is insufficient to either judge or exhibit proficiency. Here, the hiring or the promotion process becomes extremely crucial.

But when those processes are compromised, as is often the case in India, the academia starts rotting. There is a strong case for instituting a serious tenure system as well as a post-tenure review in India. Trustees, boards of governors or executive councils must play their strategic roles in protecting the purpose of the university, ensuring oversight and enforcing accountability. The government must seek reports from them on the growth of the institution and its quality, as they are the 'guardians' of the university (Kerr and Gade 1989).

Establishing Decentralised Processes

Academic institutions work best through the decentralisation of decision-making via deans and heads of departments, while coordinating the same through the office of the provost. The same holds true for non-academic administration. This is possible if decision-making becomes process-oriented and there is a strong coordination between people and activities. Processes have to be codified, or else they will be ineffective. Organisations establish a variety of councils/groups whose role is to provide a coordination and integration function without being a centre with veto power. It should be recognised that decision-making in different areas requires domain knowledge. Institutions must acquire such expertise, especially in non-academic areas, to govern themselves better. This requires re-crafting the organisation structure of the university differently to allow the induction of high-quality non-academic administrators.

Getting the University Leadership Working

It is imperative to get out of the current state where university leadership is the least empowered entity on the campus. This has prevented capable academic administrators from wanting this role, thereby further deteriorating its stature and impact. Generally, leadership is given a mandate by their boards or executive councils to achieve certain goals in a limited time, and it is their responsibility to develop a shared vision around these goals and deliver them for the benefit of society. They also evolve policies and ideas on governance or future directions through interaction with stakeholders, and oversee their execution. They look after the intellectual, financial and social health of the institution. They balance the demands of different stakeholders and are the key interface with external stakeholders. Like any leadership position in any organisation, this is quite a challenging role. Several changes are needed to ensure that this role is performed effectively: first, the vice-chancellor has to be supported very ably by her/his leadership team and office—most offices in universities are ill-equipped to play such a role. Second, successful institutions assign neutral and wise senior professors and board members as advisors (with no executive responsibility) to the leader, to ensure that the values/traditions of the university are maintained and that wise counsel is always available. Third, universities must evolve practices of strategic planning, annual planning and reviews, and periodic assessment of the plan achievement to ensure that universities are moving ahead on the ideas and plans evolved in every department. Fourth, the role of the leader as chief executive officer has to be emphasised, given the multitude of responsibilities that s/he carries, including statutory responsibilities. Fifth, the vice-chancellor's role will become even more complex and challenging in times to come because of the increased importance of fundraising and external relationships in managing the aspirations of universities. This will entail training the leadership team, and require an able development team and decentralisation of decision-making to free the leadership from day-to-day operations. Sixth, the government and private promoters will have to work through the boards to influence the leadership and their activities rather than interfere directly in the affairs of the university. And last, the compensation of the vice-chancellor must be commensurate with the responsibility, and must be made significantly higher than what is currently offered. Only then can we expect to attract high-quality people to such positions.

Managing Scale

The big challenge facing Indian institutions is managing large enrolments. Rigid control by regulatory agencies have led to an imbalance in the size of the campus: on the one hand, we have a large number of institutions that individually have inadequate enrolment. On the other hand, we have university systems with affiliated colleges that have an unmanageable number of students. This dilemma has to be resolved in favour of quality. Beyond a point, the university has to open more regional campuses to manage a reasonably sized population within its system. This would be the evolution of a multiple-campus university system with perhaps a limited set of programme offerings pertinent to the university's spatial location. There are two big challenges in managing scale: how to maintain the student-teacher ratio while growing and how to fund academic initiatives (including faculty development) to increase the impact of the institution. The solution lies in crafting a financial model to provide for this investment with a significant increase in research funding by the government (from various ministries) to universities, which will include funding for graduate students, resource generation by universities (especially through university services), and participation of the society in university funding (and this will require tax benefits/savings). New institutions need to be set up as well to address India's low gross enrolment ratio.

Developing a New Financial Model for the University

Universities, whether public or private, urgently need to rework their financial model. As the number of universities and students grow, the old model of financing based on a prescribed ratio of students, staff and activities will need to be revisited. This has had two effects: one, where the responsibility of doing newer things has been left to the discretion of the funding agency, thereby taking away local initiatives; and two, when most of the funding comes from a single source, the responsibility to the larger society diminishes (even if the funding is public). Raising funds from a variety of sources has the effect of democratising priorities, and also places this initiative in the lap of academia. There is no substitute for philanthropic participation in higher education. Each university should be helped to develop an endowment. A one-time grant for universities to set up their endowments will be necessary. The financial model will require setting aside a separate corpus for capital expenditure and maintenance, financial aid and research. Moreover, each institution will need to increase the compensation of its employees in order to attract the best talent. This will require seeking higher fees from those who can afford it and financial aid for those who cannot, yet have the merit to get admitted. Government subsidies on loans will be required to provide low interest, collateral-free educational loans to students. Providing quality education requires a high investment of resources. To support this quality, the fees will need to be increased, while at the same time providing very deep and significant need-based financial aid. Any society that seeks to develop will need to invest such resources in educating its citizens.

The key question in India always remains: Will we be able to execute any of the above changes in the governance system? The key lies in developing a pilot model through a 'lead institution implementation' strategy to test how cold the water in the river is by first putting a toe in before wading through. The country must embark on the reform by selecting a set of lead institutions to implement the change. Designing the change process will be necessary for any success.

CONCLUSION

Indian academic institutions suffer from an ineffective state of governance. Sometimes it seems as though all the foundation stones of the modern university have not been laid yet (or have been removed by ignorant vandals), since many of the key governance processes that help to run and renew academic institutions are noticeable by their absence. There have been several reasons for the same—poor understanding of what makes the university work on the part of both the government and the academia, a high propensity towards control by the bureaucracy, violent intrusions in its autonomy by politicians, poor leadership at the university, self-preservation by the faculty and a poor understanding of their role, and a very tenuous engagement of society with the university. The university has to be virtually reconstructed if quality is to be restored.

Fortunately for India, we are in a phase of expansion that will see the establishment of new institutions that can become models of experimentation with new governance structures. The same may be true for some key quality institutions in the country. They can then become role models for a large-scale restructuring of higher education in India. The tendency, however, is for organisations, caught up in the euphoria of the expansion phase, to ignore making fundamental changes, which might return to haunt them later. One hopes that the Indian higher education system does not miss this opportunity of the century.

NOTES

1. Note that we will be using the terms 'university' and 'institution' interchangeably and to mean the same, that is, an academic organisation, unless specifically mentioned.

2. The National Knowledge Commission Report (2009), although aimed at broader issues of knowledge generation and its application, also examined the state of higher education, especially its governance by the state (National Knowledge Commission 2009).

3. A few who have raised issues of broader institutional management have done so in the context of specific institutions, like Anubhai (2011). However, these are recollections and analyses of archival material on the Indian Institute of Management, Ahmedabad.

4. This may be considered the glorious period of contemporary Indian science, with contributors like C. V. Raman, J. C. Bose, S. N. Bose, P. C. Ray, Meghnad Saha, Birbal Sahani, Homi Bhabha, S. Ramanujam, S. S. Bhatnagar, etc.

5. Interestingly, this was an exception and not the norm in the development of US universities, which was further perfecting the multiversity by dismantling 'the walls around the campus'.

6. Globally, trustees and boards have played a significant role in ensuring that the university remained true to its purpose. They have played roles that range from the selection of the president (that is, the vice-chancellor) of the university, to fundraising, to oversight.

7. Carnegie Mellon University (similar to other universities globally) deploys a senior faculty advisor to an incoming president to support him and help understand and navigate the culture, processes and people of the new university. The installation of president is elaborate and a purposeful overlap is created with the tenure of the outgoing president. Corporate organisations often use Board members as mentors to a new chief executive.

8. Protests by the faculty of Delhi University on the implementation of the semester system and four-year undergraduate programmes are examples.

9. Globally, able administrators move from one leadership position to another in different institutions, thereby using their experience to improve governance.

10. See an expanded version of this chapter (Chandra 2012) for a detailed description of the issues and questions that arise from their

discussion of the three views of governance. These questions are pointers to the hypothesis that need to be developed and empirically verified with data from Indian institutions.

11. Promotion at most government institutions in India is done through a nation-wide advertisement, allowing anyone from any institution to apply for the position, including candidates from the university under consideration. At each level, the candidate is appointed afresh. This is in contrast with the evaluation of an internal candidate for promotion, where s/he is the only candidate considered. In the former, promotion is done once a vacancy at that level occurs. In the latter, which is a global practice, it is assumed the pathway for promotion for each faculty always exists, and will happen once the internal faculty meets the merit requirements for the new position.

REFERENCES

Anubhai, P., *The IIMA Story: The DNA of an Institution* (Noida: Random House India, 2011).

Bess, James L. and J. R. Dee, *Understanding College and University Organization: Theories for Effective Policies and Practice*, Vol. I (Virginia: Stylus Publishing, 2007).

Bok, D., *Beyond The Ivory Tower: Social Responsibilities of the Modern University* (Cambridge: Harvard University Press, 1982).

Chandra, P., 'Governance in Higher Education: A Contested Space: Making the University Work', Mimeo, Indian Institute of Management Bangalore, 2012.

Deshpande, J. V., 'AICTE as Politicians' Handmaiden', *Economic and Political Weekly* 35 (49), 2000, pp. 4307–08.

Freedman, J. O., 'Presidents and Trustees', in Ronald G. Ehrenberg (ed.), *Governing Academia* (Ithaca, NY: Cornell University Press, 2014), 9–27.

Garvin, D. A., 'Building a Learning Organization', *Harvard Business Review* 71 (4), 1993, pp. 78–91.

Hatekar, N., 'Changing Higher Education Scenario in India', *Economic and Political Weekly* 44 (38), 2009, pp. 22–23.

Kadane, J. B., 'A Perspective on Faculty', in Daniel P. Resnick and Dana S. Scott (eds), *The Innovative University* (Pittsburgh: Carnegie University Press, 2004) 51–62.

Kapur, D. and P. B. Mehta, 'Indian Higher Education Reform: From Half-Baked Socialism to Half-Baked Capitalism', CID Working Paper No. 108, Centre for International Development, Harvard University, 2004.

Kerr, C. and M. L. Gade, *The Guardians: Boards of Trustees of American Colleges and Universities* (Washington, DC: Association of Governing Boards of Universities and Colleges, 1989).

Kothari, D. S., *The Report of the Education Commission chaired by D.S. Kothari* (New Delhi: Government of India, 1970). Available at www.dise.in.

National Knowledge Commission, 'National Knowledge Commission: Report to the Nation, 2006–2009', Government of India, 2009. Available at www.aicte-india.org.

Radhakrishnan, S., *The Report of the University Education Commission chaired by Dr. S. Radhakrishnan* (Pub. No. 606) (New Delhi: Government of India, 1962). Available at www.teindia.nic.in.

Singh, A., 'Challenges in Higher Education', *Economic and Political Weekly* 39 (21), 2004, pp. 2155–58.

Yashpal, *The Report of the Committee to Advise on Renovation and Rejuvenation of Higher Education in India chaired by Prof. Yashpal* (New Delhi: Government of India, 2009). Available at www.academics-india.com.

Contributors

Megha Agarwal is Founder and CEO, LEAP Skills Academy.

Pankaj Chandra is Chairman, Board of Management, Ahmedabad University.

Apoorvanand Jha is Professor of Hindi, Delhi University.

Sachi Hatakenaka is a higher education specialist and international consultant based in the UK.

Srinivasan Kannan is with Teamlease Skills University, Bangalore.

Devesh Kapur is the Madan Lal Sobti Professor for the Study of Contemporary India and Director, Center for Advanced Study of India, University of Pennsylvania.

Madhav Khosla is a Ph.D. candidate at Harvard University.

K. P. Krishnan is Secretary, Ministry of Skill Development and Entrepreneurship, Government of India.

Pratap Bhanu Mehta is President and Chief Executive, Centre for Policy Research, New Delhi.

Manish Sabharwal is CEO, Teamlease Skills University, Bangalore.

Sudipa Sarkar is at the Department of Applied Economics, Faculty of Law, University of Salamanca, Spain.

Jeemol Unni is Director, Institute for Rural Management, Anand.

Index